EDGAR SNOW'S
CHINA

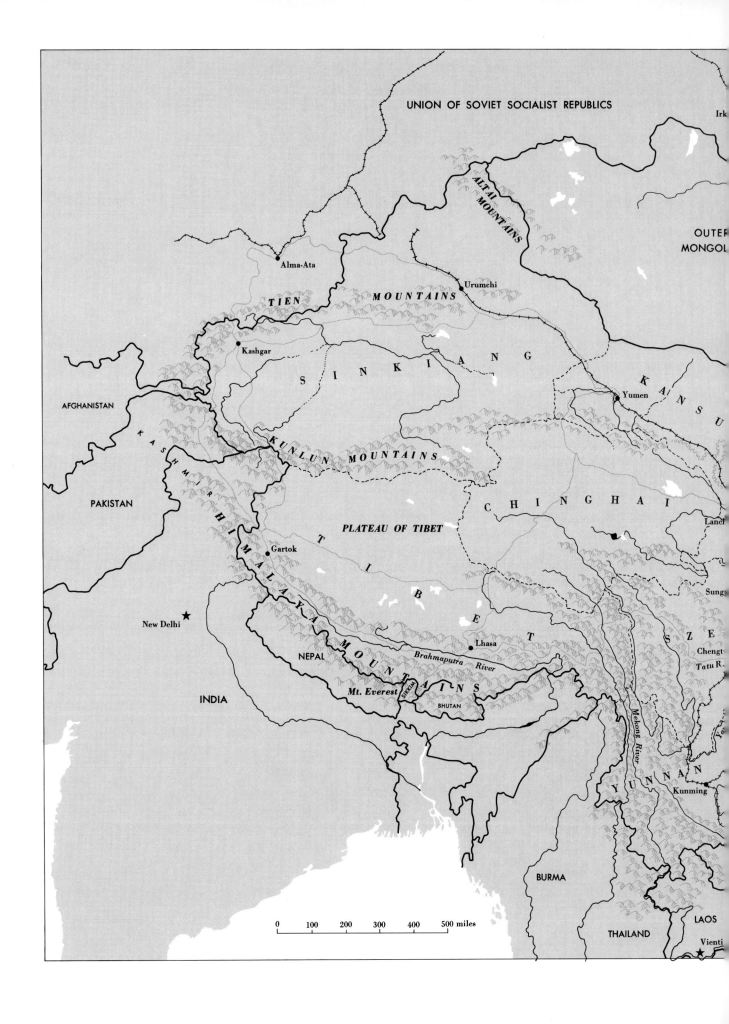

UNION OF SOVIET SOCIALIST REPUBLICS

Irk

ALTAI MOUNTAINS

OUTER MONGOL

Alma-Ata

Urumchi

TIEN   MOUNTAINS

KANSU

Kashgar

S I N K I A N G

Yumen

AFGHANISTAN

KUNLUN   MOUNTAINS

PAKISTAN

CHINGHAI

Lanc

PLATEAU OF TIBET

Gartok

T   I   B

New Delhi

E   T

Lhasa

Sung

NEPAL

Brahmaputra   River

S Z E

Chengt

Tatu R.

Mt. Everest   SIKKIM

INDIA

BHUTAN

Mekong River

YUNNAN

Kunming

BURMA

0   100   200   300   400   500 miles

LAOS

THAILAND

Vienti

Lake Baikal

TRANS-SIBERIAN RAILROAD

Ulan Bator

Amur River

Argun River

GREAT KHINGAN RANGE

HEILUNGKIANG

KIRIN

Harbin

Kirin

Changchun

Vladivostok

Ussuri River

AU OLIA

DESERT

INNER MONGOLIA

LIAONING

Shenyang (Mukden)

Fushun

Yalu River

N. KOREA

Sea of Japan

Paotou

Yellow River

Tatung

Peking

Pyongyang

Tokyo

JAPAN

SHANSI

HOPEH

Tientsin

Port Arthur

Dairen

Seoul

S. KOREA

Taiyuan

Tsinan

Lungchow

Yellow Sea

Yenan

Tsian

Tai Shan

SHANTUNG

Tsingtao

SHENSI

Yellow River

Sian

Loyang Chengchow

HONAN

Tungpei

Huai R.

Yangchow

Nanking

KIANGSU

Shanghai

East China Sea

HUPEH

Hankow Wuchang

Hanyang

Yangtze River

ANHWEI

ngking

CHEKIANG

Changsha

HUNAN

KIANGSI

FUKIEN

Chikou

CHOW

veiyang

Yutu

Taipeh

FORMOSA

KWANGSI

KWANGTUNG

Canton

Si River

Swatow

TAIWAN

HONG KONG (U.K.)

MACAO (PORT.)

AM

HAINAN

South China Sea

PHILIPPINES

EDGAR SNOW'S
CHINA

A PERSONAL ACCOUNT OF THE CHINESE REVOLUTION COMPILED FROM THE WRITINGS OF EDGAR SNOW

BY LOIS WHEELER SNOW

Random House
New York

*Grateful acknowledgment is made to the following for permission to reprint previously
published material:*

American Mercury: Excerpts from an article by Edgar Snow which appeared in the
August 1930 issue of the *American Mercury.* Reprinted by permission of the American
Mercury, P.O. Box 73523, Houston, Texas.

Grove Press, Inc.: Excerpts from *Red Star Over China* are reprinted by permission of
Grove Press, Inc.

Harvard University Press: Excerpts reprinted from *Random Notes on China* by Edgar
Snow. Originally published by Harvard University Press. Reprinted by permission of
Harvard University Press. Two maps adapted from *The Communist Conquest of China*
by Lionel Max Chassin, translated from the French by Timothy Osato and Louis
Gelas. Copyright © 1965 by the President and Fellows of Harvard College. Reprinted
by permission of the publishers.

Nation Associates, Inc.: Excerpts from five articles by Edgar Snow which appeared in
the *Nation* magazine. Reprinted by permission of Nation Associates, Inc.

Adaptation of a map from *Red China Today* by Edgar Snow. Copyright 1961, 1962
by Edgar Snow. Copyright 1970 by Random House, Inc. Adaptation of map 18 from
A History of the Chinese Communist Party, 1921–1949 by Jacques Guillermaz. English
translation Copyright © 1972 by Methuen & Co. Ltd.

Random House, Inc.: Excerpts from the following books by Edgar Snow: *Far Eastern
Front;* Copyright 1933 and renewed 1961 by Edgar Snow. Excerpts from *The Long
Revolution;* Copyright © 1971, 1972 by Lois Wheeler Snow. Excerpts from *The Other
Side of the River;* Copyright © 1961, 1962 by Edgar Snow. Excerpts from *The Pattern of Soviet Power;* Copyright 1945 by Random House, Inc. Excerpts from *People
on Our Side;* Copyright 1944 by Random House, Inc. Excerpts from *Red China Today*
(Revised and Updated Edition of *The Other Side of the River*) ; Copyright © 1961,
1962 by Edgar Snow. Copyright © 1970 by Random House, Inc. All reprinted by
permission of Random House, Inc.

Saturday Evening Post: Three excerpts from articles by Edgar Snow which appeared
in the *Saturday Evening Post.* Reprinted from the *Saturday Evening Post,* Copyright
1937/1949/1954 by the Curtis Publishing Company.

Whitney Communications Corporation: Excerpts from an article by Edgar Snow
which appeared in the December 6, 1931, issue of the New York *Herald Tribune,* and
an excerpt from an article by Edgar Snow which appeared in the December 17, 1933,
issue of the New York *Herald Tribune.* © I.H.T. Corporation. Reprinted by permission.

Library of Congress Cataloging in Publication Data
Snow, Edgar, 1905–1972.
Edgar Snow's China.
Includes index.
1. China—History—Republic, 1912–1949.   2.   Communism
—China.   1.   Snow, Lois Wheeler.   II.   Title.
DS774.S58   1981   951.04   80-5267
ISBN 0-394-50954-4

Manufactured in the United States of America
2 4 6 8 9 7 5 3
First Edition

Design: Robert Aulicino

For *Peter, Frederic, Harris—*
and Inge and Anna

Contents

Foreword

Most of this book is by Edgar Snow. Because he is not here to put it together, I have done it in my own form and way. Many of the photographs were taken by him; all the text is his, culled by me from the books, letters, diaries, and newspaper and magazine articles he wrote as a foreign journalist in China from the time he reached Shanghai in 1928, until he watched from afar the victory of obscure "bandit men and women" when the country's civil war came to an end in 1949. Those victors included people he had known in the war-torn, tumultuous cities and in the vast, sprawling stretches of countryside, as well as in the loess-hill cave towns where outlawed leaders (for whose heads, severed or in place, the Kuomintang offered millions of dollars reward) had been joined by students, artists, workers, peasants and soldiers in common battle against foreign invaders and a "rich man's government which continued to feast as poor men starved and died."

He had been part of that. I know it only from his words, from the films and photographs he collected, and from the participants and onlookers I met during the twenty-five years I shared with him. This attempt to show through his eyes and written words the sequence of China's revolutionary course, and the people engaged in that strife, is mine merely in effort. The substance is Edgar Snow's. This he left in my care, and I have used a part of it to provide a background for those people —many born after the events—who would like to understand better the past of today's awakened giant. The result is not intended to be a history of China's revolution. It is an account of one man's efforts to *report* that revolution, a chronicle of his response to a country he saw fighting to unshackle itself from feudal bonds and crippling backwardness—a China diminished in pride and strength through foreign aggression and choked by its government's betrayal of its own revolution and an arrogant denial of its citizens' rights.

For well over a decade before the emergence of the People's Republic of China, Edgar Snow had, as an outside observer, unusual contact with those people and their leaders. He knew both the Kuomintang, which had inherited and subsequently misused the principles of the Nationalist government's founding father, Dr. Sun Yat-sen, as well as the Communists, who, fighting for those principles, albeit in the context of Chinese Marxism, gained the support of multitudes and achieved a radically different kind of revolution. His personal, intimate story is history witnessed as it unfolded. It is a direct outcome of traditional—if not always typical —American journalism, from a citizen of the "show me" state of Missouri.

I first met the author in 1946 at a Manhattan after-the-theater party given by actors, artists and writers, for Russian war relief—he, a well-known correspondent; I, a young actress whose Western roots had been transplanted to flourish forever (I thought at the time) in the city of New York. I knew him as the author of *Red Star Over China*, which I had read years before in the painstaking process of investigating the library my brother had built up to supplement the family's leather-covered editions of Dickens, Shakespeare, Thackeray and black-bound encyclopedia arrayed in well-worn rows in our Stockton, California, living room. Brother Ray's collection included some fascinating strangers: Dostoyevsky, Boccaccio, Théophile Gautier (whose enticing name was bestowed on at least one member of each generation of our pet goldfish), Faulkner, John Reed—and Edgar Snow. As readable as an epic novel, *Red Star* founded my interest in China, though my main concentration, however, in those years of Hitler, Franco, Mussolini, Hirohito and World War II, was on establishing myself as a Broadway actress. It was in this role that I married the returned war correspondent and became steadily more interested in international concerns. I continued work in theater, films and television until the then almighty hand of Senator Joseph McCarthy put a halt to both Ed's and my professional activities. Seeking less restrictive conditions, we moved, with our two children, to Switzerland. The change ended my cherished career as an actress, but Ed fared better. Newspapers and magazines abroad welcomed his knowledge and experience. Communications with Chinese citizens engaged in diplomatic and other normal affairs in European capitals (forbidden at that time in the United States) led to return trips to the People's Republic (also forbidden to almost all Americans in those years of hostility and mutual fear between the two countries). Our son Christopher and our daughter Sian ("Western Peace," in Chinese) grew up, therefore, on the shores of Lake Geneva and the forested slopes of the Swiss Jura, while I (slowly) forsook further ideas of Hollywood and Broadway. During this period Ed renewed his contacts with the China he had last seen in the early 1940s. On October 1, 1970, we were there—I for the first time—the two of us standing beside Mao Tse-tung on the great height of Peking's Tien An Men, sharing the cheers received by the Chinese leadership from the multitude thronged below in the enormous square. Above the crowd a gigantic sign urged the peoples of the world to "Unite to defeat the U.S. aggressors and all their running dogs!" It was an astonishing moment: our presence there among the Chinese heads of state carried a message of important change and Ed was the instrument through which those leaders chose to forecast that future.

Born in Kansas City, Missouri, in 1905, Ed was the youngest of three children. His father owned a small printing company which allowed the family modest living conditions and started off the third child's absorption with the printed word.

"My father," Ed wrote in his autobiography, "believed in making my brother and me work, on Saturdays and during vacations, 'to learn that money represents labor.' When I was nine I began to help carry packages from the Snow Printing Company to the *Kansas City Star*, a glamorous building with a great living heart in its pressroom. There I worshipped the editors from afar." And there in those early days the seed was planted which produced the young journalist years later in a country as far removed from his Midwestern birthplace as China.

Working summers as a not yet teen-age office boy for the Katy Line railway provided him with weekend passes for trips to the Ozarks and a beginning interest in travel. That led to greener pastures at age fourteen when, Ed recalled, he accompanied two schoolmates

in Bob's new Model T touring car, an adventure of which I managed to keep my parents in the dark until we were well on the way. For most of the trip we followed the then unpaved Santa Fe Trail, which over long stretches disappeared altogether in the sand and boulders. Bob joined his parents in Santa Monica; Charlie and I, having spent all our money, had to bum our way home. If I had not seen the Pacific that summer I might never have fixed so firmly in my mind the ambition to sail across it. And if I had not bummed my way on freight trains up the coast of California, and through the Feather River Canyon and the Royal Gorge of Colorado, I would not have known, so early, the taste of rough adventure, the infinite variety of nature and man, and the kindness of strangers to an adolescent just discovering that he had the muscle, if not the brains, to do a man's job in the world.

That autumn when I went back to high school I discovered in *Les Misérables* some "foreign" characters who reminded me of some of the workers and unemployed—just "bums" to respectable people—whom I had met and come to like during my summer's adventure. Hugo opened up a strange new world of ideas and great moral and political issues for me and involved me in history in a faraway and stirring time. It was only now that reading became vicarious travel for me and the second best thing to action. My early Wanderjahr and its consequences probably did more to shape my life than all my formal education. "A man's life," says the Chinese proverb, "is a candle in the wind."

The shape of Ed's life was global. He viewed the world as a whole, he embraced people and ideas from many lands, he knew the "have-gots" and the "have-nots," the mighty and the poor. A projected "year's travel round the world" after college stretched out to a lifetime of activities and relationships that kept him both in the mainstream and off the beaten path during the sixty-five years he spent on this troubled, and to him, often beautiful planet. China, and China's revolution, was a dominant factor in Ed's development. Arriving in the "Celestial Kingdom" in 1928, he remained, the first time, for well over a decade—fascinated by the history and heritage, held by the people and their time-hewn problems, intrigued by the rumblings of revolution heard in the distance beyond most foreigners' unconcern. When he sought out that revolution, and saw it up close, he responded, as a reporter and as a human being, to one of the most unusual and profound shake-ups in history.

Though Ed covered and wrote about vastly different, far-flung areas—India, Burma, Indochina, Iran, Arabia, Africa, Europe, Mexico and the Soviet

Union—in and out of war,* the name Snow became particularly identified with China. He describes his feelings about that personal association as he left thirteen years after his arrival, to return to the United States in 1941:

I would still be for the cause of China; in the main the cause of the Chinese was on the side of truth, of right and justice. I would be for any measure which might help the Chinese people to help themselves, for in that way only could they find themselves. But I would never again imagine that I personally was anything more to China than an alien corn adrift on vast tides of history with a logic of its own and beyond my power to alter or my birthright to judge.

Yet China had claimed a part of me even if I could make no claim on her. In place of my youthful ignorance of meanings of words and statistics there were real scenes and personalities—until famine now meant a naked young girl with breasts a million years old, and horror meant an army of rats I saw feasting on the suppurating flesh of still-living soldiers left helpless and untended on a charred battlefield; until rebellion meant the fury I felt when I saw a child turned into a pack animal and forced to walk on all fours, and "Communism" was a youthful peasant I knew fighting to avenge the execution of fifty-six members of his clan-family, held jointly responsible when three of its sons joined the Red Army; until war was the slit belly of a girl ravished and thrown naked before me on the streets of Chapei, and murder was the yellow corpse of an unwanted baby tossed onto a garbage heap in an alley near the Ministry of Health; until Japan's "anti-Communist leadership in Asia" was the feet and arms of orphan girls buried in the debris of a building bombed before my eyes, and inhumanity the laughter of idle men in silk watching one beggar choke another to death in a street fight in Szechuan over a handful of leftover rice; until I had seen dark frozen fear and cowardice in myself and courage and resolution in lowly men and women I had once childishly supposed my inferiors.

* As a reporter Edgar Snow represented at various times the Chicago *Tribune*, the London *Daily Herald*, the New York *Herald Tribune* and the New York *Sun*. His reports appeared in *Life* and the *Saturday Evening Post*, for which he became a world correspondent and an associate editor.

Yes, I would be part of that. And part of me would always remain with China's tawny hills, her terraced emerald fields, her island temples seen in the early morning mist, a few of her sons and daughters who had trusted or loved me, her bankrupt cheerful civilized peasants who had sheltered and fed me, her brown, ragged, shining-eyed children, the equals and the lovers I had known, and above all the lousy, unpaid, hungry, despised, peasant foot-soldier who in the mysterious sacrifice of his own life alone now gave value to all life and put the stamp of nobility upon the struggle of a great people to survive and to go forward.

After the founding of the People's Republic Ed returned to China on three long visits—singular events for an American during those years of armed support for Chiang Kai-shek on Taiwan and the quarantine placed by the United States government on the newly born country. Civil war had ended and the revolutionaries had come to power. But the country had been plundered and impoverished, and faced new problems that compounded those existing from the past: lack of enough productive land, and food to fill the millions of bellies; industries impaired, communications disrupted or destroyed; families sacrificed to the ravages of war and uncontrolled nature. The treasury, and treasures, of China had been shipped away by alert Kuomintang leaders long before their fall, and more loot had been ripped off by others fleeing at the last minute to Hong Kong, Taiwan or Riverdale, New York. To flush out hidden enemy agents, to eradicate gangsterism and criminals who fed off the vulnerable, to rehabilitate prostitutes and drug addicts, to furnish housing, provide education, build up and dispense medical care, to pull together the millions of disparate citizens, to salvage the weak, to reach the remote, these endless obstacles had to be surmounted by the new government.

In 1960 Ed returned to China for his first visit since the end of World War II. For a decade, no other American correspondent had been there, and he would remain, for almost a decade more, the only one. He saw the Chinese coping with and surviving the effects of external embargo and internal hardship, and encountered a China engaged in new battles, standing up against adversities and isolation, armed mainly with the tremendous labor power of its hard-working citizens. But few Americans understood—few, even, were interested in understanding—the realities of an enormous Communist China they saw as a giant threat to their security and well-being. Secondhand reports pictured millions of "blue ants" starving to death under maniacal leaders bent on taking over the "civilized world." The United Nations meekly followed the United States in ostracizing the one fourth of humanity who lived in the People's Republic, and anyone who wrote with objectivity and knowledge on the subject was looked upon as a partisan and proselytizer. Over the years, while the United States denied the real China's existence, Ed had conversations lasting many hours with Mao Tse-tung, Chou En-lai and others in the party hierarchy, as well as with the people, high and low, whom he met on trips which reached far into the provinces and hinterlands. He questioned, probed, discussed and wrote extensively about what he saw and heard, though with the exception of two books published in the United States,* this information—and this unique and close American link with Chinese leadership—was discounted or disparaged by much of the American press† and by most of the American government. Numerous overtures made by the People's Republic to reopen communications with the United States had been rebuffed, and by 1960 Ed's return to China was, in his words, "strenuously opposed by the Eisenhower Administration, as had been true of every effort made by Americans on a non-official level who understood something of the historical contradictions, and their portent for the U.S.A." Once back in Peking, Ed realized that certain Chinese leaders were hopeful that his visit "might help build a bridge or two," though they clearly stated their doubt that the United States was interested in bridge building. Reflecting on that, Ed wrote:

I thought they exaggerated the resistance of Washington to the introduction of useful information. When I returned to the United States, however, I had to revise my opinion;

* Red China Today (New York: Random House, Vintage Books, 1971), and The Long Revolution (Random House, 1972).
† Look magazine sponsored the trip to China in 1960 but published only one of three contracted pieces. Magazines of limited and special circulation, The Nation, New Republic and Monthly Review, quite often carried Snow's articles during those years. It was Le Nouveau Candide in Paris which first brought out his articles in 1964–65 and the Milan weekly Epoca, the series from 1970. These had wide distribution and attention throughout Western Europe and in Japan.

the official wall was a great deal more solid than I had supposed. After a brief colloquy with Dean Rusk, the newly appointed Secretary of State [of the Kennedy Administration], I was left with the impression that the Chinese had been right. . . . It would take a long time and very much hard work by the "alert and knowledgeable citizenry" to break out of the trap. That it would change, that it was gradually changing, was becoming evident. There would be strong counterattacks against agonizing attempts to reach an objective understanding, which would be denounced as appeasement. The way ahead was hard but the bridges could, and ultimately must, be built.

All that was "pre–Ping-Pong." In 1971, when the American table-tennis team was unexpectedly invited to visit Peking—and accepted the invitation—the resulting thaw affected the freeze on America's most directly informed China reporter. Life magazine eagerly seized the opportunity to publish an article by Edgar Snow in which he revealed that Mao Tse-tung had personally informed him Richard Nixon would be welcome to visit China, "either as a tourist or as President."

It was Ed's last "scoop." His reporting stopped when he died of cancer the very week the then President began his journey to Peking—an almost unbelievable irony, considering the careers of the two men. Ed was not only aware of the significance of the presidential voyage, he was also aware of the "triumph of lies and slander, spearheaded by McCarthy and Nixon, which charged Roosevelt, Marshall, Stilwell, Truman, Acheson and loyal men of the U.S. Foreign Service with betrayal of our country and 'selling China to the Russians.'"

After Ed died, I took half of his ashes to China to be buried in a small green garden on the campus of Peking University. This had once been part of Yenching, where he had taught journalism and learned from the political courage of Chinese youths that history can, indeed, be changed. Later, in the United States, I placed the remaining ashes in the garden of a friend's home beside the Hudson River, according to a request Ed left on a piece of paper he meant me to see when he was no longer here. He had written:

I love China. I should like part of me to stay there after death as it always did during life. America fostered and nourished me. I should like part of me placed by the Hudson River, before it enters the Atlantic to touch Europe and all the shores of mankind of which I felt a part, as I have known good men in almost every land.

Premier Chou En-lai and his wife, Teng Ying-chao, along with other Chinese and foreign friends, attended the ceremony in Peking. Chinese representatives to the United Nations and different friends and family performed equally simple and beautiful rites in New York.

Ed was joined in death in 1976 by three of China's best-beloved "Red bandits"—Chou En-lai, Chu Teh and, finally, Mao Tse-tung. Their long-held hope was fulfilled several years later when other sometime Chinese "bandits," led by Vice Premier Teng Hsiao-ping and Foreign Minister Huang Hua, traveled to Washington, D.C., to formalize recognition and friendship between the Chinese and American peoples and governments. It was a time for rejoicing—perhaps, who knows, even for those "out there," where kindred souls may have echoed an ethereal "ganbei."

Because of my husband's special experience with China's past, I have put together relevant excerpts from his writings to provide some firsthand insight on the why and how of the birth of the People's Republic of China, recorded by a man who was on the scene during its gestation. "Behind its revolutionary choice of today," Ed noted, "lie reasons of history quite unlike those which made the United States and Western Europe."

In composing this book, I have taken material quite freely out of context—paragraphs out of chapters, sentences out of paragraphs, and at times, I have deleted words from sentences for continuity's sake. I have sometimes changed present-tense verbs to past tense, to avoid confusion between what took place when the author was writing about events he had just witnessed, and what is happening today. I trust that in doing this I have not distorted or changed any original meanings, even though such selectivity does result in major simplification that could only be prevented if I used the whole—an obvious impossibility in view of the size and scope of this presentation.

In *Red Star Over China* and the other Snow books, the Wade-Giles system of transliteration (romanization) is used. I have changed this to what can be called "modified Wade-Giles"—that is, dropping the aspirates employed to aid in pronunciation in that system (as in Teng Hsiao-p'ing) but keeping the hyphen (as in Mao Tse-tung). I made the decision not to use the new *pin yin* method, which is now employed in China and in most current foreign translations of the Chinese language, simply because to do so would drastically alter the original text.

For those who are interested in reading the works from which these excerpts have been taken, at the back of the book there is a list of Edgar Snow's eleven books. Many public libraries can supply a complete accumulation of his detailed reporting.

A word about the photographs. They come from different sources. A good many were taken by Ed himself. He photographed first as a "tourist," then as a journalist—always as an amateur—from his arrival in China. His was the first pictorial account made of the newly arrived Red Army in far northwestern China in 1936. A great regret to him was the limited amount of film he was able to bring with him on the hazardous journey that took him into the life of those people who were to become the founders of a new China. That any of the photographed results returned with him was a near miracle. On that visit, the Chinese Communists also allowed him to copy a few rare photographs which survived the Long March and which show some of the people and events in the Kiangsi soviets (1928–35), prior to the enforced retreat from the Southeast to their new base in Shensi.

The photograph on the jacket cover has a story behind it. In Peking, in 1979, I visited the home of my good friends Gladys and Yang Hsien-yi. By sheer coincidence that evening I met a young worker, Fu Ching-sheng, a relative of the Yangs, who had come to present them with a woodcut of Edgar Snow against a background of scenes out of *Red Star* times. It is Ed's entrance into the folk art of China. Lu Hsun, China's most prestigious modern writer, fathered the woodcut movement in his country. He encouraged young artists to take up the art as an easy and inexpensive way to record and reflect the life of the people and the time. That Fu Ching-sheng, worker-artist, chose an American journalist as his subject is implicit recognition of the role of Edgar Snow as a friend of the Chinese people and recorder of their revolutionary struggle.

Friends contributed generously. They make up a group of international personalities intimately associated with China's revolution; among them are Rewi Alley, Ma Hai-teh, Chou Su-fei, Anna Wang Martens, James Bertram, Israel Epstein and Frederic Dahlmann. It was to Anna Martens that Mao

Tse-tung said, "If you haven't had lice yet, you don't understand China." Anna understood; so did all the abovementioned. The American theater photographer Joseph Abeles, who found himself in unfamiliar drama (and lice) in World War II, allowed me the use of his pictures of Kunming at that time.

The People's Republic of China was equally generous. Under the auspices of the Chinese People's Friendship Association and its president, Wang Ping-nan, I was given access to museums and photo archives in Peking, where most records of the revolution are available. China Photos, the Museum of Revolutionary History, *China Reconstructs* magazine, and the Military Museum were the principal contributors. The Chungking Photo Archives supplied photographs of that important wartime locale. I was wonderfully assisted by Hao Po, who herself took many photographs from the Yenan days on through the 1949 victory, and by my hostesses, Yu Shih-liang and Pu Nin.

Inge Morath accompanied me to China in the spring of 1979 to lend her keen professional eye to the complex task of choosing from the hundreds of pictures that the Chinese put for our selection. On our return to the United States she, in spite of her own pressing work, continued with invaluable pictorial help and advice as the book took on its present form.

Though I alone am responsible for the selection of text, I owe a debt of gratitude to those who helped me in that selection or who, in various ways, assisted in the shaping of this undertaking. John Service and Edmund Clubb were of particular encouragement and help from the beginning, as was a host of friends who especially include Harris Russell, Peter Entell, Frederic Dahlmann, John Fairbank, Anna Wang Martens, Mark Selden, Jean Highland, Trudie Schafer, Mary Heathcote, Jean Pohoryles, Hans Maeder, James Bertram, Israel Epstein, Norma Chan, James Peck, Achilles Demain, Frank Taylor, Douglas and Marie Gorsline, Jack Belden, my sister Kashin Wheeler, and my son and daughter, Christopher and Sian Snow.

Lois Wheeler Snow
New York, N.Y.

Chronology

1911

Republican revolution (the "First Revolution") overthrows Manchu power in Central and South China. At Nanking, Sun Yat-sen declared president of provisional government, first Chinese Republic. Student Mao Tse-tung joins rebel army; resigns after six months, thinking "revolution over."

II. The Republic and the Warlords (1912–27)

1912

Rulers of Manchu Dynasty formally abdicate. Sun Yat-sen resigns in favor of Yuan Shih-kai, as president of the Republic of China. Peking is its capital. Kuomintang (Nationalists) dominates first parliament, forms cabinet. Italy takes Libya.

1912–14

Provisional constitution and parliament suspended by militarist Yuan Shih-kai, who becomes dictator. European war begins.

1915

Japan imposes "Twenty-one Demands," their effort to reduce China to vassal state. Yuan Shih-kai accepts most of the demands. Cabinet resigns. Japan seizes Tsingtao, a German concession in China. Yuan Shih-kai attempts to re-establish monarchy, with himself as emperor.

1916

Second (Republican) Revolution; overthrow of Yuan Shih-kai by "revolt of the generals" led by Tsai O. Era of warlords begins.

1917

Peking "shadow government" declares war on Germany. Generalissimo Sun Yat-sen, heading separate provisional regime in Canton, also declares war. In Hunan, Mao Tse-tung becomes co-founder of radical youth group. The October Revolution occurs in Russia.

1918

End of World War I. Mao Tse-tung becomes assistant to Li Ta-chao, librarian of Peking University.

1918–19

175,000 laborers sent overseas to help allies, 400 "Work-Study" students include Chou En-lai.

1919

May Fourth Movement. Nationwide student demonstrations against Versailles Treaty award of Germany's China concessions to Japan. Beginning of modern nationalist movement.

1920

League of Nations established.

1921

Chinese Communist Party formally organized at First Congress, Shanghai. Mao is chosen secretary of CP of Hunan. Revolution in Mongolia.

1923

Sun Yat-sen agrees to accept Soviet aid and form united front with CCP. Communists may now hold joint membership in Kuomintang, led by Sun.

III. Nationalist Revolution; KMT-Communist United Front (1923–27)

1923

At Third Congress of CCP, in Canton, Mao Tse-tung elected to Central Committee and chief of organization.

1925

Sun Yat-sen dies. Chiang Kai-shek becomes commander in chief.

1926

Nationalist Northern Expedition launched from Canton under supreme military command of Chiang Kai-shek.

IV. First Communist Nationalist Civil War (1927–37)

1927

Stalin victorious over Trotsky. Mao Tse-tung calls poor peasants "main force" of revolution, demands confiscation of landlords' land. In April, Chiang Kai-shek leads anti-Communist coup, "beheads party"; Communists reduced, by four-fifths, to 10,000. Mao leads peasant uprising in Hunan (August); defeated, he flees to mountain stronghold, Chingkangshan.

1928

Chiang Kai-shek establishes nominal centralized control over China under Nationalist government (a Kuomintang, one-party dictatorship). Mao and Chu Teh form first "Red Army" of China.

1929

Mao Tse-tung and Chu Teh conquer rural territories around Juichin, Kiangsi, where a soviet government is proclaimed. Communist Politburo, dominated by Li Li-san, remains hidden in foreign-controlled Shanghai. Stock market crash in New York.

1930

Conflict between Mao's "rural soviet movement" and Politburo leader Li Li-san, who favors urban insurrections. Red Army led by Mao and Peng Teh-huai captures Changsha, capital of Hunan, then withdraws. Second assault on Changsha a costly failure. Li Li-san discredited by Moscow. Chiang Kai-shek launches first major offensive against the Reds. Mao Tse-tung's wife and sister executed in Changsha. Gandhi leads nonviolent civil disobedience in India.

1931

Spain declares a Republic. Meeting underground in January, in Shanghai, Central Committee of CCP elects Wang Ming (Chen Shao-yu), general secretary and chief of party. All-China Congress of Chinese Soviets, convened in deep hinterland at Juichin, elects Mao Tse-tung chairman of the first All-China Soviet Government, Chu Teh military commander. In September, Japan begins conquest of Manchuria; Chiang Kai-shek suspends his third "annihilation campaign" against Red Army. End of Great Famine (1929–31) in Northwest China; estimated dead, five to ten million. Wang Ming goes to Moscow. Po Ku heads Shanghai Politburo.

1932

Japan attacks Shanghai, defended by Nineteenth Route Army; unsupported by Chiang Kai-shek, it retreats to Fukien province. Chiang authorizes Tangku Truce, to end Sino-Japanese hostilities. He renews offensive against Kiangsi soviet; Reds declare war on Japan. Police in Shanghai International Settlement help Chiang Kai-shek extirpate Red underground. Politburo chiefs Po Ku, Lo Fu, Liu Shao-chi and Chou En-lai join Mao in Kiangsi soviet. Roosevelt elected President of U.S.

1933

Nineteenth Route Army rebels and offers alliance to Reds, which is rejected. Chiang Kai-shek destroys Nineteenth R.A., begins a new campaign against Soviet China. Hitler becomes Chancellor of Germany.

1934

Second All-China Soviet Congress re-elects Mao Tse-tung chairman, but party leadership falls to "Twenty-eight Bolsheviks." Red Army changes tactics and suffers decisive defeats. Main forces and party cadres retreat to West China.

1935

Politburo meets in Tsunyi, Kweichow, in January; elects Mao Tse-tung effective leader of the party and army during Long March to Northwest China. In July, Kiangsi Red forces reach Szechuan and join troops under Politburo member and party co-founder Chang Kuo-tao, driven from soviet areas north of Yangtze River. In enlarged meeting of Politburo, Chang Kuo-tao disputes Mao's policy and leadership. Red forces divide; Mao leads southern forces into new base in Northwest China, after one year of almost continuous marching, totaling 6,000 miles. (Chang Kuo-tao follows him a year later.) Japan demands separation of two North China provinces, under "autonomous" regime. December 9 student rebellion in Peking touches off wave of anti-Japanese national patriotic activity. Italy seizes Ethiopia.

1936

Mao Tse-tung, interviewed by the author in Paoan, Shensi, tells his life story and his account of the revolution, and offers to end civil war to form a united front against Japan. Mao lectures to the Red Army University; his *On the Tactics of Fighting Japanese Imperialism* and *Strategic Problems in China's Revolutionary War* become doctrinal basis of new stage of united front against Japan. Spurning Communists' offer of a truce (first made on August 1, 1935), Chiang Kai-shek mobilizes for "final annihilation" of Reds in Northwest.

The Sian Incident, in December: Chiang Kai-shek "arrested" by his deputy commander in chief, Chang Hsueh-liang, exiled Manchurian leader. Marshal Chang insists that Chiang accept national united front against Japan. Following Chiang Kai-shek's release, and undeclared truce in civil war, Kuomintang opens negotiations with CCP and its "anti-Japanese government" based in Yenan, Shensi.

V. "United Front" against Japan: The Great Patriotic, or Anti-Japanese, War (1937–45)

1937

In July, Japan massively invades China. Agreement signed for joint Nationalist-Communist war of resistance against Japan. Chinese Soviet Government dissolved but continues as autonomous regional regime; Red Army becomes Eighth Route and New Fourth armies under Chiang's nominal command. Mao writes theoretical works, *On Contradiction* and *On Practice*. Italy leaves the League of Nations.

1938

Mao outlines Communists' wartime political and military ends and means in *On the New Stage, On the Protracted War* and *Strategic Problems in the Anti-Japanese Guerrilla War*. Chang Kuo-tao goes over to Kuomintang. Mao becomes undisputed leader of Party. Japanese armies overwhelm North China. Nationalists retreat to west. Communists organize partisans far behind Japanese lines. Nazi Germany annexes Austria and Czechoslovakia.

1939

Mao's *On the New Democracy* outlines class basis of united front, intimates future coalition-government structure. Rapid expansion of Communist cadres and military forces. Hitler-Stalin pact. Germany attacks Poland. With outbreak of European war, China's struggle begins to merge with World War II. Yenan blockaded by Nationalist troops.

1940–41

Breakdown of practical cooperation between Communists and Nationalists follows Chiang Kai-shek's attack on New Fourth Army. Chen-Yi becomes its commander. After Pearl Harbor, Kuomintang relies on American aid, while Communists vigorously expand guerrilla areas.

1942

CCP "rectification" campaign centers on Wang Ming and Moscow-trained "dogmatists"; Mao's "native" leadership enhanced.

1943

Mao Tse-tung credited (by Liu Shao-chi) with having "created a Chinese or Asiatic form of Marxism." Attraction of "New Democracy" proves widespread among peasants and intellectuals; Kuomintang morale and fighting capacity rapidly decline. Chou En-lai claims 800,000 party members, a half-million troops and trained militia, in "liberated areas" exceeding 100 million population. Fascism collapses in Italy. By decree, Stalin abolishes the Comintern.

1944

U.S. Army "observers" arrive in Yenan, Communist "guerrilla" capital. Allied landing in Normandy. President Roosevelt re-elected.

1945

Seventh National Congress of CCP (April) claims Party membership of 1,200,000, with armed forces of 900,000. Germany defeated. Russia enters Far Eastern war; signs alliance with Chiang Kai-shek's government. Mao's report *On Coalition Government* becomes formal basis of Communist demands to end Kuomintang dictatorship. After V-E Day, Communist-led forces flood North China and Manchuria, competing with American-armed Nationalists. U.S. Ambassador Hurley flies Mao Tse-tung to Chungking to negotiate with Chiang Kai-shek. Yalta Pact promises Taiwan to China. Death of Roosevelt. Truman uses atomic bomb on Hiroshima. End of World War II.

VI. Second Communist-Nationalist Civil War (1946–49)

1946

Nationalists and Communists fail to agree on "coalition government"; in July renewed civil war, called by the Communists the War of Liberation, also the Third Revolutionary Civil War, begins. Under Soviet Russian occupation, Eastern Europe "goes Red."

1947

Mao's *The Present Situation and Our Tasks* outlines strategic and tactical plans, calling for general offensive against Nationalists. Truman Doctrine proclaimed for Greece and Turkey.

1948

Despite U.S. aid to Nationalists, their defeat in Manchuria is overwhelming. Yugoslavia is expelled from Cominform, postwar successor to the Comintern.

1949

As his armies disintegrate, Chiang Kai-shek flees to Taiwan. Over the rest of China, the People's Liberation Army is victorious. In March, the Central Committee of the CCP, led by Mao, arrives in Peking. Atlantic Pact (NATO) proclaimed. U.S. "White Paper" blames Chiang's "reactionaries" for "loss of China."

EDGAR SNOW'S
CHINA

Edgar Snow in 1929, at Tai Shan, the birthplace of Confucius, with a young descendant of the ancient sage.

1

BACKGROUND TO REVOLUTION: FROM CONFUCIUS TO MAO

To attempt to condense China's long history into a brief chapter may be an affront to scholars but excusable as a service to readers unfamiliar with the rudiments of that history. Confucius thought that if he showed a man one corner of a thing, he should be able to discover the other corner for himself.

The stage which has witnessed what is to some "the world's oldest continuous civilization" and to others "the world's continuous tragedy" is a multinational country with an area of about 3,705,000 square miles; that is, a country 90,000 square miles larger than the United States. China reached its present boundaries (including Tibet, Turkestan and Inner Mongolia) many centuries ago; in times past the empire was larger than today. Two thirds of the People's Republic, however, is mountainous, desert or land otherwise unfit for cultivation. In 1960 slightly less than 12 percent of the total area was utilized as cropland and there were formidable problems to be overcome before substantially more marginal acreage could be brought under cultivation. By contrast, 17 percent of the area of the United States was cropland and a large portion of an additional 22 percent (in grassland pasture) could readily be cultivated. With close to four times as many people as the United States, the Chinese had to feed themselves on 40 percent less cropland. In order to equal American agricultural output, *per person*, China would have to raise her product per acre to almost six times as much—if confined to the present cropland area—as the American output per acre.

If one superimposed a transparent map of China on a map of the United States, the

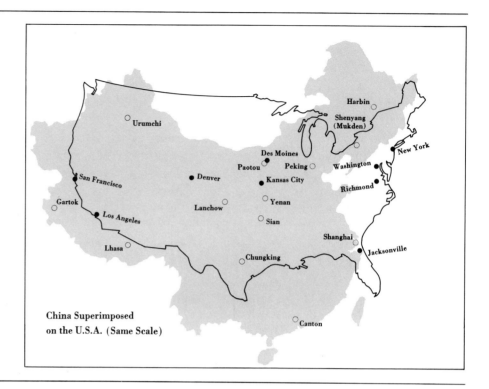

China Superimposed
on the U.S.A. (Same Scale)

two countries would correspond fairly closely in latitude and dimensions. Both lie mainly in the temperate zone. In the south, China would extend into northern Mexico and the Caribbean, and in the northeast it would reach far into Canada. China's southernmost point (the island of Hainan) would be at Haiti, and her westernmost area (Sinkiang or Chinese Turkestan) would reach a little beyond San Francisco. Shanghai would lie near Jacksonville, Washington would correspond to Peking, New York to Shenyang in Manchuria, and Los Angeles would be somewhere in western Tibet. The topographies differ greatly. China is landlocked except for her eastern seacoast. The world's highest mountain ranges and plateaus rim her southwest and western borders, and in the north lie the Mongolian desert and a frosty frontier shared with Soviet Siberia.

Until the nineteenth century the Pacific shut China off from, rather than connecting it with, the outside world. China looked inward and was a land power, not a great maritime nation. Mountains and desert both sheltered and isolated her from continental neighbors and Europe. Contacts with the West existed but made little impact on the civilization that grew up along the Yellow River—whose origin, on that superimposed map, would be somewhere around Denver, and its exit near Richmond, Virginia. China developed in almost total isolation from the West. The term Chungkuo, which the

Chinese still call their country, means Central Realm. The Ptolemaic conception of the world remains deeply imbedded in Chinese psychology even today.

Legendary Chinese history begins more than five thousand years ago. Dates of the beginning and end of the Shang and Chou dynasties are debatable, but writing on oracle bones and on bamboo offers an increasingly authentic record from the later Shang Dynasty (1523 B.C. onward). The classical period in which the civilization acquired characteristics preserved into our times was the Chou Dynasty (1027–249 B.C.) and Kung Fu-tze, or Confucius (551–479 B.C.), was its outstanding personality. His teachings gradually became state doctrine, and after the Later Han Dynasty (A.D. 23–220) Confucianism dominated the social and political thinking and the whole form and style of Chinese civilization for twenty centuries.

Lao-tzu (whose name means "Old One"), a whimsical mystic said to have been a contemporary of Confucius, preached a rival philosophy of Tao, or "The Way," of harmony with nature, which has little in common with the Confucian doctrines. Lao-tzu's teachings embraced a concept of the unity of opposites and dialecticism which had similarities with Platonism and many points in common with Hindu and Buddhistic philosophy. Lao-tzu was not a religious teacher, but his thought was corrupted and combined with traditional geomancy in what became the native religion of China, Taoism. The dialectical nature of the *Tao Teh Ching*, which contains the essence of the "Old One's" philosophy, suggests analogies with the schematic analytical methods of dialectical Marxism. (The authenticity of writings attributed to both Confucius and Lao-tzu is much disputed by scholars. Lao-tzu is far from established as a historical person.)

Confucius was not a religious teacher either. With some reservations it may be said that China was never essentially a religious country so much as a nation ruled by morals, ethics, conventions and philosophy. "Respect the spirits," Confucius is reputed to have said after a dialogue with Lao-tzu, "but keep them at a distance." He was China's first great reformer, a humanistic, practical codifier of the inherited wisdom of the ancients. He sought to "remold" everybody from ruling princes to peasants into "superior men," although he showed less interest in reforming nobles and aristocrats than in "undertaking to make men of humble background into 'gentlemen' able to hold their own in the halls of state with the most polished courtiers," according to one outstanding Confucian scholar and biographer of the sage, Professor Herrlee Glessner Creel. "Confucius himself wished to become a man of perfect virtue and to teach others without weariness."

Confucius lived when the Chou Dynasty was breaking up into the "Warring States," and Chou sovereignty was only nominal over some five thousand petty principalities somewhat comparable to the contemporary city-states of Greece. Chinese scholars revere Confucius for having edited the classics and having written the *Spring and Autumn Annals,* a work of literature as influential as the Bible and equally disputed as absolutely reliable history. A generation or more ahead of Periclean Greece, Confucius concerned himself with the same problems of human intercourse. His social and political teachings were moralistic, benevolent, traditional, realistic and authoritarian in contrast with the dynamism of the ideal republic and other lively abstractions of Socrates, Aristotle and Plato. All were equally concerned with the qualities of virtue in rulers and the attainment of an ideal society, but Confucius found answers very different from those of the Greeks.

He prescribed a code of behavior between all members of the family in which women obeyed and deferred to men, younger brothers to elder brothers, sons to fathers, and patriarchs to men of superior rank. All men rendered homage to the emperor, who was regarded as an embodiment of Confucian virtue and innate wisdom and moral superiority, the Head of the Great Family or Nation. Dynasties rose and fell, but the Confucian pattern was changeless. Administration under the emperor lay in the hands of a small Confucian-scholar class, access to which was in theory democratic. Anyone who could pass the examinations could qualify, and open opportunity represented the ideal of equality. In practice this meant a monopoly of power held by a gentry-scholar class over peasant masses organized in the family system and kept in order by filial piety, ancestor worship and imperial edicts.

Confucianism provided China with the world's most stable system of bureaucratic power. It was natural for the Chinese to look upon it as the only "correct" method of regulation of human relations and to regard themselves as superior men. China was never challenged by any advanced civilization until modern times; though sometimes defeated by culturally inferior tribes, she always ended by civilizing and absorbing them. Chinese civilization made original advances in the arts, science, industry and agriculture, and Europe borrowed many of its inventions. Treating their immediate neighbors as vassals, the Chinese conceived of the rest of the world as barbarians.

Capsulated Chinese history inevitably leaves the impression that nothing really happened after the Chou and Han dynasties. That would be as erroneous as to assert that in Europe nothing happened after Pericles until Copernicus was born. Immensely important changes, refinements and creative contributions to human culture continued despite long interregnums of regression under barbarian conquerors. As instances become relevant, I shall cite a few as we proceed. For the moment, three examples of Western loss through isolation from the Middle Kingdom: the Chinese were using elaborate water clocks six hundred years before one was independently invented in Europe; water-powered armillaries were turning in China three hundred years before Copernicus; and the Chinese invented printing roughly five centuries before Gutenberg produced movable type. China lost much from isolation also: for instance, Europe invented the mechanical clock in the fourteenth century, but it did not reach China until the seventeenth century; and although China invented gunpowder hundreds of years before the West, she failed to develop the uses of her marvelous firecrackers in time to avoid prolonged humiliation at the hands of the Christians.

For centuries China had some contacts with the West, but nothing her merchants and travelers reported changed her opinion of Europe's inferiority. Occasional envoys were received as representatives of vassal states, and a few early Jesuit missionaries at the Manchu court were tolerated more as curiosities than as cultural equals. China's isolation from the West was finally broken in the nineteenth century, when she was invaded from the sea. From the 1840s onward, the British and French wars forced China to permit the importation of opium and other trade with the West. Britain took Hong Kong and Kowloon, and extended her control over Burma and Nepal, which had been tributary vassals of Peking. In 1883 France defeated China and ended her suzerainty in Indochina. During the latter half of the century the waning Manchu power was repeatedly humiliated by violence, as China's major ocean and river ports fell under foreign control and she became a semicolony not of one nation but of all the major industrial and naval powers. A series of territorial and political concessions gave the foreigners effective control over China's trade and she seemed destined to be divided among them like India and Southeast Asia.

In the middle of the last century there occurred the Taiping ("Heavenly Peace") Rebellion, a titanic effort to overthrow the corrupt Manchu Dynasty and establish a revolutionary power. The rebellion, which reached the walls of Peking, was led by an able Chinese Christian convert, Hung Hsiu-chuan, who proclaimed himself the younger brother of Jesus Christ. Members of the Peace Corps today might tolerate a revelation of this nature by a promising nationalist in the "back lands," but it was too much for our rigid nineteenth-century missionaries. They disowned their most promising convert as a sacrilegious impostor. They were even more shocked by some of his Christian reforms. Although there is no evidence that Taiping leaders had ever heard of Marx or the *Communist Manifesto*, they had some points of similarity. Reformers in Chinese history from pre-Confucian times had reported (e.g., Rites of Chou) early egalitarian societies in which land was held in common and production and distribution were shared by all. Taiping leaders made attempts to establish this kind of primitive communism. Land was distributed, with priority given to men between sixteen and fifty. Slavery and the sale of women and children were abolished together with foot-binding, prostitution, arranged marriages and polygamy. The importation of opium was prohibited, and torture and cruel punishments were supposedly forbidden. Armies participated in production and tilled fields in common, much as on the state farms (as distinct from communes) of New China.

After fourteen years of civil war, said to have cost forty million lives, the rebellion was finally defeated by the armies of Tseng Kuo-fan, a Chinese scholar-general from Hunan. He was helped by Western mercenaries, first led by an American adventurer, Frederick Townsend Ward, and later by General Charles Gordon and other regular British army and navy officers, supported by the British government. Tseng was helped still more by decay and corruption among Taiping leaders, who failed to abide by their own principles. But the suppression of the Taiping rebellion was a Chinese victory, and the Manchu Dynasty thereafter was held hostage to the Chinese reactionary landlord-gentry-scholar class, by whom it was assimilated. The victory also increased the subservience of the Manchu Dynasty to Western imperialism, until it finally collapsed from inner rot, more than from outer assault, in 1912.

Japan had meanwhile joined the imperial overlords; in 1895 Japan defeated China, seized Taiwan, and ended China's suzerainty in Korea. With financial support from the United States, Japan fought Russia over the Chinese territory of Manchuria and defeated her. She took over the Russian naval base at Port Arthur, Dairen, and Russian railway rights and concessions in south Manchuria—all of which had been pried from Peking. Czarist Russia retained Siberia (annexed the previous century), railway concessions in north Manchuria, and a protectorate over Mongolia—where, however, Peking's sovereignty was still nominally recognized.

All through these years the reformist spirit and patriotism of the Taipings continued to seed the underground revolutionary movements, as it later also persisted throughout the Nationalist and the Communist periods. In 1900 the secret societies provided the leadership for the fanatical anti-foreign Boxer Rebellion. When the Boxers were crushed by an Allied invasion of Peking, the European powers, Japan and the United States together imposed crushing indemnities on the dynasty which robbed it of all remaining prestige. By the time it faded away not only the major powers but small states such as Belgium, Holland and Portugal had become part of the Western dominance which made China a semicolony. The United States took no territorial concessions but fully shared in the whole system of unequal treaties by securing for its nationals all the privileges of the "most favored nation"—a euphemism also reflected in John Hay's so-called Open Door doctrine, of equal rights for all, in trade and exploitation. Under the unequal treaties, foreign nationals had extraterritorial rights which enabled them to reside and do business in China while remaining accountable only to their own courts.

Following the demise of the Manchu Dynasty, attempts were made to set up a parliamentary republic, for which the nation was wholly unprepared. Western-educated Sun Yat-sen, an exiled hero of the national independence movement, was elected president of the provisional republican government.

Sun Yat-sen and the Chinese Republic

When, in 1912, China became a republic, it was in name only. There is something profoundly charming, in retrospect, about the whimsical audacity with which the young revolutionaries proclaimed the end of an ancient theocracy. Perhaps one percent of China's population at that time knew what *min kuo* (republic) meant. Long after Emperor Pu Yi abdicated, a certain vagueness concerning the term prevailed in the mass mind of China.

A friend of mine told a story to illustrate the extremely limited horizon of the Chinese peasant. He went one day into a small village to lecture on nationalism and the principles of statehood advanced by Dr. Sun Yat-sen, "father of the Chinese republic." At the conclusion of his talk, to which the village elders listened attentively, a white-haired, bearded patriarch arose and expressed the curiosity that all keenly felt. "I have lived in this village seventy years," he declared. "I know every important man within fifteen *li* [five miles] of here, and yet none by this name Sun Yat-sen. Tell us, who is he?" That is comparable to an American asking, "Who is George Washington?"

Sun Yat-sen lacked armed forces and was obliged to defer to the former chief of the imperial troops, Yuan Shih-kai. When Yuan subsequently proclaimed himself emperor he was quickly overthrown by rival militarists. Disunity and chaos reigned as provincial satraps struggled for supremacy and the foreign powers vied with each other to control them. Meanwhile, Sun Yat-sen and the Kuomintang, or Nationalist party, made alliances with various warlords. Repeatedly Sun failed to establish a stable basis for a successor to the weak, corrupt, semipuppet and largely impotent warlord-dominated governments at Peking.

Dr. Sun was spurned by all the foreign powers until after World War I, in which the Peking government had, as a result of great pressure from the United States in particular, joined the Allies. China had expected that the defeat of Germany would result in the rendition to her of Germany's colonial holdings in Shantung; at Versailles the Allied Powers revealed that they had (except for the United States) signed secret treaties awarding the Shantung concessions to Japan. All Chinese patriots were bitterly disillusioned. These included many youths who had volunteered for service in Europe and had gone there as leaders of China's labor corps. (Chinese were then considered unfit material for soldiers.) Among the members of this Work-Study movement who became prominent in

Sun Yat-sen was elected president of the Chinese Republic in 1911 and later served as director of the Kuomintang ("National People's Party") until his death in 1925.

Mme. Sun Yat-sen

She was born in Shanghai (in 1893), the second of three sisters, of whom the youngest was Soong Mei-ling (Mme. Chiang Kai-shek), in a family originally from Hainan Island. After the death of Dr. Sun his widow remained a member of the Central Executive Committee of the Kuomintang but continued to uphold a pro-Communist, or leftist, interpretation of his principles, and declined office in Chiang Kai-shek's government.

Mme. Sun was the conscience and the constant heart of a "still unfinished revolution." It required great moral and physical courage for her to resist the pressures put upon her to compromise with her own conception of the role assigned to her by history.

"How, exactly, did you happen to fall in love with Dr. Sun?" I asked her after some years of friendship.

"I didn't fall in love," she said slowly. "It was hero worship from afar. I wanted to help save China, and Dr. Sun was the one man who could do it, so I wanted to help him. I went to see him in exile in Tokyo and volunteered my services. He soon sent me word in Shanghai that he needed me in Japan."

They were quietly married the day after her arrival. She was barely twenty, he about forty-eight, with ten years to live. She became his private secretary, began to learn cryptography,

Dr. and Madame Sun Yat-sen sailed from Japan to Tientsin in 1924.

and was soon doing all his secret coding and decoding.

"Everything he planned," said Mme. Sun Yat-sen, "he saw as a means for betterment of the life of the masses. The emancipated workers and peasants were the pillars on which he meant to build a new and free China. He clearly recognized that these two classes were our basis of strength in our gigantic struggle to overthrow imperialism and effectively to unify our country."

The China Ching-ling believed in was a China where the lowliest coolie would walk like a man, and yet a China of the world. Through her I met the thought and sentiment of China at its best. Knowing Ching-ling early made me comprehend that the Chinese people were capable of radically changing their country and quickly lifting it from bottom place to the rank its history and multitudes merited in the world.

Soong Ching-ling, who married Dr. Sun Yat-sen in Japan in 1914, was a graduate of Wesleyan College, Macon, Georgia.

Mao Tse-tung looked younger than thirty-one when he posed for this photo in 1924. He was already a member of the Central Committee of the Kuomintang in Canton and the Chinese Communist Party, of which he was a founder.

Red China was Chou En-lai. Mao Tse-tung helped recruit worker-students but at the last moment he chose—a fateful decision—to stay in China.

One result of the resentment aroused by the Versailles Treaty was the May Fourth Movement of 1919, led by Chinese students and intellectuals, in which Mao Tse-tung participated. It had important cultural results—a reform in the written language and rejection of many remaining influences of Confucianism—as well as political consequences. In awakening the patriotism of the nation to resist and finally defeat Japan's effort to reduce China to an outright colony (through the Twenty-one Demands of 1915) students and intellectuals demonstrated an astonishing moral and political power and foreshadowed an end to warlord rule. By exposing the hypocrisy and cynicism of the Versailles powers, the movement opened all China to the inflow of revolutionary ideas stemming from the anti-imperialist Russian revolution. At this time Sun Yat-sen turned to Lenin for help and there at last he received it.

Soon after seizing power, the Bolsheviks had made generous overtures toward China. These included voluntary renunciation of the unequal treaties, the return of territorial concessions, and an offer of joint operation of the Chinese Eastern (Manchurian) Railway. Moscow maintained relations with the foreign-dominated Peking regime, but meanwhile Lenin's correspondence with Sun Yat-sen opened another prospect. It led eventually to the Bolshevik implementation of a new strategy to promote world revolution by supporting colonial nationalist leaders.

As late as 1919 the first writings of Lenin appeared in Chinese and it was not until 1920 that the first complete translation of the *Communist Manifesto* was published in China. Out of the intellectual ferment germinated by changes within China and by the October Revolution, the Kung-chantang, or Chinese Communist Party, arose in 1921.

Following the entente between Dr. Sun and the Bolsheviks (represented by Adolf Joffe) in 1923, the Nationalist and Communist parties formed a united front. Its platform was Dr. Sun's *San Min Chu I*, or "Three Principles of the People." These principles were known as "nationalism, livelihood and democracy." In brief, somewhat oversimplified terms, they meant national liberation and unification; restoration of China's economic independence and the regeneration of rural life; and universal education and enlightenment of the whole nation in preparation for a modern, popular government.

Late in 1924 Chou En-lai became Chiang's deputy director of the political department of Whampoa Academy. Chou's real boss was the Russian adviser, General Vasili Bluecher, known as Galen. Under the skillful guidance of Galen, and of the Russians' chief political adviser, Mikhail Borodin, Chou built up a circle of cadet disciples known as the League of Military Youth, which included future generals of the Red Army.

"Paradox of a strange alliance": In 1926 Chou En-lai, like Mao, was a high official in both the Kuomintang and the Communist Party.

Sun Yat-sen seized a base in Canton and the Russians sent money, arms, military advisers and experts in revolutionary techniques of political organization and propaganda. The Communists were permitted dual membership in their own party and the Kuomintang. In his last days (1925) Dr. Sun said of the principle of livelihood, "It is socialism and it is communism." Chiang Kai-shek, a Japanese-educated officer and one of Sun Yat-sen's young followers, was sent to Moscow and received special training there. Following Sun's death, Chiang Kai-shek was groomed as his successor by the Russian advisers.

Chiang Kai-shek

Chiang Kai-shek, the son of a middle-class merchant and landlord, grew up near Ningpo, in the small village of Chikou, where he was born in 1887. Chiang's father died when he was nine, and he was trained by his mother, a devout Buddhist and a stern disciplinarian. Although he became a Methodist after his marriage to Soong Mei-ling, his ethics remained semifeudal and Confucianist.

Apparently Chiang made up his mind early to be a soldier, but he did not enter Paoting Military Academy until he was twenty. He studied there only a few months; then he entered Shimbu Gakko, a

Chiang Kai-shek visiting the Ming Tombs in Nanking.

military school in Japan, where he graduated in 1909. In Japan he met Sun Yat-sen and joined the Kuomintang, and he returned to China in time to see the capitulation of the Manchu Dynasty. Thereafter he worked with Sun in futile attempts to intrigue among and overthrow one provincial warlord or another. Disgusted at repeated failures, he withdrew from politics in 1917 and went into business in Shanghai. He emerged to join Sun Yat-sen's entourage once more when the Kuomintang found a powerful ally in Soviet Russia.

Nationalist troops, led by General Chiang Kai-shek, commander in chief of the "Northern Expedition," conquered and united all China south of the Yangtze River. For the first time, thousands of Chinese volunteered for a Chinese army. The northern warlords seemed to be crushed almost by sheer weight of numbers. Their rabble troops fled without fighting the enspirited Southerners. Everywhere the common man began to interest himself in politics; the advance was hailed as a revolt against warlord tyranny. For a time the peasant, the workers, the millions who labor, saw something to fight for— and they joined in the struggle.

In 1927 the Nationalist revolution, under the supreme military leadership of Chiang Kai-shek, was victorious over most of China. In the same year Generalissimo Chiang broke with the Communist party and made membership in it a capital offense.

By 1928 four fifths of the Chinese Communist Party had been exterminated. Forced underground, its urban leaders continued to observe directives from Moscow, while Stalin headed the Comintern, but attempts at proletarian insurrections were disastrous failures. Meanwhile Mao Tse-tung had gone to the deep hinterland, in Hunan, to begin a guerrilla movement with its base in the peasantry. For ten years a civil war as savage as the Taiping Revolution—and still claiming direct historical descent from it—raged across South China. The basic "Three Principles" remained the common heritage of both the contending parties. The Communists brought to them a Chinese Marxist interpretation of thoroughgoing social revolution, while Chiang Kai-shek struggled to retain private ownership as the unalterable fundament of all three principles.

Throughout this whole epoch following the demise of the Manchu Dynasty, China's "traditional society" underwent a continuous disintegration. What Chiang attempted was to replace it with a capitalist state in China under a military dictator-

Chiang Kai-shek was the first commandant of Whampoa Military Academy, China's West Point, where both Kuomintang and Communist youths were trained as officers.

The Palace Clique

Because the men who held power in the Nanking regime were family relatives, it was called the "Soong Dynasty"; Chinese also dubbed it "Ching I Se," or "Pure One Color" —a royal flush. There were, of course, sincere and thoughtful men in the Kuomintang, but their function was reduced largely to that of apologists; they could get no real control of policies.

Soong Mei-ling (*right*), sister of Madame Sun Yat-sen, married Chiang Kai-shek on December 15, 1927.

Chiang had a wife and a legal concubine before he married Mei-ling. Ching-ling did not blame Chiang for that. She had herself married a divorced man and the father of a son about her own age. What she never forgave was Chiang's "betrayal of the revolution" in 1927 and her sister's "betrayal" in lending the Soong name to it.

"He has set China back years," she said, "and made the revolution much more costly and terrible than it need have been. In the end he will be defeated just the same."

It is not unfitting that his name, Chieh-shih (Kai-shek) means "boundary stone," a fixed image indeed. In a time of utmost chaos he was often concerned with form, convention and propriety, and inwardly concerned with prevention of change. He was not a great tyrant, only a petty one; he failed not because he was Caesar or killed too many people but because he killed too few of the right people; he never understood that his worst enemies were inside his own camp. Chiang was not resolute, only obstinate; not wise, only obsolete; not disciplined, only repressed; not original, only a scavenger among the relics of the past; and not ruthless, merely vain—as none knew better than the greedy parasites who surrounded and finally consumed him.

The "palace clique" included Chiang Kai-shek and his wife, Soong Mei-ling; their brother-in-law, H. H. Kung; Sun Fo, the only son of Dr. Sun Yat-sen, who was older than his stepmother (Soong Ching-ling); T. V. Soong, the younger brother of Mme. Chiang; and Mme. Chiang's elder sister, Soong Ai-ling —Mme. Kung. Each member of the "Dynasty" had his or her own "sub-court" of near and distant cousins, aunts, uncles, friends and assorted acolytes and parasites.

As far as is publicly known, no member of the Chiang-Kung-Soong family ever filed a personal income tax report.

Usually either Dr. Kung or Dr. Soong was finance minister. Chiang obviously preferred Dr. Kung, who had no party prestige and never openly opposed Chiang's demands; but Dr. Kung knew nothing about modern banking.

Periodically Chiang had to call in T. V. Soong to untangle the resulting chaos.

"T. V." certainly had a good grasp of modern banking practices; he also had a vague attachment to liberal political sentiments which Chiang detested. Although he finally sided with the counterrevolution, he sympathized with his favorite sister, Mme. Sun Yat-sen, the only revolutionary in the family. But as a "practical business man" from Harvard he had to stomach Chiang Kai-shek, whose methods he despised. He lacked the substance to be either a revolutionary or a dedicated reformer.

Dr. Kung had the shrewd rural-exchange merchant's eye out for quick profits in personal side deals, for which he and his wife became notorious. Although the Kungs perhaps did more than any other single family to demoralize all Chinese officialdom, and their selfish behavior became more septic as the war dragged on, they were more conspicuous only because they were on top.

T. V. Soong

Sun Fo

H. H. Kung

Mme. Kung

ship. It is a mistake to assume that his struggle with the Communists was over either the restoration of "traditional society" or its final destruction. "Traditional society" had already been shattered by the impact of foreign industry, science and capitalism. The struggle between the Reds and Chiang Kai-shek was quite simply over whether China's modernization was to be achieved by private enterprise under the dictatorship of a very weak bourgeoisie, or by a proletarian revolution, led by the Communist party, to establish public ownership over the basic means of production and to mobilize "the whole people" and their immense labor power.

Chiang Kai-shek and his bureaucracy were not elected but seized power. Before the Japanese occupation, the Kuomintang (membership about two million in 1938) held the cities against the Communists with armed garrisons, police and some foreign help. As far as the peasant majority was concerned, "government" simply meant the Kuomintang-appointed county magistrate who ruled as of yore in collusion with the landlord-gentry of the district and their local armed guards—10 to 20 percent of the population.

In the contest between Chiang and Mao, time was decisive. Modern capitalism had begun more than a century late in China. As the nation reluctantly accepted the superiority of science and mechanized industry, intellectuals despaired of ever catching up by emulating the nineteenth-century West and using its agonizingly slow and painful method of "capital accumulation" through the private exploitation of labor and national resources. Even so, Chiang might have won against the Communists had they not received "providential" help from Japanese imperialism.

When Mao said that imperialism had "prepared the material as well as the moral conditions" for Communist victory in China, he spoke literal truth. It was not the Communists but Japanese imperialism whose deep penetration and occupation of urban China (1937–45) crippled the bourgeoisie and destroyed Kuomintang morale. In doing so, it opened the countryside to the proselytization and organization of the peasantry by the Communists. Japan's war, originally launched under the slogan "To eradicate Communism in East Asia!" had the double effect of destroying Western colonial dominance in China and making it possible for Mao Tse-tung to arm the massive peasant fist of a renewed Taiping Rebellion—this time led by Marxists, not Christians.

February 17, 1928: "Dear Folks, Your unworthy son is now a deck boy on the S.S. *Radnor . . .*"

② ARRIVAL IN CHINA 1928

When I first reached Shanghai I was every youth, full of curiosity and wide open to the world. I could have been anyone of my generation of America moved westward, like my forebears, by the pull of some frontier dream, some nameless beckoning freedom, seeking fortune or following knowledge "like a sinking star" beyond the sunset.

I was twenty-two and I had picked up a few dollars in Wall Street speculation which gave me just enough of a stake, I thought, to finance a year of parsimonious traveling and adventuring around the world. I planned to return to New York after the year, make a fortune before I was thirty, and devote the rest of my life to leisurely study and writing. It really looked that easy in 1928.

I set out for the Pacific by way of the Panama Canal, spent three months in Hawaii and Japan, and went on to Shanghai. I had, on my itinerary, allotted six weeks to China. I was not to see America again for thirteen years.

At Shanghai I presented a letter of introduction from Walter Williams, dean of the School of Journalism of the University of Missouri, to John Benjamin Powell, editor of the *China Weekly Review*, and correspondent of the *Chicago Tribune*.

"Why don't you stay in Shanghai and help me put out the *Review*?" Powell asked. "I'm publishing a special edition in a few months—a 'New China' edition to show the diehards that the Nationalists are here to stay. China is about to become really independent and we have to face it. I want somebody with a fresh outlook to put this edition together for me."

My outlook was fresh enough, if fresh meant green. "But I know nothing about China," I answered. "Besides, my schedule says six weeks in China, no more."

"Well, Shanghai is China, even though there are plenty of people here who don't know it," he laughed. "Spend your six weeks here and then leave. My guess is that you'll like it and stay."

"All right," I said, "let's get started. Where does New China begin?"

It took me and my Chinese assistants three months to fill up the two hundred pages of that special edition with copy and advertising. I got little cooperation from the American businessmen in Shanghai or from the consulate. They mostly considered Chiang Kai-shek a Communist and looked at the *Review* askance for defending him. I crammed prodigiously from Powell's big library of Orientalia and shamelessly cribbed background for my reporting. The more I read the more enamored I became.

I discovered what antiquity meant and the dramatic contradictions it posed for the very young China I saw struggling to find its place in the modern world.

"Sampans, junks and fishing boats float in Soochow's canals. After dusk pleasure boats offer the stranger the hospitality of the city."

Edgar Snow, Shanghai, 1929.

Peking's modern buildings form today's skyline behind the ancient golden roofs of the Forbidden Palace.

Before my first task was completed Powell offered me a job as assistant editor of the *Review* and I accepted. I saw all the storied places in the lower Yangtze and along the Grand Canal: Lake Taihu's islands and the mulberry trees and silk filatures around its green shores; the temples and the pagodas of West Lake at Hangchow; Yangchow's graceful bridges and Marco Polo's image in that town, where he governed for three years under Kubilai Khan; Soochow, the Venice of China, veined with canals and celebrated for its pleasure boats and exquisite singing girls; the great Ming walls of Nanking, and the majestic Purple Mountain where Sun Yat-sen is entombed; and then all the wonders of the North: the sacred mountain of Tai Shan, the birthplace and temple of Confucius, and the native town of Mencius. Finally Peking, which I was later to call "home," city of golden roofs and marble altars, of wine-colored walls and shaded temples and palaces, of magnificent acacia trees and perfect vistas. . . . a city nobly conceived and nobly made, a treasury of art, a place of gentle birth and of more knavery than downright wickedness; a city of warm vivid springs and shadowed autumns, and of winter sunshine shimmering on snow-covered trees and frozen lakes; a city of eternal compromise and easy laughter, of leisure and family love, of poverty and tragedy and indifference to dirt; and yet a place of unexpected violence, where rebellious students coined the fighting slogans of a nation, and blinding Mongolian dust storms swept down from the Gobi Desert, leaving the graceful roofs strewn with the oldest dust of life.

I did a series of article-supplements describing the tourist attractions of towns and cities along the Chinese railways. Powell wanted to persuade Americans that it was safe to travel in China again, and Sun Fo, Minister of Communications, enthusiastically endorsed his idea. Minister Sun promised me all possible help.

"Now that the Reds are suppressed," Sun Fo told me, "there's no more antiforeignism. The revolution is over, the country is unified, and you'll see how peaceful and friendly the people are. Just publish the facts."

Before my travels were over, I saw that the country was far from unified, and began to doubt that the real revolution had begun.

Snow in China as assistant editor of Shanghai's English-language journal, the *China Weekly Review*.

"... the knotted rickshas with their owners fighting each other for customers and arguing fares ..."

3

SHANGHAI
1928-1930

Where trade and commerce are more important than lives and human rights.

Shanghai seemed a continuous freak circus with all manner of people performing almost every physical and social function in public: yelling, crushing throngs spilling through every kind of traffic, precariously amidst old cars and new ones and between coolies racing wildly to compete for ricksha fares, gingerly past "honey-carts" filled with excrement dragged down Bubbling Well Road, sardonically past perfumed, exquisitely gowned, mid-thigh-exposed Chinese ladies, jestingly past the herculean bare-backed coolie trundling his taxi-wheelbarrow load of six giggling servant girls, carefully before singing peddlers bearing portable kitchens ready with delicious noodles on the spot, lovingly under gold-lettered shops overflowing with fine silks and brocades, dead-panning past village women staring wide-eyed at Indian policemen, gravely past mah-jongg ivories clicking and jai alai and pari-mutuel betting, slyly through streets hung with the heavy-sweet acrid smell of opium, sniffingly past restaurants and brightly lighted sing-song houses, indifferently past aloof young Englishmen in their Austins popping off to cricket on the Race Course, snickeringly around elderly white gentlemen in carriages with their wives or Russian mistresses along the Bund, and hastily past sailors looking for beer and women—from noisy dawn to plangent night the endless hawking and spitting, the baby's urine stream on the curb, the amah's scolding, the high falsetto of opera at Wing On Gardens, where a dozen plays went on at once and hotel rooms next door filled up with plump virgins procured for wealthy merchants in from the provinces for business and debauch, the wail of dance bands moaning for slender bejeweled Chinese taxi dancers, the whine of innumerable beggars and their naked unwashed infants, the glamour of the Whangpoo with its white fleets of foreign warships, its shaggy freighters, its fan-sailed junks, its thousand lantern-lit sampans darting fireflies on the moon-silvered water filled with deadly pollution.

In this river are gray or white ships, lean and slenderly fashioned of steel, with armored decks on which there are guns turned westward into China. These are the foreign watchdogs: American, British, French, Italian and Japanese cruisers, destroyers, submarines and aircraft carriers that patrol the Whangpoo, the Yangtze and the coasts of China. In the threat of their cannon, poised so gracefully, is the explanation of Shanghai's security. Stationed ashore are French, American and Italian marines, British Tommies and Japanese bluejackets; their bayonets form a rim of steel around the [foreign] Settlement. They guard the largest foreign investment in any city in the world.

A beggar woman nursing her child on a Shanghai street.

Above: American sailors guard the U.S. Navy recreation grounds. *Left:* Foreign ships in Shanghai's Whangpoo River harbor.

"There were, as everybody knows, two Shanghais: a foreign-ruled city, made up of the French Concession and the International Settlement, taken from China nearly a century ago; and the Chinese-governed Greater Shanghai." *At left:* An empty park in the International Settlement looks like a transplant from Europe. The street scene (*right*) was more typical.

The Concessions

The French Concession was run by a handful of French *propriétaires* and the Settlement by an equally narrow oligarchy. Though Chinese paid nearly all the taxes, they could not own land in their own names and had to hire foreigners to serve as dummies in the land register.

The Settlement was still so "secure" that creaking wheelbarrow loads of solid gold and silver bars were openly rolled from bank to bank, often only a pompous Chinese clerk as escort, by muscled coolies grunting and grinning proudly under their rich-man's burden.

In Shanghai there is for the most part no mixture. Generation after generation, the British have stayed British, the Americans have remained "100 percenters." In Paris the foreigner enjoys learning French; in Berlin he must acquire German; in New York the American dialect is considered essential. But in Shanghai he does not learn Chinese. It is believed that the study of Chinese weakens the fiber of the mind, and the few foreigners who do master the language are pointed out as eccentrics. In Paris, Berlin, New York, the foreigner is subject to the laws of the country; in Shanghai he is immune from all but his own consular jurisdiction.

East meets West: A Chinese beggar approaches a foreigner in a ricksha.

Right: Shanghai's race-course, 1930s. "At first I mistook Shanghai for China. The bizarre contrasts of very old and very new, the sublime ugliness of the place, its kind of polyglot glamour (all nations poised for crisis there), and its frank money-is-all vulgarity held me in puzzled wonder."

Below: "The moral basis of Shanghai society was traceable to Britain's victories in the Opium War of the 1840s and 1850s. Generation after generation of Westerners enjoyed life to the full"—like the dinner celebrants marking some forgotten occasion.

Perpetual Poverty

All the legwork, and often most of the brain-work, in foreign business offices was done by Chinese assistants, and office hours were short. Lunch was called tiffin, and it went on for two or three hours. After an hour or two back at the office the average American or Englishman or Frenchman was ready to call it a day and go home or drop in at his club for a swim or shower and a "peg" or two before his valet dressed him for dinner. Life was a round of parties; food and liquor were very cheap even for the very best, and credit was unlimited.

In the Shanghai Settlement are the tallest buildings in Asia, the most spacious cinema palaces, and more motorcars than in any Eastern metropolis, or in all other Chinese cities combined. Here are the great Chinese department stores, the powerful foreign financial houses like the Hong Kong & Shanghai Banking Corporation, the Chartered Bank of India, Australia & China, and big branches of the National City and Chase banks of New York. In the Settlement are head offices of the vast American and British tobacco concerns that arrived, spread and prospered with the missionaries (whose headquarters also are here) and threaten to outlast them in China. There are the "blue-blood" British firms like Arnold's, Jardine & Matheson's, Sassoon's, and others that got their start in China with the opium

traffic inherited from the notorious East India Company, that won an Indian Empire for Britain. And here are the newer, more aggressive American firms; they represent hundreds of American factories with everything for sale, from rivets to machine guns and bombing planes.

A mendicant with rotting feet.

Without homes or families, children old enough to walk were old enough to beg.

Snow described "the beggars on every downtown block . . . the jungle free-for-all struggle for gold or survival and the day's toll of unwanted infants and suicides . . . the peddlers and their plaintive cries . . ."

Soochow Creek in Shanghai, 1928.

A home in Soochow Creek.

As a plea for help, people often wrote down the story of their miserable conditions for passers-by to read.

Above: The Great World Amusement Center in Shanghai, 1930s: ". . . the hundred dance halls and the thousands of taxi dolls; the opium dens and gambling halls; the flashing lights of great restaurants, the clatter of mah-jongg pieces . . . the myriad short-time whores and pimps busily darting in and out of alleyways . . ."

Right: Coolies gambling.

Diversions

Left: The Bund—Shanghai's Great White Way.

Below: Mei Lan-fang, the internationally renowned Peking opera actor noted for his portrayal of women.

Above: A 1930s Shanghai wedding.

Right: Shanghai's "Times Square" offered some enticing wall displays for passers-by.

Workers

Right and below: Human beings, like these dock workers, were little better than beasts of burden, and possibly worse off. "I stepped back into the Middle Ages," Snow wrote. "Yet industrialization was entering."

Left: A dormitory where children slept in a match factory.

Above: Many slept on the streets.

Below: A child worker, identified only by a number.

Above: "Surplus" market: The characters on the child's jacket read: "My name is Chen Feng-ying, a girl for sale."

Left: Little boy and girl slave workers.

The cities of China used to swarm with prostitutes, and the sale of women was a thriving industry. Girls as well as boys were sold to brokers for indentured labor, and pretty girls found ready buyers as concubines, teahouse waitresses or common street *piao-tzu.* The more talented and stronger became singing girls and sometimes emerged as prosperous house mothers, but the great multitude had a short life as cheap prostitutes and slaves of their owners and procurers.

Shanghai has been accused of many things. Repugnant to some, its fascination for others lies in its very crudities, its stark and frank carnalities. Over it hangs the promise of gold and Gehenna. Never drab, it burns with the primal longings of an animal heart. It is as swift, as sudden, as elemental as the jungle, its appetite ever-ravishing, always unappeased. It has at once the charm and the futility of a mistress who never knows repletion.

North of Soochow Creek, in the Hongkew district, factories rear belching stacks that darken the sky. Shanghai is the largest manufacturing town in Asia. In the busy cotton mills, the flour mills, silk filatures and lesser industries, more than 200,000 Chinese workers find employment. Their average wage is the equivalent of no more than twenty American cents daily.

I remembered the hundreds of factories where little boy and girl slave workers sit or stand at their tasks twelve or thirteen hours a day, and then drop, in exhausted sleep, to the dirty cotton quilt, their bed, directly beneath the machine. I remembered little girls in silk filatures, and the pale young women in cotton factories—all of them, like most factory contract labor in Shanghai, literally sold into these jobs as virtual slaves for four or five years, unable to leave the heavily guarded, high-walled premises, day or night, without special permission. And I remembered that during 1935 more than 29,000 bodies were picked up from the streets and rivers and canals of Shanghai—bodies of the destitute poor, and the starved or drowned babies or children they could not feed.

There is a perpetual famine among the hundreds of thousands of poor in the great city, just as severe, maybe worse, than famine in the farm country.

Yet there are thousands more ready to work if jobs can be found—an abundance of cheap, competent labor. And owners of the mills, British, Japanese and Chinese, ruthlessly suppress strikes, suppress labor organization. They fight down the demands of the workers, whose feeble cry for a better wage, a higher scale of living, is smothered under the weight of their own numbers and the urgent demand for bread.

Soong Ching-ling

During the thirties when Mme. Sun lived in Shanghai, she supported whatever opposition existed to Chiang's dictatorship. This once included her stepson, Sun Fo, who openly denounced Chiang as a "usurper" who had "ruined the party." He said that under Chiang "every local government, every provincial and municipal government is rotten to the core." Sun Fo accused Chiang of "betraying all the party's principles" and ridiculed claims that he was Dr. Sun's "chosen heir," adding that his father "never trusted him." But Sun Fo patched things up and took office under Chiang again and Ching-ling broke with her stepson also.

Ching-ling was not easy to meet. It was not convenient for her to see many strangers; for one thing, her home was constantly guarded and watched by Kuomintang plain-clothes men and French police. I first visited her modest two-story foreign house on Rue Molière in the French Concession. It was, with its excellent English and Chinese library, about all the property Dr. Sun Yat-sen had left to her. Many millions had passed through his hands in the cause of revolution, but he had died a poor man.

Left to right: The American writer Agnes Smedley; George Bernard Shaw; Mme. Sun Yat-sen; Tsai Yuan-pei, former president of Peking University; and Lu Hsun.

China's "Gorki"

Already revered as a scholar, teacher and great writer when I met him [in Shanghai] in 1930, Lu Hsun was a short, dark figure in his fifties, with bright warm eyes and a moist brow; he was incurably tubercular and had not long to live. Surprisingly, he had to stay in the French Concession in hiding, and most of his books were banned by the Kuomintang. Lu Hsun was not a Communist; only an ultra-conservative Confucian eye could discern anything very dangerous in his satire and humor.

His message to Chinese youth rings with an appeal to logic. "Think, and study the economic problems of society," he advises, "travel through the hundreds of dead villages, visit the generals and then visit their victims, see the realities of your time with opened eyes and a clear mind, and work for an enlightened society, but always think and study." Only the resurgent, educated youths, he believes, are capable of diagnosing China's fundamental diseases. "Reared in a class which is fast decaying, they alone can understand it, destroy it, and create an intelligent order."

When I was living in Shanghai I began working with Yao Hsin-nung on a translation of Lu Hsun's "True Story of Ah Q," which remains the most influential single piece of fiction produced in the republican era, as Lu Hsun was its most important writer.

"Ah Q" is the story of a typical illiterate coolie whose experiences, during the first revolution, show the utter failure of that event to reach the people. Constantly baffled, seeing everything through a mirage of ignorance and superstition, knowing words and not their meaning, Ah Q goes from one humiliation to

Lu Hsun, speaking to a meeting of students, shortly before his death in 1936.

another, but each time philosophically rationalizes his defeats into victories and emerges as "the Superior Man." (See Confucius, see Nietzsche, see Walter Mitty.) Even when he is executed for a crime he did not commit, Ah Q goes to his death cheerfully singing, from a Chinese opera he did not understand, " 'After twenty years I will be reborn again a hero.' "

Communist intellectuals saw in Lu Hsun's story both an allegory of China's degradation in the world and the message that until they themselves carried out revolution to the illiterate peasantry, China would never recover her lost greatness.

"Before the republic the people were slaves," as Lu Hsun himself put it. "Afterward, we became slaves of ex-slaves."

"Now that you have had the second Nationalist revolution," I asked him, "do you feel there are still as many Ah Q's left as ever?"

Lu Hsun laughed, "Worse. Now they are running the country."

She embraced all revolutionaries as her own, and through her personal intervention saved many lives. Among her failures the one that most saddened her was the immolation of six young Chinese, members of a league of left writers—historians, novelists, short-story writers and poets led by Lu Hsun. Six of the best known were made to dig their own graves. Then they were bound, thrown into the pits, and buried alive, an old Chinese punishment for subversives.

"That," said Ching-ling bitterly, "is our Christian Generalissimo—burying our best young people alive. Evidently in his Bible studies he has not yet reached the Corinthians."

Opium dens like the one above were controlled by Tu Yueh-sheng (*right*), head of the Green Circle gang. In 1927 Chiang used Tu's gangsters to help wipe out the Communist Party in Shanghai.

Counterrevolution

Opium is sold in the Settlement in much the same way that liquor is sold in the United States. In the French Concession, where no effort at concealment is made, it is purchasable at more than two hundred different establishments. The French Municipal Council is alleged to derive an annual income in excess of 8 million taels from the opium merchants, prostitution, the pari-mutuels and "squeeze." Opium smoking is the one illicit pastime that has not won acolytes among Shanghai Americans; it makes them deathly sick.

Tu Yueh-sheng [was] the Al Capone of the French Concession. Old Tu got his start "squeezing" the opium merchants while on the police force of Frenchtown, an estate to which he rose from being a sweet-potato vendor. In ten years he managed to achieve high place in the *Ching* and *Hung pangs*, Chinese gangs which control much of the illicit opium traffic in the Yangtze Valley. They are said to contribute annually the equivalent of about U.S. $20,000,000 to the French authorities, who permit them to use the Concession for headquarters in the direction of their various enterprises. Tu is a gentleman now, wears silk gowns, rides in expensive limousines, and calls the Nanking officials by their first names.

It was Lin Yu-tang who pointed out to me the humor of the situation when Chiang Kai-shek made Tu Yueh-sheng his "chief of the bureau of opium suppression," and decorated him with the Order of the Brilliant Jade. Tu and his gangsters ran the underworld in Shanghai so closely that not a brothel could solicit trade, not an opium smoker could dream in peace, not a shopkeeper could turn an honest profit, without the *pang* collecting tribute. By the mid-thirties, kidnapping, assassination and procurement each had its price.

I also learned how Tu Yueh-sheng had saved Shanghai from the Communists. In March 1927 the Nationalist revolution leftist organizers staged an insurrection and forced the Northern warlords to retreat from the Chinese-ruled parts of Shanghai before revolutionary troops reached the city. Nearly the whole working class was organized and ready

Suspected Communists, rounded up in April 1927.

Left: Kuomintang police arrest Shanghai workers and students after the May Day celebration in 1930. *Right:* Severed heads in cases swing from Shanghai singposts under a bilingual speed-limit sign.

to welcome Chiang Kai-shek. Upriver, however, Chiang was about to expel the Communists from the Kuomintang and civil war threatened. An American city manager hired by the Settlement Council secretly offered Tu Yueh-sheng five thousand rifles, armored cars and safe conduct through the Settlement, to attack and destroy the "commune" that had taken over the surrounding area. Chiang's supporters among the Chinese bankers in Shanghai financed the operation.

Escorted by foreign police, Tu's gunmen poured into the workers' homes and factories in a surprise night attack. Between five and ten thousand youths were slain, including many Communists and Socialists (left-wing Nationalists).

Chiang overthrew the two-party alliance and government and set up his own regime in Nanking. He got the support of the banking, industrial and landholding families in the lower Yangtze, the powerful gangs of Shanghai, and, of course, the sanction of the Foreign Powers. After that, Nanking's labor policy remained consistently despotic and treacherous. During the decade of effort to achieve "unification by force," the Kuomintang closely cooperated with the foreign police and with Chinese and foreign factory owners in Shanghai and ruthlessly suppressed the struggle of labor for its political and economic rights. Repeatedly the foreign authorities called in the Kuomintang's gangster allies to "mediate" disputes inside the Settlement. Repeatedly the Settlement police, run

by the British, arrested Chinese labor leaders and handed them to Nanking for imprisonment or execution.

The counterrevolution drove Soviet advisers from the country and descended upon mass organizations with a violence particularly savage in Hunan, where numerous peasant leaders and intellectuals were executed. Chiang Kai-shek emerged supreme, and the Communist party was driven underground.

Onlookers at a public execution ground view the work of Chiang's firing squads.

Mother and child, rural China, 1930s.

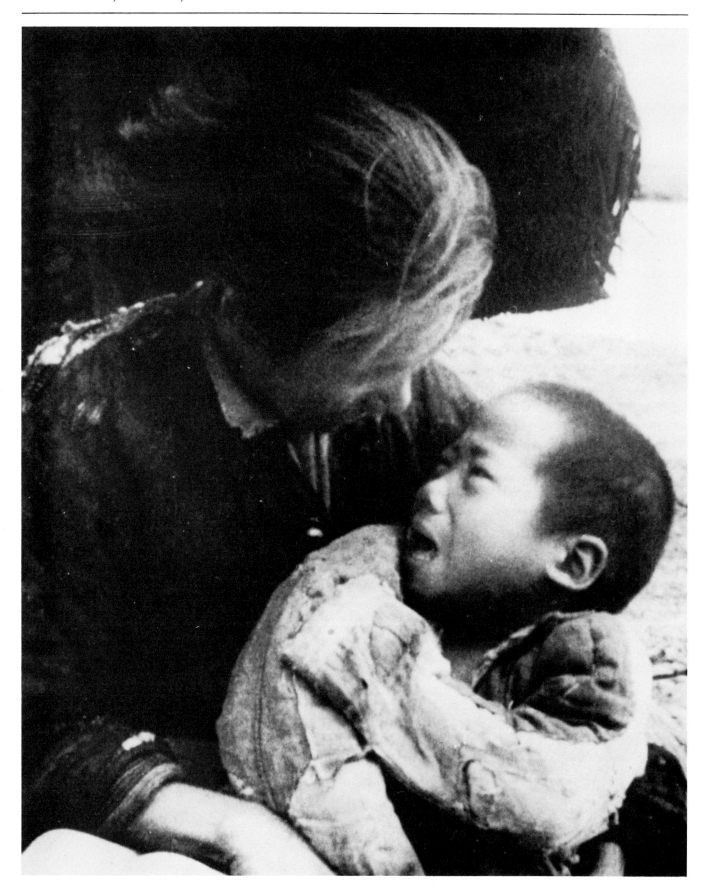

4

RURAL CHINA: FAMINE, FLOOD AND FEUDALISM

"I believe," says the young page in Mark Twain's Recollections of
Joan of Arc, *"that some day it will be found that peasants are people.
Yes, beings in a great many respects like ourselves. And I believe that
some day they will find this out, too—and then! Well, then I think they
will rise up and demand to be regarded as part of the race, and that by
that consequence there will be trouble."*

Vast libraries exist to "explain" China, and probably the most enlightening words in answer to the question Why Did China Go Red? are those of the man who led the nation to where it is today, Mao Tse-tung. Why Mao himself and other Chinese intellectuals were logically pushed toward Marxism rather than nationalism-capitalism is abundantly clarified in Mao's life story as he related it to me, and in testimonials of many other Red leaders which I later gathered. A careful study of such information as early as 1938 could hardly have failed to suggest that the whole national experience of China made a Communist victory inevitable unless the Kuomintang underwent a miraculous transformation.

When Marx's stirring call to arms first began to be read by young people in China after the First World War, they did not see in it an analysis of conditions in Europe of February 1848, but a true description of their own immediate environment. In China, with its child and female slave labor, its twelve- to fourteen-hour day, its starvation wages and the absence of any protection against sickness, injury, unemployment and old age, and no serious possibility of collective bargaining, why should people have questioned Marx's prophecies right down to 1947?

The old security under the clan-family and the guild systems had collapsed and now the have-not was literally worth no more than his price tag in the market, "purely as a means of production." Back of the defenseless position of labor lay of course the breakup of the old agrarian economy under the impact of Western imperialism and the bankruptcy of handicraft production brought on by machine products. Capital levies in the form of ever rising taxes and usurious interest rates, and the consistent plunder of public revenues by thieving bureaucrats and militarists, had by the twenties and thirties reduced the solvent landowning tillers to a minority. Aided by famine and war, this ruined economy threw millions of "surplus" sons and daughters of degraded peasant families onto the swollen labor market of unemployed. The biography of almost every Red soldier I met revealed him to be a direct product of this mass rural bankruptcy.

The Great Drought 1929

At the end of my first year abroad I was about as far from home as I could get. I was in the baking city of Saratsi, south of the Gobi Desert. There in the Northwest I saw children dying by the thousands in a famine which eventually took more than five million lives. It was an awakening point in my life and remained the most shocking of all my experiences with war, poverty, violence and revo-

A country boy drinking from an open water trough.

The dry stream bed of the Black River, in the drought-stricken region of Suiyuan in northwest China.

lution until, fifteen years later, I saw the furnaces and gas chambers in which the Nazis, too impatient to wait for mere starvation, exterminated six to seven million people.

Saratsi formerly was one of the wealthiest trading centers of Inner Mongolia. But in 1924 began the long delinquencies of the Rain God. Today the demon famine has spread his fingers over virtually a fourth of prodigious China.

It was a weird landscape swept of every growing thing as if by volcanic ash from a newly erupted earth. Even the trees had been stripped of their bark and were dying. In the villages most of the mud-brick houses were collapsing. Their few timbers had been pulled out and sold for the coppers they would bring.

Last-ditchers still sat or lay on their doorsteps, scarcely conscious. I saw a naked twig-armed child, his belly a balloon from a diet of leaves and sawdust. He was trying to shake back to life his naked father, who had just died on the road. We came upon a couple of young women as thin as the dried baked ducks dangling before a Chinese meat shop. They were the same color and just as naked, with their withered breasts hanging like deflated paper sacks. They had fainted on a village street where those who could still walk dragged past, not noticing them.

For many blocks the streets were bordered with men and women and children in the last reaches of starvation.

In their hands they had little wooden rice bowls, or tin cans, or battered tea pots. They were waiting for the Salvation Army free soup kitchen to open, and it was difficult to understand how they could sit there so quietly, anticipating what would probably be the first bowl of decent food they had tasted for weeks.

It was almost unbelievable that human beings could survive with so little flesh clinging to their frames.

Numbers of children who had been kept alive on weeds and herbs too long showed the telltale signs of famine. Their faces were puffed and their eyes, in which lingered no trace of the alert curiosity so characteristic of Chinese children, were watery.

But these were not the most shocking things, after all. The shocking thing was that in many of those towns there were still rich men, rice hoarders, moneylenders and landlords, with armed guards to defend them, while they profiteered enormously. The shocking thing was that in the cities—where

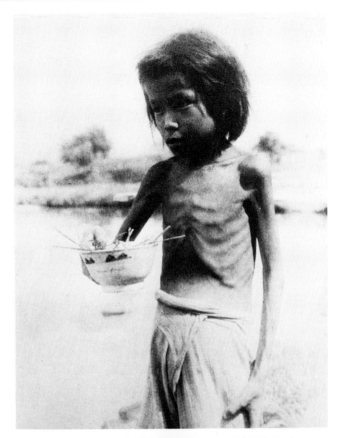

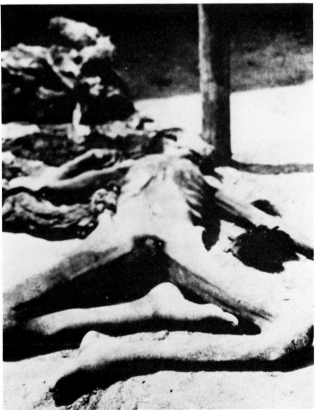

Famine victims. *Above:* A child beggar. *Below:* A body, stripped of clothes, lies along a roadside. "Corpses frequently disappeared before they could be interred," Snow wrote, "and human flesh was openly sold in some villages."

officials danced or played with sing-song girls—there were thousands of tons of wheat and millet which could not be shipped to the starving because in the Northwest there were militarists who wanted to hold all of their rolling stock and would release none of it toward the east, while there were other Kuomintang generals who would send no rolling stock westward because they feared it would be seized by their rivals.

While this famine raged, a flock of vultures descended upon this benighted country, and purchased from the starving farmers thousands of acres for the taxes in arrears, or for a few coppers, and held it to await tenants and rainy days.

Above: Where railroads existed, scores of hucksters stood behind the station retaining fence waiting for the occasional train to bring customers for their nuts, pastry or candies.

Left: A typical main street in almost any country town.

Flood 1939

An agonizing death has overtaken approximately 900,000 Chinese who lived in the treacherous river valleys of central China. Twelve million homes have been destroyed and 55,000,000 people are affected. The blow falls in the wake of droughts that have denuded whole provinces; of famines the results of which still invalid the once magnificent Northwest; of sieges of locusts; of fourteen civil wars that have sabotaged the economic structure of the nation; of ubiquitous thievery, pillaging, banditry; of a two years' struggle with the Communist revolution; of terrorism under a militaristic regime which for callous indifference, tyrannous oppression and ruinous incompetence has not been surpassed anywhere in this era.

In other days, if the crops were destroyed by evil *feng-shui* [wind-water] there was enough left until the next planting. When the rains were good the canals were full and all down the valleys the stout buffalo turned the archaic water wheels that mois-

A North China peasant family in the 1930 famine.

A child collecting bark—to fill an empty stomach.

tened the friendly earth. The farmer, with his buckets of water slung from a yoke carried over his shoulder, moved over his scrap of ground, chanting his strange, patient cry of labor. Life seemed kind. But in recent years predatory creatures have roamed the land. Officials legitimize extortion on an unprecedented scale, calling it "taxation." Soldiers take their share of loot and spoils. Bandits operate widely. The granaries are empty. Little silver is held by anyone but the landlords and usurers, and they make no display of it.

Summer passes and the peasant looks with troubled eyes toward the future. Anger against his oppressors rankles in his breast, yet he does not quite know where to place the blame. One day cool sudden winds cause him to look upward apprehensively at a darkling sky.

The downpour continues for many days. At the elders' hut he hears that the Gold Sand River [Yangtze] is now ten miles wide. Then, in the night hour of the fox, he is awakened by a dull throbbing sound. His old woman jumps up, shouting, "It is the call to the dikes!" And both of them, wading across the fields, see in the darkness the splashes of yellow light from lanterns. Thousands of men bring baskets of mud, bricks, stones and sticks to reinforce the bulwark against the swollen tide. Suddenly, where it is believed strongest, an old portion of the embankment gives way. There is a race for life. Women and children clamber to the roofs of huts, or onto anything that rides the waves. Hundreds perish as the terrific surge moves inexorably to destroy.

The waters flatten out, and as far as you can see there is one vast yellow waste dotted with corpses, tiny islets, the heads of trees, rooftops or the mocking soar of temple roof denting the sky. The peasants' pigs, cows, chickens and buffaloes drown before him. Nothing is left.

Thousands more will die this spring. Hundreds expire as I write this. Others, cut off from the mainland, cringe from death and hope for salvation. Some of them have waited for days, some for weeks, with practically no food and with only the yellow flood to drink. Around them more closely draws the dark embrace of death.

Paralysis of the Yangtze meant paralysis of China, for the great "River of Golden Sand" is the lifeblood and the sinew of what poets called the Central Flowery Kingdom. Rehabilitation after such a disaster was not a question of days, but of months and perhaps years.

The Child Miners

The Kochiu mines (in Yunnan), largest and most profitable enterprise, and semi–government-controlled, operates almost exclusively with child labor. The only limitation placed on the workers is that they be able to carry the baskets of metal required of those who would earn the thirty cents a day. It is distressing to learn that for many years the chief engineer here was an American. The present engineer is German. In Kochiu nearly all children become hunchbacked. The shafts are shallow and it is impossible to walk upright.

There are nearly 50,000 miners in the Kochiu shafts, of whom over 60 percent are slaves. Forty percent die of arsenic poisoning after three or four years. In a few months their skin turns nearly green, the arsenic eating into their bodies very rapidly. The average wage paid is around $20 yearly. Compensations to parents of the miners, when any, are two or three dollars for deceased offspring.

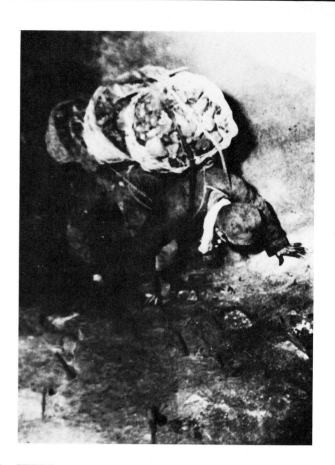

The Oppression of Women

Confucius taught the inequality of all things, and specifically of the sexes. "Women are human," he admitted, "but lower than men."

"It is the law of nature that woman should not be allowed any will of her own."

"Poor peasants formerly sold their daughters to pay off debts to landlords or to raise cash [Colonel Li Hsin-kung told me]. If parents waited too long to betroth their daughters, then the landlords sometimes claimed first rights. After that, who would marry them? Marriages to strike a good bargain, to acquire land, to pay off debts, to gain family position, to buy sons out of the army, without consulting the feelings of the betrothed, with great differences in ages and temperaments—this is what caused misery in the family."

It was not just aristocratic women who had "lily feet"; almost all women in North China endured foot binding. Early marriage by arrangement was a constriction of another sort, and the teen-age mother (*above, right*) a typical victim.

A peasant (*right*) encounters the city.

"Why Don't They Revolt?"

In most districts in the interior the only roads are cart tracks, worn deep through centuries of use, impassable for wheeled traffic. The vast majority of rural folk rarely see, never use, a train, airplane, automobile, radio, electric light or newspaper. From 80 to 90 percent of them are totally illiterate, and are almost incredibly poor.

In places as much as 80 percent of the arable soil is concentrated in the hands of as little as 15 percent of the population. The average farm holding is so small that landlordism on the scale now developing means the complete destitution, or reduction to the status of serfs, of the poor peasants.

Tax collectors had police powers and could imprison any peasant for failing to pay taxes and rent. The tenant who did not wish to go to jail had to borrow from the usurer—not infrequently incarnated in the selfsame landlord and tax collector. Principal and interest sometimes compounded at repayment at as high as 400 percent in six months, or 700 percent a year. Land taxes were in instances collected sixty years in advance.

Probably the average farming family earns a livelihood from less than two acres of soil. The family's average annual income does not exceed $240 in Chinese currency, the equivalent of about $60 in American money. The average farmer makes little more than the hired Chinese laborer. The latter's magnificent daily wage is now under twenty cents in Chinese money, or about four cents American.

Children in Yunnanfu are used for hauling extraordinary loads. One day out on the road to Talifu I met an old woman leading a dozen juveniles laden with enormous loads of wood. One of them, frailer than the rest, had fallen down weeping and refused to go on. The old lady stood over her and beat her with a hunk of wood. Not one of the passers-by intervened, although I noticed one or two had the decency to avert their heads. I prevailed upon the irate woman to leave the child alone; we lightened her load. I gave her a dollar—which the old lady doubtless removed from her before the day was done.

"Why don't they revolt?" I asked myself. "Why don't they march in a great army and attack the scoundrels who can tax them but cannot feed them, who can seize their lands but cannot repair an irrigation canal? Or why don't they sweep into the great cities and plunder the wealth of the rascals who buy their daughters and wives, the men who continue to gorge on thirty-six-course banquets while honest men starve?" I was profoundly puzzled by their passivity. For a while I thought nothing would make a Chinese fight.

I was mistaken. The Chinese peasant was not passive; he was not a coward. He would fight when given a method, an organization, leadership, a workable program, hope—*and arms*.

Of all Mao's writing, probably none is more important for a student of history than his *Report on an Investigation into the Peasant Movement in Hunan*, written in February 1927. Mao listed "Fourteen Great Deeds." Greatest of the "deeds" was that the poor peasants had at last actually organized—a miracle in itself—against "the local bullies," "the bad gentry," and "the corrupt officials." Among the other good deeds were smashing the political prestige of the landlords; compelling them to audit accounts; forcing them to make contributions to the starving; parading the most brutal oppressors through the streets; prohibiting usury, grain hoarding, speculation, excessive rents; taking over the offices of police chiefs and electing magistrates; taking command of the landlords' militia; eliminating banditry (by bringing bandits into the peasant associations!); overthrowing feudal clan tyranny of rich over poor; fining oppressive landlords and helping themselves to their provisions; ridiculing superstitious practices; ending male tyranny over women; spreading knowledge of the "Three Principles"; prohibiting gambling, opium smoking, sumptuous feasts, expensive weddings and elaborate funerals; sponsoring mass education for illiterates; organizing marketing and credit cooperatives; and building roads and irrigation ditches financed by "contributions" from the landlords.

One of the most remarkable things about Mao's report was that it scarcely mentioned Western imperialism, the major preoccupation of Comintern strategy of the time; almost its entire emphasis was on the necessity to overthrow landlord-gentry oppression in order to liberate the peasantry from "feudalism" and inequality.

A woman in a rural marketplace with two children for sale.

Such was Mao's vision of good and evil in the countryside. Such became the program of history's first Communist-led revolution based on the poor peasantry as its "vanguard."

Mao's faith in the peasant as the main engine of social revolution developed from objective experience and was not shared by the Russians. Orthodox Marxists elsewhere also continued to believe that a Communist movement could not succeed without an organized industrial proletariat as its main insurrectionary force. In the beginning the Chinese agreed. After their initial disasters (1927–30) in urban insurrections, when the party was all but destroyed, they had no choice but to fall back on the rural areas, where Mao and Chu Teh set up the first peasant sanctuaries. Real events thenceforth made the peasants virtually their sole material and mass support. Out of them came the strength which finally carried the Communists to national power, with minimum help from the heavily policed urban working class.

Mao Tse-tung speaking to a poor-peasants' meeting in Kiangsi province, 1933.

" 'Whoever wins the peasants will win China,' " Mao Tse-tung told me in 1936. " 'Whoever solves the land question will win the peasants.' "

"Nothing is more significant of the nature of Manchuria's past than the Great Wall of China. At Shanhaikuan, westward from Dairen, it comes down to the sea to end a rambling career of more than 2,000 miles from its beginning on the edge of far Turkestan. The 'problem of Manchuria' today was old for China when the wall was built, 23 centuries ago. The most stupendous visage of masonry on earth, the only man-made thing that could be seen from the moon, it was in a respect the world's greatest fiasco. For it did not keep out the barbarians of the north; it delayed, but did not prevent, the successive conquests of China."

A poster proclaims the establishment of Manchukuo
—the Japanese name for occupied Manchuria.

5

MANCHURIA 1931: THE REAL BEGINNING OF WORLD WAR II

For the Japanese generals in Manchurian command, the horizon beckoned, illimitable and romantic. As it stirred the blood of conquistadores in the past, so it excited the Yamato-descended samurai. Using the weapons of our thoroughly modern "civilization" they were in reality the standard-bearers of a state still semifeudal in structure, and imbued with a love of feudal emprise.

Historically Manchuria has been the birthplace of Asiatic conquerors. There seems to be, innate in the natural geography of the land, something that impels men to drive southward and westward. That impulse, long ago, swept the Tungus outward from their tribal home along the Yalu River. It drove the virile Liaos ("Iron Men"), the Chins ("Golden Horde"), the Tartars, the Mongols, and finally the Manchus, each in successive waves, to ride down below the Great Wall, ravage and vanquish China, and rule Eastern Asia.

"Blood and Iron" Baron Gi-ichi Tanaka, leader of the militant Seiyukai party, and spokesman for the military, came into control of the Japanese government. He at once announced his intention to follow a "strong policy" against China, and his subsequent acts proved it. The *Tanaka Memorial* was believed prepared following a conference held in June 1927, when high civil and military officials from the empire assembled to make recommendations regarding future policy in Asia. The advantages of Mongolia and Manchuria, this document explained, were not merely in scarcity of population in a country three times as large as Japan, but with a third of her population; they also have greater undeveloped wealth in mines, agricultural possibilities and timber than any land. This document, with its very detailed recommendations for combined economic and military penetration into Manchuria and Mongolia, supposedly formed the basic plan for positive action intended to be commenced as soon as practicable. It was to prove an almost unerring guide to the march of Japanese imperialism. For in Tokyo the army and navy, separately commanded by the emperor, and responsible to him alone, had prepared to

Chang Hsueh-liang (*left*), "The Young Marshal," ruler of Manchuria 1928–31, and Chang Tso-lin, "The Old Marshal" (1873–1928).

realize just such a plan as the *Memorial* succinctly indicated.

Chang Hsueh-liang's policy was to restrict Japanese economic and political expansion in Manchuria and in time to break down Japan's "special position" entirely. In Chang, for the first time, the Japanese had to deal with a man who, through influences and environments under which he lived in China, was more Chinese than "Manchurian." The ethical direction of his rule bent more and more toward interdependence with China, though he released no real authority.

To comprehend the "Young Marshal" you must know something of that wise, wily, energetic Sino-Manchurian "Old Marshal" Chang Tso-lin, who presented him with Manchuria as a patrimony. By the time Japan declared war on Russia and chose Manchuria for the field of contest, Chang Tso-lin was chief of a large, well-organized bandit force. Lured by promises of liberal reward from the Japanese, he threw in his lot on their side and came out of the war with the strongest army in Manchuria. Before the collapse of the Ching Dynasty in 1912 he held power of life and death over the greater part of South Manchuria.

Following the [first] revolution, Chang Tso-lin was ordained with the title of governor, bestowed by the Caesar-minded Yuan Shih-kai, dictator of the new regime in China. When in 1917 Yuan attempted an imperial restoration with himself as emperor at Peking, Chang helped bring about his

ruin. Through Yuan's failure to mount the Dragon Throne, Grand Marshal Chang was enabled to extend his influence south of the Great Wall.

The Old Marshal's life was no couch of cherry blossoms. He lived in constant fear of assassination. He felt somewhat more at ease when his son Hsueh-liang took command of the bodyguard. Young Chang was twenty-one years old.

A breezy, handsome youth who liked Western style and custom, he wore imported clothes and drove European racing cars at top speed through his father's cities; he acquired a passion for gambling and the opium-smoking habit. He became the singing girls' delight and the Old Marshal's great problem.

From 1926 till 1928 Chang Tso-lin ran a government in North China and Manchuria which was recognized by the Powers. Ousted finally from Peking by the drive of the southern Nationalists, he retired north of the Wall. As his train crossed a bridge over the Japanese-owned South Manchuria Railway a bomb exploded directly over his private car. Both the Nationalists and the Japanese were credited with the assassination. Nanking denied it. Tokyo did not.

It was uncertain who would succeed him. Two powerful generals seemed more likely candidates than the callow son of the Grand Marshal. But Chang Hsueh-liang solved the matter with a coup d'état of his own. At Nanking the Nationalist government rejoiced. The youth's control of Manchuria was given official approval. Nanking gave him the rank of governor general, a courtesy which the elated Young Marshal returned by "recognizing" Nanking.

The "Mukden Incident"

On September 18, 1931, a few feet of track allegedly were blown up on the South Manchurian Railway conveniently near the Japanese garrison at Mukden. An express train shortly afterward passed over the spot without damage, but the "incident" was the excuse for punitive action which ended with the Japanese conquest of Manchuria, the richest part of China. But the "Mukden Incident" was not a beginning so much as the end product of a half dozen earlier wars and "unexpected" results and "issues" created by them. Protean social and political forces which exploded in Japan's aggression were mixed with the moral and political convictions of a sense of divine mission to correct ancient wrongs.

The Mukden invasion deeply stirred many Chinese, and economic retaliations commenced. For a while it seemed that the Kuomintang and the Nan-

king government might become regenerate, might restore popular faith by rallying, organizing and consolidating the disillusioned nation in a program of resistance against Japan. But the correct brand of leadership was not to appear; Nanking remained invertebrate.

Nevertheless, thousands of patriotic students, small merchants, intellectuals, rose now and in the cities led demonstrations against the Japanese. "Heaven is high and the Emperor is far away," but despite their indifference to political pyrotechnics the Chinese began to demonstrate that they still possessed a certain racial solidarity in passive resistance. Could the boycott, too, be broken by the

Peddlers offering wet towels for rent to Chinese government troops.

Japanese mounted soldiers enter Shenyang, Manchuria, 1931.

sword? The Japanese were soon to attempt it at Shanghai.

When General Honjo came into Mukden he adopted the measures of war against the populace and the former government. Officials who had not fled were arrested; a few were killed; most of them were released and put out of the country; some were retained to be used in the new Japanese-organized administration. The military seized control of government offices, including the provincial bureaus of finance, industries, post office and communications. They took over Chinese railways, telegraphs, the American-built radio station, the telephone, light, power and salt administrations. Chinese who participated in this reorganized scheme of things became known as "puppets" because they held their jobs, of course, only as long as they carried out instructions of the Japanese advisers.

When the invasion commenced, Young Marshal Chang was in Peking and in no condition to meet this crisis alone. He leaned heavily on Nanking and on his blood-sworn "elder brother," Chiang

Chiang Kai-shek (*center*) meets a delegation of students protesting Japanese aggression, in Nanking, November 1931.

Letter from the Front

"I had an interesting trip to Manchuria last month. It was cold in Dairen, colder in Mukden and below freezing in Harbin. I went up to Tsitsihar, where it was ten below—in November. I felt like a couple of stalactites when I left the place. Six of us went up on the Chinese Eastern Railway the same day the Japanese occupied the town, which is the capital of Heilungkiang province. There were still numerous bodies spread over the fields and various parts of what were once Chinese soldiers: arms, legs, hands, feet, etc. They were all frozen; some of the bodies had been devoured partly. There are many wolves and wild dogs, always hungry. The snow was covered with their bloody tracks. Despite the fact that 5,000 Japanese drove back 20,000 Chinese, and annihilated nearly a thousand, the latter put up a better fight than anyone expected. Those northerners are tall and strong limbed, used to the cold and are full of courage. Against them the Japanese had eight giant air bombers, tanks, heavy artillery, armored cars, and all under the operation of a highly efficient, well-disciplined army. The Chinese were mostly recruited from bandits and peasants, had no airplanes, and only light artillery. But they managed to kill more than 200 Japanese before the latter obliterated their front line trenches." (Letter to brother Howard, Shanghai, Dec. 7, 1931)

Rolling stock destroyed by Japanese invaders, Shenyang, September 18, 1931.

Kai-shek, who urged reliance on the League of Nations. As a result Chang lost his homeland after only token resistance was offered by his retreating troops. The sacrifice enabled the Generalissimo to hold his own shaky regime together in Nanking and begin a new annihilation campaign against the Reds. That was how the Manchurian troops, known as the Tungpei Army, moved south of the Great Wall into China proper.

Attack on Shanghai

It was dark midnight, January 28, 1932.
Suddenly Japanese rifle and machine-gun fire laced Jukong Road up which I hurried from the Shanghai North Station. I saw a figure stop and fall. Beyond, a Chinese soldier dropped to his knees, crawled inside a doorway, and commenced firing.

Above: A district of Shanghai destroyed by Japanese bombs, 1932. *Below:* "Harvest" is the title Snow gave to this photograph of bombing victims, which he took in Shanghai, 1932.

The street emptied like a drain; iron shutters closed as if clams lived inside, and the last light disappeared.

In that stinking alley, the "greatest" battle since World War I was beginning.

Outrage piled on outrage: cases of banditry, kidnapping, homicide and brutality. Obviously certain Chinese had been marked well in advance; these were leading merchants or businessmen who had declined to trade with Japanese. Some were abducted, not to be heard of again; their families were attacked and often wiped out completely. I saw a helpless old Chinese woman dragged from her home and kicked in the face. The reign of terror instituted by these Japanese run amok was not to be effectively checked for days.

This extraordinary conduct was not sanctioned by the entire Japanese community. The more intelligent were shocked and alarmed by the crimes committed. Certain Japanese consular officials were especially embarrassed, but they were powerless to interfere.

"There was the fresh corpse of a fallen Japanese aviator I saw right after a Chinese soldier pulled out his smoking heart, leaving behind a deep dark wound the shape of a perfect cross, cut by bayonet; and the smell of smoking flesh slapped against the steel sides of a bombed troop train around which naked youths, their clothes blown off and their bodies roasted whole, were plumper than ever in their meagerly-fed lives. I remember, too, the surrealist rag-doll men in their rough cotton-padded blue gowns hanging where the Japanese had left them after using them for bayonet practice; and the heat of skies of a city that the great arsonist burned for a month, to 'maintain law and order,' while dancing as usual went on in the Settlement sanctuary."

A Japanese sailor displays the head he has just cut off the body of a Chinese.

The Nineteenth Route Army

"The Chinese," said Japanese Admiral Kenkichi Shiozawa, "respect nothing but force." Shiozawa took everything into consideration except the Nineteenth Route Army.

I had met many Chinese generals, but never one who inspired trust and confidence. Tsai did. The rough grace of his manner, his habit of direct speech, the Spartan simplicity of his dress and his surroundings, all impressed me. Tsai was never under any illusion regarding the mechanical superiority of the Japanese forces. "The Japanese have every device of modern warfare," he said. "They have tanks, armored cars, heavy artillery, airplanes and a fleet of the best warships in the Orient. We have practically nothing but rifles and machine guns. But our resistance here is to establish a principle: the right of any people to defend themselves against invasion threatening the very existence of their nation. Men of my army know this and that is why they fight with a great spirit."

Made up largely of soldiers who participated in the Nationalist advance which, in 1926, nearly succeeded in uniting North and South, the Nineteenth Route Army is perhaps the oldest modern army in China. Its nucleus was trained at Canton by Russian Communist advisers when the Kuomintang was allied with the Communist party of China. Unlike other Chinese armies, it did not impress men; they had all enlisted voluntarily.

The "Nineteenth" was the best army in the lower Yangtze Valley, a "new" army, the product of the Nationalist revolution. Its commanders had sided with the Generalissimo against the Communists but they had their own system of left-wing nationalism, political indoctrination and morale. Although officers and men were alike indignant when Chiang capitulated to the Shanghai ultimatum, they were good soldiers and began obeying orders to withdraw. When the Japanese attacked, however, they turned in their tracks in passionate self-defense. Within a day or two the whole country offered them unprecedented moral support. Thousands of youths flocked to volunteer. The battle was fought over every street and block of the metropolis. Only after thirty-four days of operations, which involved a large part of the Japanese fleet, scores of naval bombers, 65,000 Japanese troops, and extensive operations far on the flanks of the city, did the Nineteenth Army retreat—with about half of its original force of approximately 45,000. Chiang Kai-shek himself never entered the battle.

General Tsai Ting-kai, commander of the Nationalist government's 19th Route Army.

The Nineteenth Route Army
defending Shanghai,
January 28, 1932.

The Japanese charge that among the Nineteenth were many Communists is true. That was denied by the Chinese government, which pointed to the fact that the army had been fighting Communists in Kiangsi before coming to Shanghai. It was in Kiangsi, as a matter of fact, that many of the rank and file had come into contact with Communist peasants and had been converted. At the conclusion of the Shanghai hostilities, that element was to become so influential as to necessitate the entire reorganization of the army, and the elimination of hundreds of such revolutionary youths.

The "Nineteenth" was later liquidated by the Generalissimo after the shattered remains had retired to Fukien province. There Chiang kept it bottled up and carefully watched for an opening. Its disgruntled commanders rebelled and organized a "reformed" and "revolutionary" Kuomintang. They even sought an anti-Japanese alliance with the Chinese Red Army, which had already formally "declared war" on Japan. But the Communists blundered and thereby saved Chiang. Divided by arguments over whether they could trust such an alliance, they lost time. Chiang attacked by surprise and broke up the Nineteenth before it could unite with the Reds. He was then able to turn all his energy to the suppression of what he described as his "first and worst enemy."

The Chinese Boy Scouts were made dispatch bearers—doctors and nurses offered services behind the lines, while hundreds of civilians contributed food, sweets, clothing and books to men at the front. One music house gave nearly its entire stock of gramophones, so that afterward, between spasms of machine-gunning, you often heard them grinding out the latest jazz. When one day I saw a fastidious Chinese singing girl I knew bearing a stretcher behind the Chinese lines I concluded that something at last had shaken China.

Getting Away with Murder

After more than a year's procrastination the League of Nations began definitely and finally to turn against Japan. For the first time in history a nation had stood trial before a tribunal of other nations and a judgment had been rendered against it. But, fatal weakness of the League, who would enforce its judgment?

Japan could not have chosen a better time to strike. America seemed paralyzed with the Depression. In Britain unemployment also was a grave matter. The nation's finances were in a perilous state. She was engaged in a futile effort to end the Indian agitation for independence. France was absorbed with revolt in Indochina. In Germany there were violent social and political conflicts, where six million unemployed clamored for relief. The whole Western capitalist world appeared mated with disaster unless some new scheme were devised to control the social and economic forces it had created and which threatened to crush it. Soviet Russia alone appeared to have found such a scheme, and experiment with it involved the nation's entire energy, resource and application. China as usual was in a state of turmoil.

"Ex-Emperor Henry Pu Yi, whose dethronement in 1912 ended 268 years of Manchu rule in China. At the age of six he had been sitting on the Dragon Throne in the Forbidden City when the first revolution forced his abdication. He lived in exile in Tientsin until the Japanese spirited him off to set him up as the puppet emperor Kang Teh of Manchukuo."

America vacillated, never did make up her mind, not then, and not up to the eve of Pearl Harbor. When America did little but moralize against Japan in 1931, Chiang also did nothing. Nonresistance and "reliance on the League of Nations" became his policy. The League also did nothing. Italy and Germany, rising new aggressor states of the West, now took their cue from the East.

"On September 15, 1932, just three days before the first anniversary of the Japanese invasion at Mukden, H.I.J.M. Hirohito's 'Own Ambassador,' General Nobuyoshi Muto, signed the Protocol at Hsinking which accorded full and formal recognition to the independent government of 'Manchukuo.' The ceremony was sanctified in the palace of Pu Yi, to whom the Chinese writing brush used by the signators was presented as a souvenir."

Pu Yi and wife.

Pu Yi 1960

In Peking, at a cocktail party, I found myself talking to a thin, hollow-chested guest who gazed out of lashless eyes behind heavy-rimmed glasses. He had a bad haircut and was the most simply attired person there. If he had not been munching hors d'oeuvres and holding a glass of wine, I would have thought he had wandered in by mistake. Yet he looked vaguely familiar.

"What kind of work are you doing now?" I probed.

"I am a gardener," he said. "I work in the botanical gardens of the Academia Sinica."

"Oh, you're a horticulturist?"

He replied, through an interpreter, in self-accusation: "My crime helped to cause the deaths of millions of people. I should have died for it. Instead I have been given a chance to repent and to work for socialist construction. I am happy for the first time in my life because for the first time I am doing something useful."

Here was indeed a sinner wearing his re-molded thoughts on his sleeve.

"You are," said the Chinese beside me, "speaking to the former Manchu emperor, Hsuan Tung." The boy emperor—Pu Yi. He was now fifty-four. Captured by the Russians in 1945, he had been returned to China only a few years ago. Pu Yi had been kidnapped by the Japanese and I asked him now if after all he should really feel guilty.

"Oh, yes," he told me. "I worked willingly with them. I felt ashamed to have lost my family's power and I believed the Japanese would help restore it. Any other country would have killed me. Instead, they have let me work at what was always my hobby—gardening."

Someone later told me that the best of it for Pu Yi was that he had finally been able to divorce two of the three wives to whom others had married him.

"And today you support socialism?" I asked.

"Yes, certainly!" he said. "Socialism is good." He proposed a toast which was on everybody's lips that day: "To the friendship of the Chinese and American—people!"

Beginning and end are like a circle, says the *Chuang-tzu*; where there is end there is the beginning. Pu Yi had reached the end.

Pu Yi with Edgar Snow in Peking, 1960.

From left: Chou En-lai, Chu Teh and Mao Tse-tung, in northern Shensi.

6

MAO AND HIS CIRCLE 1927-1934

Under the military stewardship of Chiang Kai-shek the Kuomintang inevitably alienated most of the mass support which it had won on the basis of Dr. Sun's broadly socialistic principles. Control of the government retroverted to the hands of the not very intelligent members of the military caste, poorly educated, socially backward, worshiping power, privilege and wealth, some intellectually subnormal, and in political outlook Machiavellian. The destruction of people's organizations removed restraints from such militarists, and the reaction, wherever it held real power, established a "White" terror. Even "intellectual Communism" became, in most districts, a capital offense. Thousands of adherents of the more democratic and progressive elements were imprisoned or shot; the word massacre is not inaccurate to describe the executions which took place. These attacks were conducted as a crusade against the "Red menace," but in the élan for "purgation," modern liberal thought also became the target. Dr. Sun's sacred texts were badly besmirched.

The Nanking government sanguinarily crushed the labor-union movement in China, which had been enjoying a salutary independent growth. It cracked up the various unions of peasants struggling for political enlightenment, and to free themselves from the lethal system of usury and landlordism that militarism had fastened upon them. Peasant and worker leaders were executed wherever the militarist went. Elementary rights of citizenship were curtailed. Regional military satraps again entrenched their control of what courts existed. Intellectuals were threatened with violence, and their demand for constitutional government was hushed. Political philosophy differing from the brand of the generals (who sanctimoniously continued to worship Dr. Sun Yat-sen) was regarded as heresy; its proponents were persecuted and killed. A break with Communist leadership, as handled by General Chiang, nullified all the early achievements of the Northern Expedition and left regional militarism and foreign imperialism entrenched throughout China. The Kuomintang now lost its revolutionary drive and its unity. Its program was immolated; it became the instrument of Chiang's group. Repressive methods adopted by the neo-militarists who everywhere grasped power tragically retarded natural political growths and social reforms. Their excesses in restoring full feudal and bourgeois control over government and property estranged the confidence of the workers, the peasants, the students, the scholars, the intellectuals, the patriotic youth everywhere that for a while had had faith. The more radical revolutionary elements among them, including a host of untutored but increasingly desperate farmers, joined the Communists in Central China.

With Chiang's reversion to the warlord prototype there began a series of factional party quarrels and a recrudescence of civil war. The net results were an appalling sacrifice of life and property, a sullen agrarian population for which life became more and more intolerable under the scourge of militarism, a nation shouldered with a debt so heavy as to make reduction of taxes unthinkable, and a government at Nanking mortgaged at home and abroad to imperialism, but withal in uncertain control only of four central provinces immediately surrounding the capital.

Principally in Kiangsi province but also in large parts of Hunan, Honan, Szechuan, Fukien and Anhwei, peasant armies had driven out or killed Kuomintang officials and gentry and had established soviet government. Areas which included a population of between fifty and seventy millions of peasants were thoroughly bolshevized. The movement was fundamentally a mass effort to achieve economic and social reforms.

Following the reaction in 1927, the Red Armies, accompanied by political organizers, extirpated the system of exploitation. Landlords, usurers and local militarists were liquidated. Debts were canceled, deeds torn up, and land redistributed among peasants and soldiers. Temples, ancestral temple estates, public utilities and resources were placed under state control. Child slavery was abolished, opium smoking prohibited, prostitution and concubinage ended, and the franchise extended to all peasants, workers and soldiers.

Beginning, in 1927, with the nucleus of 15,000 ill-equipped troops, the Red Armies in 1933 numbered about 90,000 men. Originally armed with little more than pitchforks and spears, surrounded on all sides by enemies, with little but the resources of the peasants to support them, the Communist party had, in Central China, achieved formidable dimensions. Red soldiers were all peasants, likewise their political leaders. Everywhere they moved they seemed to win the support of the peasantry. Even small children became their spies against Nanking.

The earth had been prepared for something new. It seemed clear that the old values would never be restored. It remained to be seen whether the movement would produce something better to replace it.

Attempts at armed uprisings in Canton and Nanchang were bloodily suppressed. Gathering together the pieces of the peasant associations—their local leadership having been decapitated by the Kuomintang—Mao launched the first armed rural insurrection, called the Autumn Harvest Uprising. By September 1927 it had developed the First Division of the First Peasants and Workers Army. Inexperienced and poorly armed, the little band was quickly surrounded and forced into disorderly retreat. Mao himself was captured by Kuomintang forces and almost beheaded. While he was being taken to the execution grounds he broke loose and fled into a swamp. Fleeing southward at night, he emerged, barefoot and with seven dollars in his pocket; he came upon friendly peasants who helped him re-establish contact with his remnant forces. Rallying about a thousand men, he retreated to a mountain stronghold called Chingkangshan (Kiangsi), and there established the first base of the new revolution.

The Red Army clung tenaciously to the mountains of South China, and civil war spread over many provinces. The Communists went about redistributing the land and organizing local workers' and peasants' governments, while Chiang went after them, bringing back the landlord system, restoring boundary stones, and executing the rebels and smashing their unions. A decade of this waste took a terrific toll in lives of educated youths with rare qualities of leadership which China could little afford to lose.

The schoolhouse meeting hall of the Autumn Harvest Uprising in Changsha, Hunan province. "Protect Your Health" is the message written in Chinese above the numbers on the wall of the school's exercise yard.

"The Chinese Red Army made its first training base on the mountain of Chingkangshan in Kiangsi province and built defences about it. They wrote a song of nostalgia about this mountain, sung to the melody of 'I Wish I Were in Dixie.'"

Seven members of the First Central Executive Committee in Juichin, November 7, 1931. *From left:* unknown, Jen Pi-shih, Chu Teh, Teng Fa, Hsiao Keh, Mao Tse-tung and Wang Chia-hsiang. It was at this meeting that Mao was elected Chairman of the Chinese Soviet Republic and Chu Teh became commander-in-chief of the Red Army.

At the First Party Congress of the Soviet area, held on December 11, 1931, Mao is seated on the stage (*center*) with Chu Teh to his right.

Fang Chih-min (*center*) with two of his officers, prisoners of the Kuomintang.

Fang Chih-min was a leader of the Kiangsi provincial Communist party and organizer of peasant partisan warfare. He supported Mao's "peasant line" and led the first peasant detachments in the Kiangsi Autumn Harvest Uprising. He joined Mao and Chu Teh at Chingkangshan. He continued to adhere closely to Mao's views throughout the pre–Long March period. Left behind with the rear guard, he was captured by Kuomintang troops. After being paraded through the countryside in a bamboo cage, he was beheaded in 1935.

The "mass base" of the soviet movement was built upon the organization of workers' and peasants' unions, with the principal role in the hands of the "poor peasantry, the vast majority" led by the Communist party, claiming hegemony over the revolution and its ultimate "proletarian dictatorship." Its radical policy included outright confiscation of landlords' estates and their distribution among have-not peasants, and the establishment of socialist ownership over means of industrial production. Effective leadership required very strict discipline and moral codes and a readiness to share all the hardships of peasant life.

As early as the Chingkangshan period, the army had "imposed three simple rules: prompt obedience to orders; no confiscations whatever from the poor peasantry; prompt delivery to the government, for disposal, of all goods confiscated from the landlords."

The "eight disciplinary rules" were aimed chiefly to establish friendly relations with the people. Red soldiers sing them on the march:

1. Replace doors when you leave a house.*
2. Return and roll up the straw matting.†
3. Be courteous and polite to the people and help them.
4. Return all borrowed articles.
5. Replace all damaged articles.
6. Be honest in all transactions with the peasants.
7. Pay for all articles purchased.
8. Be sanitary: establish latrines at a safe distance from people's houses.

Three other duties were taught to the Red Army as its primary purpose: first, to struggle to the death against the enemy; second, to arm the masses; third, to raise money to support the struggle—all innovations for Chinese soldiers, traditionally contemptuous of the people and regarded by them as a kind of unavoidable scourge and punishment. (Good iron doesn't become a nail, said an ancient Chinese proverb, nor does a good man become a soldier.)

---

* Wooden doors of Chinese peasant houses are hung on pegs and are easily detachable; placed on wooden stools, they serve as improvised beds.
† Used for sleeping.

The Education of a Communist

Mao was born in 1893 in the village of Shao Shan, in Hunan province. His father, Mao Jen-sheng, owned 3.7 acres, which gave him the status of a rich peasant. Tiny as his acreage was, labor productivity was so low that he needed a regular hired hand; in busy seasons he took on another. He also used the part-time labor of his wife and three sons, of whom Mao Tse-tung was eldest. Once a month the father gave the hired laborers eggs with their rice, "but never meat," said Mao. "To me he gave neither eggs nor meat."

The old man regularly beat his children to secure unquestioning compliance. He was himself barely literate enough to keep books. He sent his sons to school, hoping to see them become good businessmen and help him "amass a fortune." Their teacher belonged to the "stern-treatment school" and beat his students. Mao's first remembered act of rebellion was in protest against such treatment when he was ten years old. He ran away from school but was afraid to return home for fear of another beating. He wandered "in the general direction of the city" until he was found.

"After my return to the family," said Mao, "to my surprise conditions somewhat improved. My father was slightly more considerate and the teacher was more inclined toward moderation." Mao's mother was wholly illiterate and a devout Buddhist who gave young Mao religious instruction—heavily diluted by his father's skepticism. "She was a kind woman, generous and sympathetic," said Mao. "She pitied the poor and often gave them rice when they came to ask for it during famines. But my father disapproved of charity. We had many quarrels in my home over this question." Mao and his mother "made many efforts to convert him, without success."

"There were two 'parties' in the family. One was my father, the Ruling Power. The Opposition was made up of myself, my mother, my brother and even the laborer. In the United Front of the Opposition, however, there was a difference of opinion. My mother advocated a policy of indirect attack. She criticized any overt display of emotion and attempts at open rebellion against the Ruling Power. She said it was not the Chinese way."

When Mao was about thirteen his father invited

Left: Mao Tse-tung, a student in 1914. *Right:* Mao in 1919, after graduation from normal school in Changsha.

many guests to their home. A dispute arose between them and the old man denounced Mao before everybody, calling him "lazy and useless." Infuriated, Mao cursed him and left the house, threatening to commit suicide. His mother ran after him and begged Mao to return, but he continued to the edge of a pond and stood ready to jump in.

"My father also pursued me, cursing me at the same time he commanded me to come back. He insisted that I *kou-tou* [knock head to earth] as a sign of submission. I agreed to give a one-knee *kou-tou* if he would promise not to beat me. Thus the war ended and from it I learned that when I defended my rights by open rebellion my father relented but when I remained meek and submissive he only cursed and beat me the more."

The dichotomy between his father's harsh conservativism and his mother's kindness and compassion, the sympathy established with hired peasants who supported him against his father, his resentment against male domination of his mother, and her submissiveness to fate, all reflected a generation in rebellion against blind filial piety and Confucian traditions no longer suitable for the nation's needs. An end to the feudal and patriarchal clan-family system, opportunity for the poor peasants, equal rights for women, brotherhood in a new freedom that had to be won by hard struggle for one's rights, by defending the interests of the lowly against the mighty: these were ideas which Mao's early life taught him to share with many awakening youths.

Always among the most impoverished students, Mao nevertheless managed to scrimp through five years in the Hunan Normal School [in Changsha, the capital city of Hunan], from which he graduated in 1918. In the interim, and while still in primary and middle schools, he had witnessed famines, revolts, banditry and executions. In Changsha he had seen the heads of rebels mounted on poles to strike terror into the people. As a child he had watched poor peasants, driven by starvation during famine, sack the granaries of the gentry. When leaders of the bandits were captured, their heads had also been spiked and displayed as a public warning. By now he fully understood the price of both social and national revolt.

In 1911 Mao enlisted in the republican forces after he had witnessed the seizure of Changsha. Six months later he "resigned"; the emperor had abdicated and a republic was proclaimed. "Thinking the revolution was over," he explained, "I

The head of a bandit—Red or real—stuck on a pole.

decided to return to my books." After many vacillations Mao determined to become a teacher.

It quickly became apparent that a mere change from dynastic role to military dictatorship would not end China's decline. Mao began to spend most of his limited cash on newspapers. The famous *New Youth* magazine, edited by Chen Tu-hsiu, a returned student from France, made a deep impression on Mao and other students of the time. Echoing Chen's revolutionary ideas in Hunan, Mao gathered together some friends to form a "discussion group." He built up a following among students and asserted his political leadership for the first time. Everything they did and said "must have a purpose," he told me. They wasted no words on "love or romance and considered the times too critical and the need for knowledge too urgent to discuss women or personal matters. I was not interested in women. My parents had married me when I was fourteen to a girl of twenty but I had never lived with her—and never did. I did not consider her my wife."

More unusual for Chinese students of that time, Mao and his friends became ardent physical culturists. They sought to toughen and steel themselves by taking long excursions, living in the mountains on a minimum of food, sleeping in the open, bathing in cold streams. One summer Mao and another student walked across five counties of his native province, "without using a single copper. The peasants fed us and gave us a place to sleep;

wherever we went we were kindly treated." It was always the poor peasants, Mao noted, who were generous in sharing what little they had. Discussing their lives and problems, Mao learned of hardships and injustice beyond anything he had suffered.

In these same counties, and to the homes of many of the same peasants who had sheltered him, Mao would ten years later return to launch the peasant movement which provided the first recruits for the Red Army.

Mao first went to Peking in 1918, as a delegate from the New People's Study Society. There, at the age of twenty-five, he tentatively stepped upon the national political stage. Mao had already made wide-ranging contacts and done omnivorous reading in the Changsha library. In his self-study he was guided by his favorite teacher, Yang Chang-chi. Now Mao found Yang again, as a professor at Peking National University. Through his help Mao secured a job under the university librarian, Li Ta-chao, who later became a principal founder of the Communist party. Here he also fell in love with Yang Chang-chi's daughter, Kai-hui; they were married in 1920.

Both Li Ta-chao and Mao's youthful and beautiful bride were executed a few years later, after membership in the Communist party was made a capital offense.

As an assistant librarian Mao's job was "so low that people avoided me." He lived in a little room which held seven other people. "When we were all packed fast on the *kang* there was scarcely room to breathe. I had to warn people on each side when I wanted to turn over." They could not afford wood for a fire but shared each other's bodily warmth. Among them they had one winter coat, and they wore it in turn when they wished to go out at night.

In spite of his poverty and humble occupation Mao managed to meet important leaders of the cultural renaissance, including Chen Tu-hsiu. Under his spell and that of Li Ta-chao and other senior intellectuals of that time, the impact of the Russian Revolution turned Mao toward Marxism and a commitment to socialist revolution. By the summer of 1920 Mao considered himself a Marxist, and in the following year he joined Li Ta-chao and ten others to found the Chinese Communist Party. His leadership was not to assume great national significance until 1926, but in retrospect it is clear that his experience in organizing the peasant unions of his native province came to dominate his own thinking and, ultimately, the course of the revolution.

Li Ta-chao (1888–1927), one of the founders of the Chinese Communist Party. "Li Ta-chao became, during his relatively brief life, which ended in execution by strangulation, the single most important Chinese radical political influence in his time, the first impressive Chinese interpreter of Marxism, and the first major contributor to a system or ideology which may be called Chinese Marxist thought. To say that without Li Ta-chao there could have been no Mao Tse-tung may be an overstatement, but some of the main features of Mao's thought are explicit or implicit in the writings of Li Ta-chao, which Mao implemented in action."

Chen Tu-hsiu, the first general secretary (1921–27) of the Chinese Communist Party. "In 1927 Chen was accused of 'rightism' and dropped from the Politburo. I asked Mao whom he considered most responsible for the failure of the Communist Party in 1927 and the triumph of the Nanking dictatorship. Mao placed the greatest blame on Chen Tu-hsiu, whose 'wavering opportunism' deprived the Party of decisive leadership and a direct line of its own at a moment when further compromise clearly meant catastrophe."

Tsai Ho-sen and Yang Kai-hui

Tsai probably had a greater influence than anyone else on Mao's thinking as a revolutionary "internationalist." The son of an intellectual family of Hunan, Tsai was among the first Chinese to join the Work-Study student emigrants to France in 1920 and perhaps the first Chinese to espouse the Communist cause there. Tsai Chang, his sister, accompanied him to Europe. After he returned to China, Tsai played a leading role in the Central Committee during the 1925–27 period. At the time of his arrest and execution in 1927, by order of Chiang Kai-shek, he was a member of the Party Politburo. His wife, Hsiang Ching-wu, an outstanding women's leader, was executed in 1928.

Yang Kai-hui came from a wealthy landowning family of Hunan. She was the daughter of Yang Chang-chi, Mao Tse-tung's highly respected teacher. Mao was a frequent visitor in Yang's home; in Peking he often dined with the family. Marriages were then arranged by parents; in many cases, the bride and bridegroom did not see each other before betrothal (as in Mao's first "marriage"). Yang Chang-chi obviously had advanced ideas about women's rights or he would not have provided a higher education for his daughter and permitted her to dine at the table with Mao and himself. Mao influenced Yang Kai-hui toward radicalism—and marriage to himself—in 1920. She was then twenty-five. When arrested, in 1930, she refused to repudiate the Communist party, or Mao, as the alternative to death. She was executed in the same year, at Changsha. Yang Kai-hui and Mao had two sons, Mao An-ching and Mao An-ying.

Peking, 1920. Mao (*fourth from left*) posed for this picture with some student companions, including his best friend, Tsai Ho-sen (*in fur collar, right of Mao*) and Teng Chung-hsia (*right of Tsai*) who played a leading role in the Chinese labor movement. Teng was executed by the Nationalists in 1933.

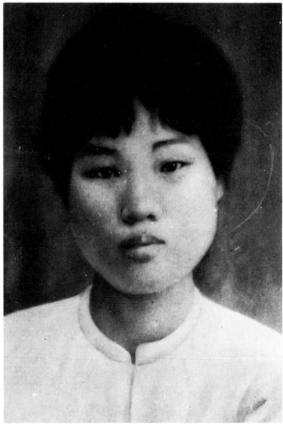

Mao's first wife was Yang Kai-hui (1901–1930). Their marriage was celebrated as an "ideal romance" among radical youths in Hunan province.

"Chu Teh, who was the Reds' commander-in-chief and Mao's military alter ego, came from a tenant peasant family in which five children were drowned at birth because of poverty. Of the Chu children who survived he was the only one educated; instead of being drowned he was given away to a childless relative who managed to get him into a school for landlords' sons."

Chu Teh congratulating a Red Army squad after a successful offensive in Kiangsi in 1923. He has removed his hat to address his troops, a practice common among the Red commanders.

The Chu-Mao Combination

Chu Teh's political fortunes pyramided rapidly. He acquired several wives and concubines and built a palatial home in the capital of Yunnan. He had everything he desired: wealth, power, love, descendants, poppy dreams, eminent respectability and a comfortable future. He had, in fact, only one really bad habit, but it was to prove his downfall. He liked to read books. He gradually understood that the revolution of 1911 had merely replaced one despotic bureaucracy of exploitation with another. What was more, he seemed to have worried about it —as anyone of feeling, living in Yunnanfu [later known as Kunming], a city of 40,000 slave girls and boys, might well have done. By 1922 Chu Teh, unburdened of wives and concubines, went to Shanghai, where he met many young revolutionaries of the Kuomintang, which he had joined.

He went to Germany, where he divested himself of all the prejudices and limitations of his traditional Chinese training. Late in 1925 he returned to Shanghai and rejoined his former superior, General Chu Pei-teh, whose power in the Kuomintang Army was second only to that of Chiang Kai-shek.

Ordered by his commander in chief to suppress the August Uprising in Nanchang [1927], in which Communist troops first began the long open struggle for power against the Kuomintang, Chu Teh instead joined with the rebels. When, after the defeat, he headed his regiment southward, the city gates which closed behind him were symbolic of the final break with the security and success of his youth.

To Chu Teh, not far away, Mao sent as delegate his brother, Mao Tse-min. He brought instructions from the party to unite forces, and news of a program of partisan warfare, agrarian revolution, and the building of soviets. When in May 1928 the two armies combined at Chingkangshan, they were in control of five counties and had some 50,000 followers. Of these about 4,000 were armed with rifles, some 10,000 being equipped only with spears, swords, and hoes, while the rest were unarmed. Thus began the famous Chu-Mao combination which was to make history in South China for the next six years.

The relationship was very close between Chu Teh, the army commander, and Mao Tse-tung, the party leader. They jointly signed all orders and for years the press referred to "Chu Mao" as the "commander leader" of the still little-known "Communists-bandits"; many people believed they were one.

Chu Teh's devotion to his men was proverbial. He lived and dressed like the rank and file, had shared all their hardships, often going without shoes in the early days, living one whole winter on squash, never complaining, rarely sick. Any soldier in the army could bring his complaints directly to the commander in chief. On the Long March he lent his horse to tired comrades, walking much of the way, seemingly tireless.

Millions knew the name of Chu Teh in China, and to each it was a menace or a bright hope, according to his status in life, but to all it was a name imprinted on the pages of a decade of history.

Chu Teh (*left*) and Mao were reunited in Yenan after the Long March. "It is difficult to imagine Mao's rise and success in the special pattern of peasant-based revolution which he developed without the unvarying loyalty and self-effacing support of Chu Teh."

Chou En-lai and Teng Ying-chao

Chou was born in 1899 in Huaian, Kiangsu, in what he called a "bankrupt mandarin family." Chou was given (at the age of four months) to the family of his father's younger brother. The brother was about to die without issue when Chou's father, to assure [his brother] of male posterity (on the family tablets), presented him with En-lai to rear as his own son.

Chou's foster mother was highly literate. Still more uncommon, she liked fiction and "forbidden" stories of past rebellions, to which she introduced Chou as a child. Thus he read most of the exciting books that also affected Mao Tse-tung as a boy. His early education was in a family school under a private tutor who taught classical literature and philosophy. At the age of fourteen Chou entered Nankai Middle School in Tientsin and fully came under the influence of the Nationalist party of Dr. Sun Yat-sen. Chou went to Japan in 1917; he became widely acquainted with revolution-minded Chinese students during his eighteen months there.

Chou En-lai at the age of twelve.

In 1919 Chou entered university in Tientsin. "During my last two years at Nankai Middle School I had received no help from my family. I lived on a scholarship which I won as best student in my class. I became editor of the Students' Union Paper, which helped cover some expenses." He managed to do that despite five months spent in

A farewell sendoff for Chou En-lai as he left Paris in 1924. Among his colleagues is young Teng Hsiao-ping (*third from right in the top row*) and Li Fu-chun (*first row, fourth from right*).

Chou En-lai, soon after his arrival in Paris, 1920.

jail in 1919, as a leader of Nankai's student rebellion which grew out of the May Fourth movement. During that period Chou helped to form the Awakening Society, a radical group whose members later became, variously, anarchists, Nationalists and Communists. One of them was Teng Ying-chao, whom Chou was to marry in 1925. The Awakening Society existed until the end of 1920, when four of its founders, led by Chou, went to France as part of the Work-Study program organized by Chen Tu-hsiu.

"In 1922 I became a member-founder of the Chinese Communist Youth League and began to work full time for that organization. After two years I went to London, where I spent two and a half months. Then I went to Germany and worked there for a year, helping to organize."

In Paris, Chou En-lai, as an unknown, impoverished "Chinaman," and a miner and waiter in part-time jobs, found a welcome only among French proletarians. In 1921 he joined other exiles in forming a Chinese branch of the French Communist Party—the year Mao Tse-tung became a founder of the home party in Shanghai. During the next four years, between work and study, he read Marxist literature, traveled Europe and helped organize party branches in Berlin, London and Marseille. On his return to China he stopped briefly for instructions in Moscow. Late in 1924 he arrived in Canton, where he became Chiang Kai-shek's deputy director of the political department of Whampoa Academy.

Ying-chao possessed one of the most astute political brains I have encountered among Chinese women.

Born in 1903 in Honan, she studied at the First Girls' Normal School in Tientsin and then graduated from Peking Higher Normal School. A radical student, she was arrested in 1919 and briefly jailed. With Chou En-lai she joined the Work-Study Plan to go to France. A member of the Chinese Communist Youth League in Paris, she returned to China in 1924, joined the Chinese Communist Party, married Chou, and was the only prominent woman participant in the Nanchang Uprising. In 1928 she went to Russia with Chou, and returned with him to China to do underground work until she entered Soviet Kiangsi, where she led the women's work department of the Central Committee. She was one of only thirty-five women who made the Long March, during which she developed pulmonary tuberculosis and had to be carried on a stretcher.

Mme. Chou shared the danger and hardships of her husband's life in an extremely close relationship since their schooldays. Her urbanity and simplicity, mixed with patriotic and revolutionary ardor, won her nation-wide respect.

Teng Ying-chao and her husband, Chou En-lai, in a rare moment of tranquillity.

Peng Teh-huai, a former general in Chiang's army and a famous Red warrior, is seated at left in this group picture taken in Kiangsi in January 1932. The other two men are unidentified except by rank: a political commissar (*middle*), later killed in action, and an army commander.

Peng Teh-huai

Peng's career as a "Red bandit" had begun when he led an uprising in the Kuomintang Army of the polygamous warlord-governor, General Ho Chien. When he was twenty-eight years old, he was already a brigade commander, and noted as the "liberal" officer who actually consulted his soldiers' committee. In the winter of 1927 General Ho began a drastic purgation of leftists in his troops and launched the notorious Hunan "Peasant Massacre," in which thousands of radical farmers and workers were killed as "Communists." He hesitated to act against Peng, however, because of his widespread popularity. It was a costly delay. Peng directed the Ping Kiang Insurrection, accumulated about 8,000 followers, and with this force he attacked and captured the great walled city of Changsha and put to rout Ho Chien's army of 60,000 men, then mostly opium smokers.

Peng Teh-huai was born in a village near the native place of Mao Tse-tung; his family were rich peasants. His mother died when he was six, his father remarried, and this second wife hated Peng because he was a constant reminder of her predecessor.

"My grandmother regarded us all as her slaves. She was a heavy smoker of opium. I hated the smell of it, and one night, when I could stand it no longer, I got up and kicked a pan of her opium from the stove. She called a meeting of the whole clan and formally demanded my death by drowning. My stepmother agreed, and my father said that since it was the family's will, he would not object. My own mother's brother stepped forward and bitterly attacked my parents. My life was spared but I had to leave home. I was nine years old, it was cold October, and I owned nothing but my coat and trousers. My stepmother tried to take those from me, but I proved that they did not belong to her, but had been given to me by my own mother."

Such was the beginning of Peng Teh-huai's life. By 1926 Peng had read the *Communist Manifesto*, an outline of *Capital* and many articles and pamphlets giving a materialist interpretation of the Chinese revolution. "Formerly," said Peng, "I had been merely dissatisfied with society, but saw little chance of making any fundamental improvement. After reading the *Communist Manifesto* I dropped my pessimism and began working with a new conviction that society could be changed."

Yeh Chien-ying

Yeh Chien-ying was born in Canton in 1898 into a merchant family. He graduated from Yunnan Military Academy six years behind Chu Teh. He joined the Communist party (1922), became an instructor at Whampoa, and remained there until the launching of the Northern Expedition in 1926. He commanded the Twenty-first Division under Chiang Kai-shek. (Chou En-lai said that Yeh left in "disgust" after Chiang's disastrous attack on Nanchang, in 1927.) In 1929 he went to Moscow, where he studied for two years. Returning to Shanghai, he went to Kiangsi and assumed important staff responsibilities. By 1936 he was chief of the General Staff of the Eastern Front and a member of the Revolutionary Military Council. He speaks Russian, German and a bit of English.

General Yeh Chien-ying, one of the ablest Communist tacticians.

Ho Lung

Born in 1896, in Hunan, Ho Lung organized armed peasant insurrections at least a decade before Mao Tse-tung tried it. His reputation as a "bandit" was well earned. A youth of sixteen, with little schooling and an empty belly, he tried to kill a government officer, then gathered a band of outlaws in the mountains. By the time he was twenty-one his 19,000 followers held eight counties. Rebels united around him, calling themselves a Peasant Army. They became so formidable that government forces were obliged to grant them amnesty and monetary rewards to disband. Ho Lung went to Changsha to ally himself with Sun Yat-sen. At Nanchang he joined the armed uprising of August 1, 1927. He then re-entered the Kiangsi-Hunan area and recruited new forces for Chu Teh and Mao. From 1927 onward he was a top army leader.

Many stories are told of his bravery as a youth: His father was a military officer in the Ching Dynasty, and one day he was invited to a dinner by his fellow officers. He took his son with him. The father was boasting of Ho Lung's fearlessness, and one of the guests decided to test it out. He fired a gun under the table. They say that Ho Lung did not even blink!

Ho Lung. "It is said of him that he established a soviet district in Hunan with one knife. Early in 1928, he was hiding in a village when some Kuomintang tax collectors arrived. Leading a few villagers, he attacked the tax collectors and killed them with his own knife. From this he got enough revolvers and rifles to arm his first peasants' army."

Intraparty Struggles

Li Li-san was a Hunanese and a returned student from France. He divided time in Shanghai and Hankow, where the Communist party had "underground" headquarters—only after 1930 was the Central Committee transferred to the soviet districts. Li dominated the Chinese [Communist] Party from 1929 to 1930, when he was removed from the Politburo and sent to Moscow. Like Chen Tu-hsiu, Li Li-san lacked faith in the rural soviets,* and urged that strong aggressive tactics be adopted against strategic big capitals like Changsha, Wuhan and Nanchang. He wanted a "terror" in the villages to demoralize the gentry, a "mighty offensive" by the workers, risings and strikes to paralyze the enemy in his bases, and "flank attacks" in the north, from Outer Mongolia and Manchuria, backed by the USSR.

The Li Li-san period was really only one phase of a struggle for power between the urban-based Central Committee and the rural-based soviets, where Mao won a dominant position. Generally Mao's disputes† with Moscow-oriented Politburo leaders revolved around his conviction that the land-hungry poor peasants were the "main force" of the revolution and that rural bases had to be built before the metropolitan areas could be encompassed and held. Those opposed to him tended to share Stalin's view of the peasants as primarily auxiliaries to be manipulated by the urban proletariat, the true "main force" of the revolution. [This was the stand of the Twenty-eight Bolsheviks.]

In 1925 the Comintern had set up the Sun Yat-sen University [in Moscow]. Among hundreds who studied there, only twenty-eight Chinese consistently

Li Li-san, shown here in 1951, was a labor organizer and in 1924 became chairman of the Shanghai Federation of Trade Unions and a political instructor of Whampoa Academy. He worked with Chou En-lai in preparing the 1927 Shanghai Uprising.

---

* "Soviet" is used here in the Chinese context. In the Chinese language it is simply transliterated *su wei ai* from the Russian term meaning "council"—as used to designate the governmental structure introduced at the time of the 1905 Revolution, and used more extensively after the 1917 Revolution, in Russia. The first Chinese soviet was set up in Tsalin, on the Hunan border, in November 1927, and the first Chinese soviet government then elected. On February 7, 1930, the Kiangsi Provisional Soviet Government was established and the following year saw Mao Tse-tung elected President of the new Chinese Soviet Republic. Mao credited the local soviets as the organizations which mobilize the masses directly and carry out practical duties.

† Mao was reprimanded three times by the Central Committee and three times expelled by it.

supported Stalin during his struggles with Trotsky, Zinoviev and Bukharin. These were protégés of Pavel Mif, who was twenty-seven when Stalin made him director of the university and chief of the Comintern Far Eastern Section, after 1927. By 1930 Mif had built them into a hardcore "professional Bolshevik" elite schooled to take over China. Once called "Stalin's China Section" by their opponents, they later came to be known as the "Twenty-eight Bolsheviks." In 1930 their leader was a youth of twenty-four named Wang Ming and his closest comrade was Po Ku, aged twenty-three.

Wang Ming was general secretary of the Chinese Communist Party and founded a politburo regime which opposed Mao Tse-tung between 1931 and 1935. He was admitted to the Chinese Communist Party in 1925. After the Kuomintang-Communist break (1927) he went back to Russia with Pavel Mif and won leadership among those Chinese students there called the "Twenty-eight Bolsheviks."

In mid-1930 Pavel Mif secretly returned to the

sanctuary of the foreign-ruled International Settlement of Shanghai with Wang Ming, Po Ku, Lo Fu, Teng Fa, and other Stalinist disciples, who were introduced into the Chinese Communist Party Central Committee. When they opposed Li Li-san, however, Li resisted Mif's maneuver and dismissed Wang Ming and others from the Politburo, with the support of Chou En-lai. Mif secured Li's recall to Moscow. He remained in disgrace and was not to return to China for some years.

In Shanghai, Chou worked with Li Li-san until the latter was held responsible for his (and the Comintern's) failures at urban insurrection. Chou recanted and called upon the party to "condemn my mistakes." That year [1931] he was sent by the new leadership to Kiangsi. When Chou became political commissar to Chu Teh's command, in 1932, his prestige in Kiangsi began to overshadow that of Mao. Perhaps it was the unequaled breadth of Chou's viable connections with all factions that committed him to the role of chief reconciler and balancer of forces rather than to bitter-end struggle for personal leadership attainable only by violent repression of one or the other element in a core dispute.

Here I could not even outline the absorbing and only fragmentarily written history of the six years of the soviets of South China—a period that was destined to be a prelude to the epic of the Long March. Mao Tse-tung told me briefly of the organic development of the soviets and of the birth of the Red Army, how the Communists built up, from a few hundred ragged and half-starved but young and determined revolutionaries, an army of several tens of thousands of workers and peasants, until they had become such serious contenders for power that Nanking had to hurl its first large-scale offensive against them. The initial "annihilation drive," and then a second, a third and a fourth were net failures. In each of those campaigns the Reds destroyed many brigades and whole divisions of Kuomintang troops, replenished their supplies of arms and ammunition, enlisted new warriors and expanded their territory.

Po Ku (*left*) and Wang Ming.

Soviet China, 1932-1934

Above: This Kuomintang plane was seized by the First Red Army Corps on the East Front in April 1932, after their occupation of Changchow in Fukien, where an entire Kuomintang division was destroyed. "The Reds captured a few of Chiang's airplanes, and they had three or four pilots, but they lacked gasoline, bombs, and mechanics."

Middle: Young Red soldiers guarding two important captives taken in battle in Kiangsi, April 1932. The prisoner at the right, a Kuomintang brigadier general, was at first imprisoned by the Reds, later joined the Red Army and became a lecturer in the Red Academy at Juichin.

Right: Mao Tse-tung (*left*) with his bodyguards in 1934.

Above: Graduation Day ceremonies were held for this class of Red Army cadets in Kiangsi in May 1932. Their shoes are of grass straw, often woven by the soldiers themselves.

Left: Following a victory over the Kuomintang's 19th Route Army, in North Fukien Province, December 28, 1933, these Red Army leaders relaxed for a photo. Among them (*left to right*): Yeh Chien-ying, Yang Shang-kun (one of the "28 Bolsheviks" who, at the end of the Long March, became acting director of the political department of the Red Army) and Peng Teh-huai. On the left of Chou En-lai (with a beard) is Li Ke-nung (head of the Political Defense Corps in Kiangsi).

Juichin, Kiangsi

Few photographs exist which show the physical aspects of Juichin, the capital of the Central Soviet Government in Kiangsi. The Congress Meeting Hall (*above*) was erected there to house the delegates who came from all other Soviet districts as well as from the underground Communist Party in the White areas. Army cadets group (*below*) for a picture in front of the Red Academy in Juichin.

Left: At the Second All-Soviet Congress in Juichin, January 25, 1934, an audience listens to a report given by Mao Tse-tung on the two years' work of the Central Executive Committee. Several million dollars worth of "heads wanted" were represented here.

Below: Delegates at the All-Soviet Juichin Congress give the Red salute after electing new Central Executive Committee members, February 1, 1934. Most of these Kiangsi photographs were printed on blueprint paper because the economic blockade by Nanking shut out such commodities as photographers' supplies.

The March Begins

Late in October 1933 Nanking mobilized for the fifth and greatest of its anti-Red wars. The Fifth Campaign was said to have been planned largely by Chiang Kai-shek's German advisers, notably General von Falkenhausen of the German army, who was then the Generalissimo's chief adviser. The new tactics were thorough, but they were also very slow and expensive. Operations dragged on for months; the effect of the blockade was seriously felt in the Red districts, and especially the total absence of salt. The little Red base was becoming inadequate to repel the combined military and economic pressure being applied against it. Considerable exploitation of the peasantry must have been necessary to maintain the astonishing year of resistance which was put up during this campaign. At the same time, it must be remembered that their fighters were peasants, owners of newly acquired land. For land alone most peasants in China would fight to the death. The Kiangsi people knew that return of the Kuomintang meant return to the landlords.

Nanking believed that its efforts at annihilation were about to succeed. The enemy was caged and could not escape. Thousands supposedly had been killed in the daily bombing and machine-gunning from the air, as well as by "purgations" in districts reoccupied by the Kuomintang. The Red Army itself, according to Chou En-lai, suffered over 60,000 casualties in this one siege. Whole areas were depopulated, sometimes by forced mass migrations, sometimes by the simpler expedient of mass executions. Kuomintang press releases estimated that about 1,000,000 people were killed or starved to death in the process of recovering Soviet Kiangsi.

Nevertheless, the Fifth Campaign proved inconclusive. It failed to destroy the "living forces" of the Red Army. A Red military conference was called at Juichin, and it was decided to withdraw, transferring the main Red strength to a new base.

The retreat from Kiangsi evidently was so swiftly and secretly managed that the main forces of the Red troops, estimated at about 90,000 men, had already been marching for several days before the enemy headquarters became aware of what was taking place. They had mobilized in southern Kiangsi, withdrawing most of their regular troops

Nanking Kuomintang government troops, sent against the Red Army, marching through Kiukiang, Kiangsi.

Communist prisoners of the Nationalist Army in Kiangsi.

from the northern front and replacing them with partisans. Those movements occurred always at night. When practically the whole Red Army was concentrated near Yutu, in southern Kiangsi, the order was given for the Great March, which began on October 16, 1934.

For three nights the Reds pressed in two columns to the west and to the south. On the fourth they advanced, totally unexpectedly, almost simultaneously attacking the Hunan and Kwangtung lines of fortifications. They took these by assault, put their astonished enemy on the run, and never stopped until they had occupied the ribbon of blockading forts and entrenchments on the southern front. This gave them roads to the south and to the west, along which their vanguard began its sensational trek.

Besides the main strength of the army, thousands of Red peasants began this march—old and young, men, women, children, Communists and non-Communists. The arsenal was stripped, the factories were dismantled, machinery was loaded onto mules and donkeys—everything that was portable and of value went with this strange cavalcade. As the march lengthened out, much of this burden had to be discarded, and the Reds told me that thousands of rifles and machine guns, much machinery, much ammunition, even much silver, lay buried on their long trail from the South. Someday in the future, they said, Red peasants, now surrounded by thousands of policing troops, would dig it up again.

After the main forces of the Red Army evacuated Kiangsi, it was still many weeks before Nanking troops succeeded in occupying the chief Red bases. Thousands of peasant Red Guards continued guerrilla fighting. To lead them, the Red Army left behind some of its ablest commanders. They had only 6,000 able-bodied regular troops, however—and 20,000 wounded, sheltered among the peasants. Many thousands of them were captured and executed, but they managed to fight a rear-guard action which enabled the main forces to get well under way before Chiang Kai-shek could mobilize new forces to pursue and attempt to annihilate them on the march.

A forest of Red bayonets: units of the Red Army make their first contact on September 19, 1935, at Yungpingtsun, North Shensi.

THE LONG MARCH
1934-1935

Adventure, exploration, discovery, human courage and cowardice, ecstasy and triumph, suffering, sacrifice and loyalty, and then through it all, like a flame, an undimmed ardor and undying hope and amazing revolutionary optimism of those thousands of youths who would not admit defeat by man or nature or God or death—all this and more seemed embodied in the history of an odyssey unequaled in modern times.

The Long March covered 18,088 li, or slightly more than 6,000 miles, and it lasted 368 days. During the first 5,000 miles the army averaged only one day of full halt and rest for every 114 miles of marching. Over the whole distance the mean daily stage covered was the equivalent of 24 miles—a terrific and probably unequaled pace for a great army and its transport to maintain over some of the most hazardous terrain on earth. En route, the fugitive rebels crossed 18 mountain ranges, 24 rivers and 12 Chinese provinces populated by more than 200 million people. They occupied 62 cities, broke through enveloping lines of 10 different provincial armies, and defeated, eluded or outmaneuvered crack forces which the Central government sent against them.

"When not in contact with the Red Army, Chiang Kai-shek's troops seemed to be very courageous [Mao told me]. They marched quickly and kept up with our long difficult marches. But when they came near us they were extremely careful. They had been used to fighting with fortifications behind them, now they had none. Four methods were used by Chiang: frontal attack, flank attack, encirclement and obstruction. We overcame him by using opposite tactics. When we wanted to go to south Kweichow, we made

The Tsunyi Conference, Kweichow, 1935.

a feint to the west; when we wanted to enter Szechuan, we went to Yunnan. In this way we exhausted and tantalized Chiang's army, and in the battles that occurred, won victory."

Moving into opium-soaked Kweichow province, the Reds captured the governor's headquarters and seized his residence at Tsunyi. There a historic enlarged Politburo conference, in January 1935, unequivocally recognized Mao's leadership. As chairman of the Politburo, he assumed supreme responsibility for strategy. Moscow-trained Po Ku and his supporters stepped down and acknowledged their errors. High among them had been turning over strategic military command to Li Teh during the fifth campaign. Now Mao's strategy (in general,

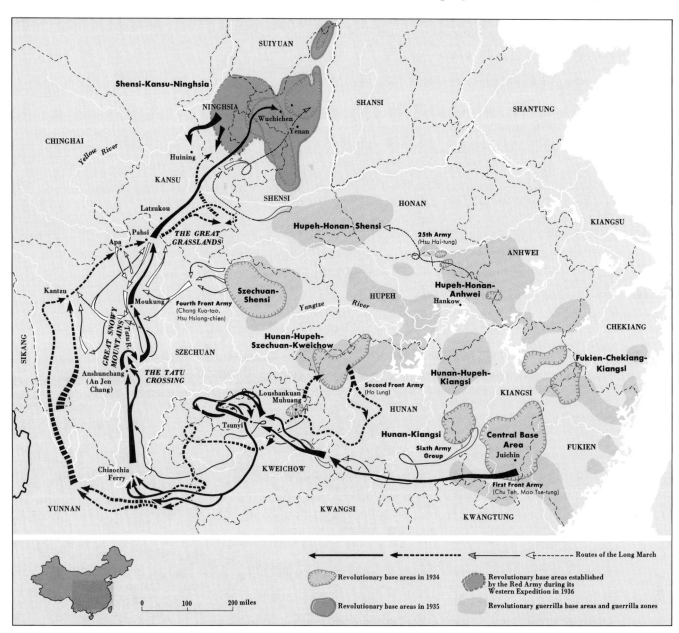

The Long March began at Yutu (Kiangsi), October 16, 1934.

one of capturing the countryside to encircle the cities) was held to have been correct. His summary of the lessons of the period, *Strategic Problems in China's Revolutionary War*, was to become a party classic.

Li Teh was the Chinese party name adopted by Otto Braun, a German Communist sent to China by the Comintern. Braun entered Kiangsi in 1933, smuggled into the Red areas in a sampan where he lay covered with cargo for many days. As a Comintern delegate he held a position of extraordinary prestige in the Central Committee revolutionary military council, and he bore a large share of responsibility for military practices followed in 1933–34.

Otto Braun was the only foreigner who made the Long March. He was married to a Chinese actress.

Left: "Camping in the grass-lands."

Below: "On the March."

Sketches of the Long March

The sketches shown were done by Huang Chen, who, from 1972 to 1977, served as Chief of Liaison of the Peoples' Republic of China to Washington, D.C. They are the only drawings created during the Long March to be preserved. Huang Chen was in his early twenties and working in the Central Red Army's propaganda section. Sometimes the only brushes he had were those he made from hemp. He made ink from soot or scrapings from the blackened bottoms of cooking pots. In 1938, copies of the sketches reached Shanghai from northern Shensi. The first edition appeared in October 1938. *Red Star Over China* had just been published in Chinese under the title *Notes on Travels to the West*. To give some indication of the content, yet not to attract the attention of the enemy, the collection of drawings was given the name *Sketches of Travels to the West.*—L.W.S.

Huang Chen (*far left, first row*) with a group of Miao aboriginal tribe people he encountered as the Red Army passed through Kweichow in southwestern China.

Far left: "A Long Marcher carrying a ration of dried food."

Left: "Red guerrillas of the Yi minority."

Far left: "Wild leaves replace tobacco."

Middle: "Er Hua-lo, a Yi chieftain who served as guide through his territory."

Left: "Baking biscuits made of Tibetan barley flour."

Tatu Ho!

West of An Jen Chang, where the gorges rise very high and the river flows narrow, deep and swift, there was an iron-chain suspension bridge called the Luting Chiao. It was the last possible crossing of the Tatu east of Tibet.

Sixteen heavy iron chains, with a span of some hundred yards, were stretched across the river. Thick boards lashed over the chains made the road of the bridge, but upon their arrival the Reds found that half this flooring had been removed, and before them only the bare iron chains swung to a point midway in the stream. At the northern bridgehead an enemy machine-gun nest faced them, and behind it a regiment of White troops.

Volunteers were called for; thirty were chosen. Soon they were swinging out above the boiling river, moving hand over hand, clinging to the chains. Red machine guns spattered the bridgehead with

bullets. The enemy replied with machine-gunning, and snipers shot at the Reds tossing high over the water. The first dropped into the current below; a second fell, and then a third. At last one Red crawled up over the bridge flooring, uncapped a grenade and tossed it into the enemy redoubt. More Reds were moving forward on their hands and knees, tossing grenade after grenade into the enemy machine-gun nest. On the southern shore, their comrades began to shout with joy. "Long live the Red Army! Long live the heroes of Tatu Ho!" The enemy was withdrawing in pell-mell flight.

Paraffin was thrown on the planking, and it began to burn.

Running full speed over the remaining planks, through the flames, the assailants nimbly hopped into the enemy's redoubt and turned the abandoned machine gun against the shore. In an hour or two the whole army was tramping and singing its way across the river Tatu into Szechuan.

Tatu Bridge. "Its crossing was the most critical single incident of the Long March. Had the Red Army failed there, quite possibly it would have been exterminated."

"Coming down from the Snowy Mountains."

Ahead lay a 16,000-foot pass over the Great Snowy Mountains of western Szechuan and range after range beyond that. They climbed on.

"On Pao-tung Kang peak alone," Mao Tse-tung said, "one army lost two thirds of its transport animals. Hundreds fell down and never got up again."

So did hundreds of the men and women who braved the trek.

The survivors finally emerged in the rich Moukung area and debouched into the Sungpan region of eastern Tibet. Here they met the Fourth Front Red Army, which Chang Kuo-tao had led up from the abandoned Red districts north of the river in the central Yangtze Valley. They had had an easier retreat and had even managed to augment their forces—estimated at 100,000. And now, in Chang Kuo-tao, Mao met the last rival to his leadership. A clash of wills which almost destroyed the party, it was described to me by both Mao Tse-tung and Chou En-lai as the most critical moment in its whole history.

Two main columns of Red forces met in June 1935, in the middle of the Long March. Mao led the southern group, Chang Kuo-tao those in retreat from north of the Yangtze. A decisive duel arose between them. Chang and his supporters refused to recognize Mao's supreme authority as "chair-

"Chang Kuo-tao (*left, with Mao Tse-tung*), a founder of the Chinese Communist Party, was Mao's most important rival for party leadership in 1934–36. He was born in Kiangsi in 1897, in a rich landlord family. Chang left the Red areas in 1938 and joined the Kuomintang at Hankow."

man," as decided at Tsunyi. Chang opposed Mao's plans to move to Shensi and wished to seek a compromise peace with the Kuomintang. He also insisted that Mao was violating the Comintern "line," that the Tsunyi Conference was illegal, and that a new Central Committee plenum must be called to unseat Mao.

The crisis was broken by two factors. First, the rapid advance of new forces mobilized by Chiang Kai-shek in Szechuan threatened to drive a wedge between the two Red columns. Second, a sudden rise in the headwaters of one of Szechuan's rapid rivers, which then physically divided the two forces, completely cut them off from each other. Chang's forces were left on the southern banks. Obliged to leave Chu Teh a virtual prisoner of Chang Kuo-tao, the main Kiangsi column now continued its northward advance under Mao Tse-tung, accompanied by Chou En-lai, Peng Teh-huai and Lin Piao. They resumed the march with only 30,000 men.

Chang divided the Red Army, keeping his troops in west Szechuan, while Mao led the First Front Army to Shensi. A year later, badly pressed, Chang was obliged to move north. While crossing the Yellow River his columns were nearly annihilated. Chang and Hsu Hsiang-chien barely managed to reach Yenan, leaving their scattered forces under the command of Li Hsien-nien. Chang left the Red areas in 1938 and joined the Kuomintang at Hankow.

Along their route the Reds provisioned themselves by "confiscating" the supplies of the rich—the landlords, officials, bureaucrats and big gentry. There were big "surpluses"—more than the Reds could carry—and these were distributed among the local poor. In Yunnan they seized thousands of hams from rich packers, and peasants came from miles around to receive their free portions—a new incident in the history of the ham industry, said Mao Tse-tung. Tons of salt were distributed. From Kiangsi they had carried Nanking notes, and silver dollars and bullion from their state bank, and in poor districts they used this money to pay for their needs. Land deeds were destroyed, taxes abolished, and the poor peasantry armed. Often the peasantry sent groups to urge the Reds to detour and liberate their districts. They had little conception of the Red Army's political program; they only knew that it was "a poor man's army." Mao told me laughingly of one such delegation which arrived to welcome "Su Wei-ai Hsien-sheng"—Mr. Soviet! These rustics were no more ignorant, however, than the

As Mao Tse-tung said to Snow, "In Szechuan, eighteen-year-old women go trouserless, too poor to buy them. If Hitler wants to prohibit nudism, in China he would have to furnish them with trousers."

"A farmhand family in Szechuan—the parents in rags, the children without clothes."

Fukien militarist Lu Hsing-pang, who once posted a notice offering a reward for the "capture, dead or alive, of Su Wei-ai." Lu announced that this fellow had been doing a lot of damage and must be exterminated.

By September they were deep in the Great Grasslands, where they saw no human habitation for ten days. Almost perpetual rain falls over these high swamplands, passable by a maze of narrow footholds known only to native highlanders, whom

Long Marchers cross the grasslands. This is one of the few photographs to survive the March.

the Reds had to capture to guide them. More animals were lost, and more men. Many foundered in a weird sea of wild grass and disappeared, beyond reach. There was no dry firewood. There was nothing to eat but wild vegetables and herbs. There were no trees for shelter; at night they huddled under bushes tied together. Worst of all, they could get no potable water. "On occasions [said Mao] men were reduced to drinking their own urine."

Part of the Second Front Army, North Shensi, after the Long March. Li Chen (*first row, right*) was the only woman commander in the People's Liberation Army. (After a united front resumed between the Kuomintang and the Communists in 1936, the Red Army was renamed the Eighth Route Army. In July 1946 the Communist forces took the name of the People's Liberation Army, a designation which remains to this day.)

August 1, 1935, Kansu. Hsu Hai-tung, commander of the 15th Red Army Corps, seated (*front row, center*), surrounded by his staff. "Hsu, once a worker in a pottery works, led the 25th Army from Honan into North Shensi in 1935. For him, dead or alive, Chiang Kai-shek offered $50,000 in a handbill dropped over Ninghsia by airplane. Hsu (and Peng Teh-huai, his superior commander) promptly ordered the thousands of handbills collected to use the blank side for paper. They then printed the 'Red Army Daily' on the side opposite the reward-offer, which was distributed to the soldiers, to their great amusement."

When at last they came down onto the Kansu plain their numbers had been cut to 7,000. Still more critical battles lay ahead before they entered the fertile Yellow River basin. After a brief rest, they broke through weak cordons of Moslem cavalry and replenished themselves. They finally united with local Red forces in north Shensi, on October 25, 1935, and wearily assessed their achievement.

In one sense this mass migration was the biggest armed propaganda tour in history. The Reds passed through provinces populated by more than 200,000,000 people. Between battles and skirmishes, in every town occupied, they called mass meetings, gave theatrical performances, heavily "taxed" the rich, freed many slaves (some of whom joined the Red Army), preached "liberty, equality, democracy," confiscated the property of the "traitors" and distributed their goods among the poor. Millions had now seen the Red Army and heard it speak, and were no longer afraid of it. Many thousands dropped out on the long and heartbreaking march, but thousands of others— farmers, apprentices, slaves, deserters from the Kuomintang ranks, workers, all the disinherited— joined in and filled the ranks.

It is impossible not to recognize the Long March as one of the great triumphs of men against odds and men against nature. While the Red Army was unquestionably in forced retreat, its toughened veterans reached their planned objective with moral and political will as strong as—probably much stronger than—ever. They declared and believed they were advancing to lead a sacred national-salvation war against the invading Japanese—a psychological factor of great importance to the rank and file. The conviction helped turn what might have been a demoralized rout into an arrival in triumph. History has subsequently shown that Mao was undoubtedly right in taking the Red forces to the strategic Northwest, a region which he correctly foresaw was to play a determining role in the immediate destinies of China, Japan and Soviet Russia.

Mao Tse-tung—"the flesh still lean on his bones from the ordeal."

On platform, right center: Liu Cui (Tsui) addresses fellow Yenching University students at a mass meeting in Peking in 1935. She is still an active leader in the People's Republic of China.

⑧

STUDENT REVOLT 1935-1936

Late in 1935 students of Yenching University spontaneously staged a street demonstration in Peking which touched off nationwide protests that probably saved North China from falling to Japan by default.

Japanese demands of November were the climax of months of infiltration into "North China." We then used the term to mean Hopei and Chahar provinces, which lay just south of the Great Wall. After the conquest of Manchuria and Inner Mongolia, Japan had momentarily halted her armed advance when the Generalissimo directed his chief of staff, Ho Ying-chin, to sign a truce which in effect recognized the new status. The agreement set up an "autonomous" or buffer area covering the two large Northern provinces, of which Peking was the capital. But even within this area the Japanese used their troops to carve out a "demilitarized zone," between Peking and the Great Wall, and put a puppet in charge.

General Sung Cheh-yuan, an old Nationalist soldier, held administrative responsibility over the Hopei-Chahar "autonomous" council. He was under such constant pressure that he had to shift officials and policies pretty much at Japanese demands. This had confusing results. For example, earlier policy had been to force opium smokers to take out licenses. Hundreds of violators of that law had been beheaded outside the walls of Peking, *pour encourager les autres*. But somehow hundreds of other "Ah Q's," exactly like those beheaded, had to be treated tenderly when they patronized the narcotics dens now elaborately protected by the Peking-Tientsin police.

At last the Japanese decided to end the farce and sever North China from Kuomintang authority completely. They called in their genius of intrigue, the misnamed "Lawrence of Manchuria," who had masterminded the "Mukden Incident," General Kenji Doihara. Doihara demanded that General Sung declare his independence from Chiang Kai-shek's Nanking government.

December 9 was chosen for the first city-wide student strike and demonstration. That was one day before General Sung was to announce the "separation" of North China from the South.

Yenching University was an upper-class institution whose students normally should have been political conservatives. But as the national crisis deepened, and class war merged with Japan's conquests in the North, a wave of radicalism began to spread there. By 1935 Yenching had unexpectedly

Above left: "No Name Lake" on the campus of Yenching University. On his death, a portion of Edgar Snow's ashes were placed in a small garden on these shores, under a marble stone inscribed by an old friend, Yeh Chien-ying.

Above middle: Kung Peng (*far left*) and Kung Pu-sheng (*top center, under the umbrella*), two sisters who became revolutionary leaders along with many other students at the time.

Above right: Wang Ju-mei, non-Communist student leader at Yenching, acted as translator-interpreter during the latter half of Edgar Snow's visit to the Northwest in 1936. He remained there, under the name of Huang Hua, and eventually became Foreign Minister and Vice Premier of the People's Republic.

Left: Students march to protest Japanese aggression and Kuomintang capitulation, 1935.

become the birthplace of student protests which touched off a nationwide "rebellion of youth."

The names of the student leaders were to become famous in China. There was not a Communist among them and yet within a few years nearly all of them would have joined the Communists, in the patriotic war against Japan.

The students of that period were neither pro-Kuomintang nor pro-Communist—merely pro-China.

For most of them it was the first concrete thinking they had done about what war with Japan would mean to them. What emerged was a series of demands on both General Sung and Chiang Kai-shek to reject Doihara's ultimatum, to end civil war, unite all factions for resistance to save China, begin "mass training and mobilization," and give people freedom to know the truth and prepare for what was coming. China must rely on herself alone, they proclaimed.

On December 9, students gathered at a dozen different gates and memorial arches throughout the city. From these their columns converged toward the main streets and joined at the wide avenue leading into the Winter Palace, where a high Kuomintang official then had offices. There the students were to meet to present their petitions to the government.

It was the first time any of us had seen mass political courage displayed by educated Chinese youths, as apart from common soldiers. The sight was exhilarating to both participants and spectators. Thousands and thousands of blue-clad youngsters marched and sang their way to the Forbidden City in defiance of both their own police and conservative parents. Nothing like it had happened in Kuomintang China for eight years.

Caught unprepared and puzzled by the presence of sympathetic Westerners, the local police made only half-hearted attempts to interfere. When an arrest was attempted, the blue-clad mass invariably surrounded the police, pressed leaflets on them and shouted patriotic slogans. Usually the baffled police retired with grins of embarrassment. Weren't they also patriots? Then the fire department was called out and hoses were turned on the paraders. The youths swept on, drenched but triumphant.

Suddenly the political gendarmes, in black leather jackets, led by a nephew of Chiang Kaishek, descended on the main column in motorcycles and sidecars with machine guns. For a tense moment the "leather jackets" leveled weapons in ready-to-fire position. A few rifles were fired in the air; the parade wavered but held. Correspondents and camera men closed in, hoping foreign witnesses would be enough to prevent a tragedy. We were. An officer threw up his hands and ordered his men to lower their guns.

Chinese shopkeepers, housewives, artisans, monks, teachers and silk-gowned merchants applauded from the streets, or ran out to get leaflets. Even ricksha coolies shouted the forbidden slogans: "Down with the bogus independence movement! Down with Japanese imperialism! Save China!"

Within a few days youth organizations sprang up in Tientsin, Shanghai, Hankow, Canton and all major cities, including even Nanking. On December 17 a second massive demonstration swept Peking and Tientsin, and tens of thousands joined the ranks. Although many were injured and nearly 200 arrested, a third demonstration was held a week later which for the first time called for an end to civil war and a "united front" to resist Japan.

As a face-saver, General Doihara was given enough support to set up a puppet regime in "demilitarized" East Hopei. Aside from its strategic value to Japan, it was extremely useful as a huge narcotics and smuggling base.

Peking's strategic position was reduced to still further absurdity by other Japanese moves, so that militarily and politically it became a curiosity which had to be seen to be believed. The Japanese almost controlled the Peking-Mukden Railway to the once Forbidden City. They had 7,000 troops stationed at various points on this line in permanent

Police (including plainclothesmen in Western-style hats) line the main streets of Peking.

Water-soaked students
capture a hose (*top*), while
black-jacketed political
police respond to orders to
retreat.

fortlike barracks at Tientsin, North China's greatest port, and inside the Legation Quarter of Peking itself. Nominally, those garrisons were stationed in accordance with the Boxer Protocol of 1901, but Japan had several times more troops than all other foreign powers combined and used them for highly illegal purposes.

The student rebellion of 1935–36 was the beginning of the end of China's nonresistance policy. Its greatest immediate impact fell on the Manchurian exiles in Peking. Manchurian University students poured into the villages to relate the facts about Japanese conquest of their homeland. Others went to Sianfu, where the exiled Manchurian leader, Chang Hsueh-liang, was deputy commander in chief of Chiang Kai-shek's "Red bandit suppression"

headquarters. Marshal Chang welcomed them and soon the whole Manchurian University shifted to Sian, which was shortly to become the scene of a rebellion that finally forced Chiang Kai-shek irrevocably into the anti-Axis camp.

Among all the causes of revolution, the total loss of confidence by educated youths in an existing regime is the one indispensable ingredient most often neglected by academic historians of that phenomenon. The profound failure of the Kuomintang to play any dynamic role of guidance or inspiration in this critical period made it a symbol of pessimism, stagnation and repression, and in the years of decision that lay ahead drove hundreds of the ablest and most patriotic young men and women to the Red banners as China's last hope.

Guardian of the Red gateway: a Red sentry at an army outpost in north Shensi, 1936.

9

RED STAR OVER CHINA 1936

Fighting in the very heart of the most populous nation on earth, the Celestial Reds had for nine years been isolated by a news blockade as effective as a stone fortress. A wall of thousands of enemy troops constantly surrounded them; their territory was more inaccessible than Tibet. No one had voluntarily penetrated that wall and returned to write of his experiences since the first Chinese soviet was established in southeastern Hunan, in November 1927.

Some people denied that there was a Red Army. There were only thousands of hungry brigands. Some denied the existence of the soviets. They were an invention of Communist propaganda. Yet sympathizers extolled both as the only salvation for all the ills of China. The Communists claimed to be fighting for agrarian revolution, and against imperialism, and for soviet democracy and national emancipation. Nanking said the Reds were vandals led by "intellectual bandits." Who was right? Or was either?

Who were these warriors who had fought so long, so fiercely, so courageously, and—as admitted privately among Chiang Kai-shek's own followers—on the whole so invincibly? What kind of man was Mao Tse-tung, No. 1 "Red bandit" on Nanking's list? Or was Mao already dead, as Nanking officially announced? Who were the many other Red leaders reported dead, only to reappear in the news—unscathed and commanding new forces? Who led the outmaneuvering, not only of all Kuomintang commanders sent against them but also of Chiang's large and expensive staff of German advisers?

How did the Reds dress? Eat? Play? Love? Work? Were women "nationalized," as

Kuomintang publicists asserted? What was a Chinese "Red factory"? A Red dramatic society? How did they organize their economy? What about public health, recreation, education, "Red Culture"?

What was the strength of the Red Army? If, as Generalissimo Chiang announced in 1935, Nanking had "destroyed the menace of Communist banditry," what explained the fact that in 1937 the Reds occupied a bigger single unified territory than ever before? If the Reds were finished, why did Japan demand that Nanking form an anti-Red pact with Tokyo and Nazi Germany "to prevent the bolshevization of Asia"?

Finally, what was the meaning of the Communists' offer to form a "national united front" in China, and stop civil war?

We all knew that the only way to learn anything about Red China was to go there. A few had tried and failed. People thought that nobody could enter and come out alive.

Then in June 1936 I heard of an amazing situation that was developing in the Northwest. Marshal Chang Hsueh-liang, in command of the anti-Red headquarters at Sianfu, had made a secret truce with the Communists and only kept up the appearance of war. With his help it would be possible, a friend told me, to travel into northern Shensi and Kansu provinces, where the main forces of the Red Army were then concentrating from all parts of China.

I went to Shanghai, where I again saw Mme. Sun Yat-sen. I sought her help. Shortly after, in the spring of 1936, it was Ching-ling who made the arrangements. In June, just as the Generalissimo announced preparations for a sixth "final extermi-

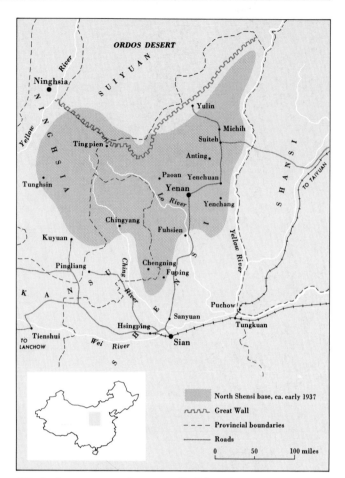

"Both the eastern and western Red frontiers were formed by the Yellow River . . . It was within this great bend of China's most treacherous river that the soviets then operated—in northern Shensi, northeastern Kansu and southeastern Ninghsia. And by a strange sequence of history this region almost corresponded to the original confines of the birthplace of China."

nation drive" against the Reds in the North, I set forth on this singular journey.

It is true there were risks involved, though the reports later published of my death—"killed by bandits"—were exaggerated. But against a torrent of horror stories about Red atrocities that had for many years filled the subsidized vernacular and foreign press of China, I had little to cheer me on my way. Nothing, in truth, but a letter of introduction to Mao Tse-tung. All I had to do was to find him. Through what adventures? I did not know. But thousands of lives had been sacrificed in those years of Kuomintang-Communist warfare. Could one foreign neck be better hazarded than in an effort to discover why? I found myself somewhat attached to the neck in question, but I concluded that the price was not too high to pay.

Mme. Sun Yat-sen in her garden.

One midnight I climbed aboard a dilapidated train—bound for "Red China." I left Peking, equipped with only a letter of introduction, written in invisible ink, to Mao Tse-tung, Chairman of the Chinese Soviet Government, a man whose head, as container of the chief brains of the Communist movement, Chiang Kai-shek assessed at $250,000, on his list of dead-or-alive rewards for Red leaders.

In the morning I inspected my traveling companions and found a youth and an old man with a wisp of gray beard sitting opposite me. The youth was on his way to Szechuan, to visit his hometown. Bandits were reported to be operating there.

"You mean Reds?"

"Oh no, although there are Reds in Szechuan. No, I mean bandits."

"But aren't the Reds also bandits? The newspapers always call them Red bandits."

"But you must know the editors must call them bandits because they are ordered to do so by Nanking. If they called them Communists or revolutionaries, that would prove they were Communists themselves."

"But in Szechuan don't people fear the Reds as much as the bandits?"

"The rich men fear them, and the landlords and officials and tax collectors, yes. But the peasants do not fear them. Sometimes they welcome them." The old man sat listening intently, and yet seeming not to listen. "You see," he continued, "the peasants are too ignorant. They think the Reds really mean what they say. My father wrote to me that they did abolish usury and opium in Szechuan, and that they redistributed the land. So, you see, they are not exactly bandits. They have principles, all right. But they are wicked. They kill too many people."

Surprisingly, the graybeard lifted his gentle face and with perfect composure made an astonishing remark. "*Sha pu kou!*" he said. "They don't kill enough!" We both looked at him flabbergasted.

Unfortunately, I had to transfer to the Lunghai line and was obliged to break off the discussion. I have ever since wondered with what deadly evidence this Confucian-looking old gentleman would have supported his startling contention. I wondered about it all the next day until my train rolled up to the new and handsome railway station at Sianfu.

A curtained car waited in front of the hotel and I saw in a corner a man wearing dark glasses and the uniform of a Kuomintang official. We drove out to the site of the old palace, where the celebrated Han Wu Ti once sat in his throne room and "ruled the earth." The Kuomintang official, who had sat without speaking during our drive, removed his dark glasses and his white hat. A mischievous grin spread over his bronzed face; one look at him showed this was no sedentary bureaucrat but an out-of-doors man of action.

He put his face close to mine—and winked! "Look at me!" he whispered with the delight of a child with a secret. "Do you recognize me? I thought maybe you had seen my picture somewhere. Well, I am Teng Fa." He pulled back his head to see the effect of a bombshell.

Teng Fa? Why—Teng Fa was chief of the Chinese Red Army's Security Police!

Teng was full of amusement at the situation. And he was overjoyed at seeing me—an American who was voluntarily going into the "bandit" areas. Did I want his horse—the finest in Red China! His pictures, his diary? He would send instructions to his wife in the soviet areas to give all this to me. And he kept his word.

Teng Fa had been a leader of the great Hong Kong shipping strike, had become a Communist, entered Whampoa, and taken part in the Nationalist revolution. After 1927 he had joined the Red Army in Kiangsi.

"Aren't you afraid for your head?" I asked as we drove back to the city.

"Not any more than Chang Hsueh-liang is," he said. "I'm living with him."

Teng Fa, 1930s.

We left Sian before dawn, the high wooden gates of the once "golden city" swinging open and noisily dragging their chains before the magic of our military pass. In the half-light of predawn the big army trucks lumbered past the airfield from which expeditions set out for daily reconnaissance and bombing over the Red lines. Opium poppies nodded their swollen heads, ready for harvest, along the newly completed motor road—a road already scarcely navigable even for our six-ton truck. The wonderful loess lands account for the marvelous fertility of these regions (when there is rainfall), for the loess furnishes an inexhaustible porous topsoil tens of feet deep. Geologists think the loess is organic matter blown down in centuries past from Mongolia and from the west by the great winds that rise in Central Asia.

To state precisely the manner in which, just as I had hoped, I did pass the last sentry and enter no man's land might have caused serious difficulties for the Kuomintang adherents who assisted me on my way. Suffice it to say that my experience proved once more that anything is possible in China, if it is done in the Chinese manner.

From poor peasant to wealthiest landlord, the people of China's northwest were tucked away in these loess hills, living in homes dug out of the hard, fudge-colored cliffs.

Chou En-lai, Paoan, Shensi province, 1936.

Chou En-lai was the first important Communist leader I encountered when I crossed the Red lines. He was in command of an East Front Red Army in a tiny cave village north of Yenan. I had just entered camp when a slender figure in an old cotton uniform came out to greet me, brought his cloth-soled shoes together, and touched his faded red-starred cap in a smart salute. He examined me intently with large dark eyes under heavy brows. His face, covered with a beard of abundant growth

for a Chinese, parted in a smile which exposed even white teeth.

"Hello," he said. "Are you looking for somebody? I am in command here." He had spoken in *English.* "My name," he added, "is Chou En-lai."

"I have a report that you are a reliable journalist, friendly to the Chinese people, and that you can be trusted to tell the truth," said Chou. "This is all we want to know. It does not matter to us that you are not a Communist. We will welcome any journalist who comes to see the soviet districts. It is not we, but the Kuomintang who prevent it. You can write about anything you see and you will be given every help to investigate the soviet districts."

He told me that the Reds wanted to end the civil war and unite with the Nationalists to resist Japan. That would not mean abandoning the revolution, he said, but advancing it. "The first day of the anti-Japanese war," he prophesied, "will mean the beginning of the end for Chiang Kai-shek."

Chou ended our first visit by tracing an itinerary for me on his hand-drawn map, noting the names of people and institutions for me to see in each place. It added up to a journey (by foot and horse) of ninety-two days—an underestimate, as things turned out. Then he saw me off, with a company of Red soldiers, on a three-day trek to Paoan, where I was to meet Mao Tse-tung.

Northern Shensi in the 1930s was so ravaged a land that it was always astonishing to find people living in its crevices at all. The soil seemed worn down, worn out, the topography all against profitable farming: nine tenths of it sloping and eroding, and the valleys so narrow that the good land there provided even landlords with no more than a poor living by our standards. Most of them were all illiterate as the peasants. This country was blighted worse than an Oklahoma dust bowl or the Texas badlands; there were very few trees, and it was arid except for swift summer floods and winter snows. Its best asset was a fine dry healthful climate. That alone probably explained why poor people could survive in their tumble-down caves infested by flies and rats (bubonic plague used to be endemic) and scratch an existence from scabby patches of grain planted on slopes sometimes as steep as 30 degrees, from which they were lucky to bring in three or four bushels an acre.

It was quite breathtaking to ride out suddenly on the brow of the wrinkled hills and see stretched out below me in a green valley the ancient walls of Paoan, which means "Defended Peace."

Right: Yangchialing, a suburb of Paoan.

Below: The terminus of the Long March, Paoan was the provisional capital of the Chinese People's Soviet Republic. Through its gates, Genghis Khan had invaded China in the thirteenth century.

tion!" At the end of the street waited a group who included most of the Politburo members then in Paoan.

It was the first time I had been greeted by the entire cabinet of a government, the first time a whole city had been turned out to welcome me. Had I been called upon to make any kind of speech I would have been unable to do so. I was overcome at the warmth of the greeting, the incredible experience of receiving it far in the interior in this little city fortified by many-ribbed ranges of mountains, and the strange thrill of solemn military music in the stillness and vastness of those mountains.

Paoan was once a frontier stronghold, during the Chin and Tang dynasties, against the nomadic invaders to the north. Remains of its fortifications could be seen flanking the narrow pass through which once emptied into this valley the conquering legions of the Mongols. There was an inner city, still, where the garrisons were once quartered; and a high defensive masonry, lately improved by the Reds, embraced about a square mile in which the present town was located.

A curious crowd lined both sides of the street before a few dozen ramshackle huts and shops. Red flags bore the hammer and sickle and the inscription "Chinese People's Anti-Japanese Red Army." Banners in English and Chinese were held aloft proclaiming: "Welcome the American journalist to investigate Soviet China!"; "Down with Japanese imperialism!" and "Long live the Chinese Revolu-

The sign reads: "Welcome American comrade offering assistance to our revolution."

Mao Tse-tung, Chairman of the Central Soviet Government and member of the Revolutionary Military Committee, as Snow first saw him.

I met Mao soon after my arrival: a gaunt, rather Lincolnesque figure, above average height for a Chinese, somewhat stooped, with a head of thick black hair, and with large, searching eyes, a high-bridged nose and prominent cheekbones. He had the simplicity and naturalness of the Chinese peasant, with a lively sense of humor. His laughter was even active on the subject of himself and the shortcomings of the soviets. He was plain-speaking and combined curious qualities of naïveté with incisive wit and worldly sophistication.

Mao was an accomplished scholar of Classical Chinese, an omnivorous reader, a deep student of philosophy and history, a good speaker, a man with an unusual memory and extraordinary powers of concentration, an able writer, careless in his personal habits and appearance but astonishingly meticulous about details of duty, a man of tireless energy, and a military and political strategist of considerable genius. Many Japanese regarded him as the ablest Chinese strategist alive.

I was quartered in a newly built mud-brick house and Mao lived in a hillside cave not far down the road. It had a single window and a door that opened on a lane guarded by a lone sentry. There I soon found myself ending every day, or beginning it. Mao invited me down regularly to have hot-pepper bread—or compote made by Mrs. Mao from local sour plums.

There would never be any one "savior" of China, yet undeniably one felt a certain force of destiny in Mao. It was nothing quick or flashy, but a kind of solid elemental vitality. One felt that whatever there was extraordinary in this man grew out of the uncanny degree to which he synthesized and expressed the urgent demands of millions of Chinese, and especially the peasantry. If their "demands" and the movement which was pressing them forward were the dynamics which could regenerate China, then in that deeply historical sense Mao Tse-tung might possibly become a very great man.

I often wondered about Mao's own sense of responsibility over the question of force, violence and the "necessity of killing." He had in his youth had strongly liberal and humanistic tendencies, and the transition from idealism to realism evidently had first been made philosophically. Although he was peasant-born, he did not as a youth personally suffer much from oppression of the landlords, as did many Reds, and, although Marxism was the core of his thought, I deduced that class hatred was for him probably an intellectually acquired mechanism in the bulwark of his philosophy, rather than an instinctive impulse to action.

There seemed to be nothing in him that might be called religious feeling. He was a humanist in a fundamental sense; he believed in man's ability to solve man's problems. I thought he had probably on the whole been a moderating influence in the Communist movement where life and death were concerned.

"Revolution," observed Mao Tse-tung, "is not a tea party." That "Red" terror methods were widely used against landlords and other class enemies—who were arrested, deprived of land, condemned in "mass trials," and often executed—was undoubtedly true, as indeed the Communists' own reports confirmed. (Mao Tse-tung's "Report on an Investigation into the Peasant Movement in Hunan" describes activities carried out by Communist-led peasants against "local bullies," "bad gentry," and "corrupt officials" for whom the "only effective suppression was to execute . . . at least some of those whose crimes and wrongdoings are most serious.") Were such activities to be regarded as atrocities or as "mass justice" executed by the armed poor in punishment of "White" terror crimes

Ho Tzu-chen

Mao's second wife was a teacher before she joined the Communists. She married Mao in 1930.

Ho Tzu-chen and Mao had two children in Kiangsi, left behind in the care of Red peasants when the Long March began. The children were never found after the war. In Shensi, Ho Tzu-chen bore Mao a daughter.

Mao had met her in the course of his campaigns across rural China. She first worked for him as secretary, and later became his wife. A shy and self-effacing woman, she worshiped Mao, hung on his every word, and watched over him as possessively as a mother hen.

Ho Tzu-chen and Mao Tse-tung.

by the rich when they held the guns? Never having seen Soviet Kiangsi, I could add little, with my testimony, to an evaluation of second-hand materials about it. The truth is that I saw little that could be called a "terror" in the Northwest and I doubt if any then existed. I must emphasize that this was a period of transition in Red policy from an all-out struggle for power and uncompromising class war to united front tactics which sought to embrace all but the most irreconcilable elements of the old owner-ruler class. Persuasion and gradualism were the practice in bringing poor peasants into participation in both land and political reformations. I have no doubt that in earlier days in the South the Reds had behaved in a more extreme and uncompromising fashion.

The Red Army

Nearly every province in China was represented in the various armies. In this sense the Red Army was probably the only national army in China.

The great mass was made up of young peasants and workers who believed themselves to be fighting for their homes, their land, their country. The average age of the rank and file was nineteen; the average age of the officers was twenty-four.

There is nothing grim about life here or about any of the people one meets. They go about remaking the world like college boys to a football match.

The world's youngest "old veterans." In Paoan, the Chinese Soviet government re-established its Red Army University. It had four sections, with about two hundred students in each. Here the First Section listens to a talk.

Red cadets in Paoan cheer for the American photographer. The Chinese Communist armies did not use the word *ping*, or soldier, to which much odium was attached, but called their men *chan-shih*, meaning fighters. They did not use the title "general," only "commander." Neither officers nor men got any salary.

Three young commanders of the First Red Army Corps.

It seems strange to see two soldiers, fully armed, walking along a path hand in hand and singing, yet that is what you see here very often. Every house rings with singing at night, laughter and good humor. Peasants come to join the Reds in singing.

The majority of the soldiers as well as officers are unmarried, or "divorced"—that is, they have left their wives and families behind them. My impression is that most of these "Red fighters" are still virgins. There were no camp followers or prostitutes with the Red troops I saw. The Reds treat the peasant women and girls with respect, and the peasantry seem to have a good opinion of Red Army morality. I heard of no cases of rape or abuse of the peasant women. Peng Teh-huai, commander of the First Front Army, who used to be a Kuomintang general, once remarked to me that the extreme youth of the Red Army explains much of its capacity for standing hardship. It also makes the problem of feminine companionship less poignant. Peng himself has not seen his own wife since 1928, when he led an uprising of Kuomintang troops and joined the Reds.

I have seen no cases at all of attack on women, old or young, and here they move about with complete freedom. They look upon the soldiers as their friends and protectors and voluntarily cook and prepare food for them, often refusing any payment. I have seen pretty young girls gladly sit down behind a bellows and pump this ancient instrument for an hour or more to flame the fire cooking the warrior's meal, talking and joking meanwhile.

"What," I asked a young soldier, "was really bitter? Not to have bread and potatoes, but to feed only on *hsiao-mi*?"

"No, that can't be reckoned bitter," he replied. "If there's no rice we eat bread, no bread we eat *hsiao-mi*, no *hsiao-mi* we eat corn, no corn we eat potatoes, no potatoes we eat cabbage, no cabbage we drink hot water, no hot water we drink cold water. But if there's no water at all? *Shih-ti*, that's bitter!"

Young women in soviet areas, northwest China.

The Reds had a very limited output of armaments; their enemy was really their main source of supply. For years the Reds had called the Kuomintang troops their "ammunition carriers," and they claimed to capture more than 80 percent of their guns and more than 70 percent of their ammunition from enemy troops. The regular troops (as distinct from local partisans) I saw were equipped

mainly with British, Czechoslovakian, German and American machine guns, rifles, automatic rifles, Mausers and mountain cannon, such as had been sold in large quantities to the Nanking government. Questioned as to the source of the Reds' munitions, Generalissimo Chiang admitted that most of them had been taken from defeated government troops.

Red soldiers with captured machine guns and artillery.

Mounts of a Red cavalry regiment of the 25th Army taken in battles with the Northeastern Army of the "Young Marshal," Chang Hsueh-liang.

Physical Fitness

" 'Sound Heart, Sound Mind, Sound Body' is a Red slogan. The Communists seem undismayed when you tell them that it is copied from the Y.M.C.A. And the Y.M.C.A. in China also had much to do with popularizing broad jumping and other physical exercises, at which the Reds are probably the most proficient of any army in China."

Far left: Broad jumping.

Left: "Environmental sanitation"—sweeping as exercise.

Far left: Grenade-throwing contest.

Middle: Basketball practice.

Left: "These Red Army University cadets are smiling at the photographer's remark that bandit tennis-players have heretofore been an unknown species. These youths called themselves 'revolutionaries' and labeled Chiang Kai-shek 'bandit' in turn."

"Hsiao Hung Kuei"– "Little Red Devils"

They were youths between twelve and seventeen and they came from all over China. Many of them had survived the hardships of the march from the South. They worked as orderlies, messboys, buglers, spies, radio operators, water carriers, propagandists, actors, grooms, nurses, secretaries, and even teachers. I once saw such a youngster, before a big map, lecturing a class of new recruits on world geography.

They wash their face and hands three times daily, they claim, but they are always dirty, their noses are running and they are usually wiping them with their sleeves and grinning. They eat well, have a blanket each, a uniform and a Red Army cap with a broken bill. They are the most loyal and optimistic of Red Army fighters—the incarnation of the spirit of the army—the boundless energy, the endless stream of youth, the eternal hope rising anew in China.

Their simple text books told of the Kiangsi soviets, of the revolution and its aims, of Marx, Lenin and Stalin, of imperialism and China, of the Japanese conquest of Manchuria, and Nanking's failure to defend the country. The youngest, a child of eight, was reading aloud a text telling of the necessity of youth the whole world over to unite and liberate the oppressed classes in a socialist revolution. This in a mountain village over 200 miles from a railway, three or four days from even a

Hsiao Kuei, nicknamed "The Little Red Colonel."

Primary school, Paoan.

motor road, where no one had ever seen an imperialist or a capitalist.

"What is a capitalist?" I asked one of them. "A capitalist," he replied, "is a man who makes other people till his land and does no work himself." I asked one of them, "What is a Kungchangtang?" "He is a man who helps the Red Army fight Japan and the White troops," he replied promptly. "Is that all?" I asked. "He also helps to fight the landlords and the capitalists."

"Are there any landlords left here?"

"No, no landlords. They have all run away or been killed."

"By whom?"

"By our Red Army."

I sat down to dinner with a section of the communications department. I ate heartily, but as usual, there was nothing to drink but hot water and I could not touch it. The food was delivered by two nonchalant young lads wearing uniforms several sizes too large, and Red caps with long bills that kept flapping down over their eyes. I called to one as he went past.

"*Wei* [hey]! Bring us some cold water."

The youth simply ignored me. I tried the other, with no better result.

Then I saw Li Ke-nung was laughing. He plucked my sleeve. "You can call him 'little devil,'" he advised, "or you can call him 'comrade,' but you cannot call him *wei*. These lads are Young Vanguards, and they are here because they are revolutionaries and volunteer to help us. They are future Red warriors."

Just then the cold (boiled) water did arrive.

"Thank you," I said apologetically, "—comrade!"

The Young Vanguard looked at me boldly. "Never mind that," he said, "you don't thank a comrade for a thing like that!"

The Reds saw to it that a man earned his new land. In busy periods the system of "Saturday Brigades" was used, when not only all the children's organizations but every soviet official, Red partisan, Red Guard, women's organization member, and any Red Army detachment that happened to be nearby, were mobilized to work at least one day a week at farming. Even Mao Tse-tung took part in this work. Here the Reds were introducing the germs of the drastically revolutionary idea of collective effort—and doing primary education work for some future period when collectivization might become practicable. At the same time, into the dark recesses of peasant mentality there was slowly penetrating the concept of a broader realm of social life.

Red-star–spangled young women in the soviet factories at Wuchicheng, north Shensi. The Chinese characters on the apron of the worker, in the middle, read: "Try Hard to Learn."

A trio of "Little Red Devils."

"Child slavery is completely abolished in the soviet districts [Mao told me]. Child slaves are immediately freed and returned to their homes. If they have no homes they are given work. They are given their share of land. If they cannot cultivate it themselves they can lend the land to others and get some rent."

The myths of "communized wives" and "nationalization of women" were too patently absurd to be denied, but changes in marriage, divorce and inheritance were in themselves extremely radical against the background of semifeudal law and practice elsewhere in China. Marriage regulations included interesting provisions against mother-in-law tyranny, the buying and selling of women as wives and concubines, and the custom of "arranged matches." Marriage was by mutual consent, the legal age had been moved up sharply to twenty for men and eighteen for women, dowries were prohibited, and any couple registering as man and wife before a county, municipal or village soviet was given a marriage certificate without cost. Men and women actually cohabiting were considered legally married, whether registered or not—which seemed to rule out "free love." All children were legitimate under soviet law.

The Pupils of Ma the Big Beard

There was a Lenin Club for every company and for every regiment, and here all social and "cultural" life had its center. They all had pictures of Marx and Lenin, drawn by company or regimental talent. Like some of the Chinese pictures of Christ, they generally bore a distinctly Oriental appearance, with eyes like stitches, and either a bulbous forehead like an image of Confucius, or no forehead at all. Marx, whose Chinese moniker is Ma Ke-ssu, was nicknamed by the soldiers Ma Ta Hu-tzu, or Ma the Big Beard. They seemed to have an affectionate awe for him. That was especially true of the Mohammedans, who appeared to be the only people in China capable of growing luxuriant beards as well as appreciating them. A corner of the club was devoted to character study, and here one saw the notebook of each warrior hanging on its appointed peg on the wall. There were three character-study groups: those who knew fewer than 100 characters; those who knew from 100 to 300;

and those who could read and write more than 300 characters. Only about 20 percent of the First Army Corps, I was told, was still *hsia-tzu*, or "blind men," as the Chinese call total illiterates.

There was a wall newspaper in every club; its contents included notices of the Communist party and the Communist Youth League; a couple of columns of crude contributions by the newly literate; radio bulletins of Red Army victories in southern Kansu; new songs to be learned; political news from the White areas; and, perhaps most interesting of all, two sections called the red and black columns, devoted respectively to praise and criticism. "Praise" consisted of tributes to the courage, bravery, unselfishness, diligence or other virtues of individuals or groups. In the black column, comrades lashed into each other and their officers (by name) for such things as failure to keep a rifle clean, slackness in study, losing a hand grenade or bayonet, smoking on duty, "political backwardness," "individualism," "reactionary habits," etc. On one black column I saw a cook criticized for his "half-done" millet; in another a cook denounced a man for "always complaining" about his productions.

Workers (*at left*) pose outside a local Lenin Club. The interior, a workers' clubroom with textbooks hanging on the wall, is festooned with bright paper decorations and a Chinese conception of Marx and Lenin.

Above: Central Post Office, Soviet Areas
Northwest Branch.

Left: Book display.

Above: Red Army reading room.

Left: Wall newspapers played an important
role in the educational system in the soviet
areas.

Living Newspapers

There was no more powerful weapon of propaganda in the Communist movement than the Reds' dramatic troupes, and none more subtly manipulated. By constant shifts of program, by almost daily changes of the "Living Newspaper" scenes, new military, political, economic and social problems became the material of drama, and doubts and questionings were answered in a humorous, understandable way for the skeptical peasantry.

Left to right: The "United Front Dance" interpreted the mobilization of China to resist Japan. "By what legerdemain they produced their costumes I do not know," wrote Snow, "but suddenly there were groups of youths first appearing as cavalry formations, next as aviation corps, then as foot soldiers and finally as navy."

Far left: An audience awaits what could be a play—or a political lecture. Latinized signs over the rude theater (improvised from an old temple) were part of the campaign to popularize the use of the Roman alphabet instead of the difficult Chinese ideograph.

Middle: Wei Kung-chih, twenty-eight-year-old director of the People's Anti-Japanese Dramatic Society, entered the revolution in 1926 and made the Long March from Kiangsi.

Left: "Barefoot, clad in peasant trousers and coats, with silk bandannas on their heads, they danced with unison and grace. Two of these girls had walked from Kiangsi, where they had learned to dance in the Reds' dramatic school at Juichin."

At the Front
A "Foreign Guest"

Although in a strict military sense all Red warriors might be called "irregulars" (and some people would say "highly irregulars"), the Reds themselves made a sharp distinction between their front armies, independent armies, partisans and peasant guards. During my travels in Shensi I had not seen any of the "regular" Red Army, for its main forces were then moving in the west, nearly two hundred miles from Paoan.

As I traveled toward the Kansu border and the front, I stayed in the rude huts of peasants, slept on their mud *kangs*, ate their food, and enjoyed their talk. Some of them refused any money from me when they heard I was a "foreign guest." I remember one old bound-footed peasant woman, with five or six youngsters to feed, who insisted upon killing one of her half-dozen chickens for me.

"We can't have a foreign devil telling people in the outer world that we Reds don't know etiquette," I overheard her say to one of my companions.

Above: Infantry waiting for an order to advance on an enemy position, near the front, in Ninghsia.

Below: The Red Army reaches the Great Wall of China. By June 1936 the Communists held a long stretch of this strategic dividing line, from extreme northeastern Shensi to far-western Kansu.

A "Little Red Devil" Grown Up

I was traveling with Fu Chin-kuei, who had been delegated by the Red Foreign Office to accompany me to the front. Like all the Reds in the rear, Fu was delighted at the prospect of a chance to be with the army, and he looked upon me as a godsend. At the same time he regarded me frankly as an imperialist, and viewed my whole trip with open skepticism. He was unfailingly helpful in every way, however, and before the trip was over we were to become very good friends.

(Fu joined the Red Army in 1930. He has the polish and aplomb of a college graduate but is entirely self-taught—or Red Army–taught—intelligent, good-humored, patient, observant and courageous. One would not believe he was an illiterate factory worker four or five years ago.)

Fu Chin-kuei.

Above: Edgar Snow at the front.

Eight "divisions" of the First Front Red Army were holding a line from the Great Wall in Ninghsia down to Kuyuan and Ping-liang in Kansu. A vanguard of the First Army Corps was moving southward and westward, to clear a road for Chu Teh, who was leading the Second and Fourth Front armies up from Sikang and Szechuan, breaking through a deep cordon of Nanking troops in southern Kansu. Yu Wang Pao, an ancient Mohammedan walled city in southeast Ninghsia, was headquarters of the First Front Army, and here I found its staff and Commander Peng Teh-huai.

I found Peng a gay, laughter-loving man, in excellent health except for a delicate stomach—the result of a week's forced diet of uncooked wheat grains and grass during the Long March, and of semipoisonous food, and a few days of no food at all. A veteran of scores of battles, he had been wounded but once, and then only superficially.

Commander Peng Teh-huai at Yu Wang Pao, an ancient Mohammedan walled city in southeast Ninghsia, headquarters of the First Front Army. He actually preferred marching to riding a horse, and in the long trek from Kiangsi, in which he led his army through a blockade of half a million government troops, walked at least 6,000 miles.

Right: "Red sentries on duty outside an encampment in Kansu; the sentry-box is camouflaged against air attack—although the Hammer-and-Sickle is very much in evidence."

Far right: "Three Red leaders at Wu Tai Shan, political center of the Shansi-Hopei-Chahar border area government."

This photograph, taken by a participant of the capture of Chi Hsien, shows the Communists about to occupy the medieval city in the spring of 1936. In Shansi the Reds met virtually no opposition from Yen Hsi-shan, China's oldest warlord. Within one month they had occupied about half the province, swelling their numbers by 15,000 recruits, many of them from Yen's "model army."

Mao Tse-tung addressing troops at Paoan, 1936.

10

THE COMMUNIST LEADERSHIP

If China had not been 80 to 90 percent peasant, if the majority of the peasants had not been poor families who stood to gain by land redistribution, and if the urban and rural owning class had not been so very small and its interests so firmly vested in an economy of scarcity, China would not have had the kind of revolution she had. But the facts were otherwise and Mao Tse-tung was their prophet. He and his party succeeded because they learned how to by-pass the owning class to form a corporative union between China's revolutionary intellectuals and the great inert peasant masses still living in the iron age.

Most of what has subsequently happened was forecast by him in his talks with me. He demanded, and said there soon would be, a cessation of class war in China and a united front to resist Japan. He outlined just the kind of "protracted war" he would and did conduct against Japan, and the manner in which it would bring the revolution to power. He forecast an early attack by Japan on the European colonies, and against the United States, and was sure that Russia too would finally be drawn into a general war to defeat Japan—and end colonialism in Asia.

He promised no easy victory. He told me to expect Japan to win all the great battles, seize the main cities and communications, and in the process destroy the Kuomintang's best forces early in the war. Then a prolonged struggle would ensue in which Red guerrillas would play the principal role, building up their forces as fast as Kuomintang strength was dissipated. At the end of the war the forces of the Chinese revolution would be far more numerous, better armed, more experienced, more popular, and would emerge as the leading power of East Asia.

He never pretended that his party aspired to anything less than ultimate complete power. He had serene confidence that Japan would bring that "opportunity" to China—had indeed already opened it.

Inwardly I often smiled at the extravagance of Mao's claims. There he sat, with two pairs of cotton pants to his name, his army a minuscule band of poorly armed youths, facing a precarious existence in the most impoverished corner of his land.

"Consult others first," "don't gossip behind comrades' backs," "exchange information," and "don't call a meeting until preparations are completed," are among Mao's precepts of leadership. Preceding any important Politburo meeting I used to see members visit Mao's cave, one by one at first, then two or three together, for discussions which lasted for several hours. When Mao called a meeting he knew how to present a synthesis to include different points of view. The full meeting usually took less time than meetings between individuals.

He had what Mark Twain called "that calm confidence of a Christian with four aces." In his case the aces were Asian Marxism, his knowledge of China and Chinese history, his boundless faith in the Chinese people, and his practical experience in "making generals out of mud."

Mao and the Hat

"You were the only person around who managed to put a hat on Mao Tse-tung," Shag* remembered [in Peking in 1960]. "His hair was very long then and he wouldn't wear a hat."

* George Hatem (Dr. Ma Hai-teh). See page 183.

"I forgot about that."

"Yes, you were taking photographs and insisted that he put on a hat. He didn't have one and you put yours on him because it was the only one that looked at all like an army hat. That was the best picture ever taken of Mao. It's been in books and papers for years, and now it's in the Revolutionary Museum."

Edgar Snow (*left*), age thirty, wearing Red Army cap; Mao Tse-tung in the same cap. "Mao was forty-three, only fourteen years older than I," Snow wrote, "but he had lived nine lives to my two."

Chou En-lai, Red Commander of the Eastern Front.

Chou En-lai

There was a kind of magnetism about him that seemed to derive from a curious combination of shyness, personal charm and the complete assurance of command. He was that rarest of all creatures in China, a pure intellectual in whom action was perfectly coordinated with knowledge and conviction. He was a scholar turned insurrectionist. He did not seem to fit any of the well-worn descriptions of the Red bandits. He seemed, on the contrary, genuinely light-hearted and as full of the love of life as the "little Red devil" who trudged manfully beside him, and around whose shoulder he had thrown a fatherly arm.

From the highest commander down to the rank and file these men ate and dressed alike. Battalion commanders and higher, however, were entitled to the use of a horse or a mule. I noticed there was even an equal sharing of the delicacies available—expressed, while I was with the Red Army, chiefly in terms of watermelons and plums. There was very little difference in living quarters of commanders and men, and they passed freely back and forth without any formality.

Chu Teh (*standing*) addresses the men and women of the Red Army.

Kang Ke-ching

Stronger than most Red soldiers, she sometimes carried weak ones on her back during the Long March, which she made entirely on foot. She is an expert shot, and before her marriage commanded a partisan detachment herself; she frequently went to the front and fought with the soldiers. She was married to Chu Teh at Chingkangshan. They have no offspring. (Chu Teh's first wife was captured at the same place by the Kuomintang. Her stomach was cut open, her skin pulled away and her breasts sliced off, then her body thrown back to the Reds.)

Tsai Chang

Tsai Chang [sister of Mao's early friend, Tsai Ho-sen] was the only woman member of the Central Committee at the front and she was one of the veteran Communist women who completed the Long March. Her grandfather was a Ching scholar; she received a classical education to a degree unusual for girls. In 1919 she ran away from home and went to France. She met her husband there—Li Fu-chun, who later became chairman of the Kansu-Ninghsia border soviet. They returned from France in 1923, both having meanwhile joined the branch Chinese Communist Party in France, with Chou En-lai. Tsai Chang fled to Russia after the counter-revolution; returning to China, she got into Kiangsi and worked there until the defeat and the Long March.

Mmes. "Chu-Mao": Kang Ke-ching, right, wife of Chu Teh, with Ho Tze-chen, wife of Mao Tse-tung, in 1938. Kang Ke-ching told Snow that "I like babies as an institution but I don't want any myself. I have to keep fit for my work in the army."

Tsai Chang (*second from right*) with three other women who also made the Long March.

Po Ku

Po Ku was one of the more personable and interesting of the Communist leaders I met, and the youngest member of the Politburo. He was above average height and very thin and wiry—literally so, for he seemed almost strung on wires, his bodily movements being jerky and ill-coordinated. He had a high nervous laugh, prominent teeth, and exophthalmic eyes which, especially behind his thick-lensed glasses, seemed to be popping out of his head. He liked to play tennis—and poker.

Born in 1908, he graduated from a Soochow technical school at seventeen, entered Shanghai University, studied English and joined the Chinese Communist Party. Sent to Russia in 1926, he, like his classmate Wang Ming, became fluent in Russian and in Marxist-Leninist doctrine. In 1930 he returned to China, helped put Wang Ming in leadership, and (aged twenty-three) became his first deputy. Po Ku was elected general secretary of the

"Liu Chun-hsien, wife of Po Ku, and director of the Women's Department of the Trade Unions. She is a small, capable, bright-eyed, very peasant-looking and extremely charming woman of 29. Born in Wusih, she worked as a factory girl till 1927, when the Communist party sent her to Russia for three years. She . . . knew Vincent Sheean; she is the Chinese girl whom he describes making a speech in Moscow at the 10th anniversary of the October Revolution, and Po Ku, whom she met there, was her interpreter."

Po Ku.

Central Committee and Politburo [in 1931]. In the protracted struggle between "Moscow-oriented" and "native" Marxists for dominance in the Chinese party leadership (which reflected differences over the relative importance of the cities and the countryside in the conquest of power), Po Ku personified the former and Mao Tse-tung the latter. At the end of the Long March, Po Ku continued in the Politburo and in 1936 was acting as chairman of the provisional Northwest soviet government.

Lin Piao

Red Army cadets standing atop the entrance gate to Kang Ta, the Military Academy at Paoan.

Lin Piao was the son of a factory owner in Hupeh province, and was born in 1908. His father was ruined by extortionate taxation, but Lin managed to get through prep school, and became a cadet in Whampoa Academy at Canton. He received intensive political and military training under Chiang Kai-shek and Chiang's chief adviser, the Russian General [Vasili] Bluecher. By 1927, at the age of twenty, he was a colonel in the noted Fourth Kuomintang Army. In August of that year, after the Right coup d'état at Nanking, he led his regiment to join the Twentieth Army under Ho Lung and Yeh Ting in the Nanchang Uprising, which began the Communists' armed struggle for power.

When Generalissimo Chiang drove the rebels from Kiangsi, in 1934, Lin Piao led the breakthrough forces of the Long March. He fought successful battles in Shansi and Shensi (1935–36) and took part in the occupation of Yenan in December 1936. His 115th Division delivered a smashing defeat to invading Japanese forces, a first proof that Chinese troops, properly organized and led, could be victorious against modern armies.

Lin Piao, director of Kang Ta.

A Red sentry, northwest China, 1938.

Teng Hsiao-ping

Teng Hsiao-ping was born in 1904 in Szechuan. After a rudimentary schooling he joined the Work-Study Plan and went to France in 1920. He did not attend school in France but spent his five years there as a worker. He learned Marxism from French workers and became a Chinese member of the French Communist Party, from which he transferred to the Chinese Communist Party. He returned to China by way of Russia, where he "studied several months." In 1927 he helped form a peasant army in Kiangsi. After the counterrevolution Teng worked in the Shanghai party underground until 1929. He then formed the Seventh Red Army at Lungchow, Kwangsi. "The Lungchow Soviet had relations with the Annamites [Vietnamese] who began the worker-peasant rebellion in 1930. French airplanes bombed Lungchow and we shot one down," Teng told the author in 1936. Combined French and Nationalist forces destroyed the Lungchow soviet movement, as well as the Vietnamese forces, but the latter maintained ties with the Chinese guerrillas. With remnants of the Seventh Army, Teng made his way through Kwangsi and Kiangsi to Chingkangshan. With his followers reorganized as the Eighth Army, he took part in the capture of Changsha in 1930. From 1932 to 1934 Teng was in the political department of the Red Army and edited *Hung Hsing* (Red Star).

During the Long March, Teng Hsiao-ping was deputy commander and political commissar of Liu Po-cheng's Twelfth Division. He backed Mao in his dispute with Chang Kuo-tao and he completed the Long March with Mao's columns. In 1936 he was Nieh Jung-chen's deputy as political commissar of the First Army Corps in Kansu.

Teng Hsiao-ping (*left*) with Liu Po-cheng, popularly known as the "One-eyed Dragon" after he lost an eye in one of many battles. Chief of staff of the Central Revolutionary Military Committee in Kiangsi, Liu led part of the vanguard forces during the Long March, then commanded the 129th Division, Eighth Route Army, at the start of the Resistance War (1937–45). Teng Hsiao-ping was associated with Liu Po-cheng throughout the war.

Nieh Jung-chen (*front right*), military commander, Shansi-Chahar-Hopei Border Region. He was a former secretary of Whampoa Academy, and was born near Chungking, in a rich peasant family. From 1931 he was in the political department of the Red Army in Kiangsi. He made the Long March and in 1936 was chief of staff of the First Red Army Corps. He became famous as an organizer of guerrilla forces in the Wu Tai Mountains, and after the Liberation War was made one of China's ten marshals of the People's Liberation Army.

The First Army Corps Staff, photographed in Yu Wang Pao, Ninghsia province. Nieh Jung-chen is first on right in the back row. *Fourth from left, first row:* Cheng Ken, Commander of the First Division, graduate of Whampoa Academy, and former aide to Chiang Kai-shek, whose life he once saved. *Extreme left:* Hsiao Hua, who joined the Red Army in Chingkangshan at age fifteen.

"As a member of the People's Political Council, a united-front consultative body set up by the Chiang Kai-shek government, Tung Pi-wu (shown above soon after he made the Long March) was the only Communist in a ten-member Chinese delegation to San Francisco in 1945 to establish the United Nations. The only high-ranking Communist to hold an imperial degree in the Classics, a loyal follower of Sun Yat-sen as well as Mao Tse-tung, widely respected among all classes in China, an extensive traveler abroad and held in high esteem among foreign Communists, Tung Pi-wu was a remarkable, durable gentleman. In 1970 Chairman Mao remarked to the author that he and Tung Pi-wu were the lone survivors (in good standing) among the founders of the Chinese Communist Party in 1921."

"One-eyed Li Ke-nung, head of the Communications Corps in Shensi. His legs had carried him over marches totalling 25,000 li. A native of Shanghai, he worked there as a clerk; later, after he joined the Communist party, he became head of the Political Defense Corps in Kiangsi. He is nervous, quick-speaking, witty, a great mimic. One of his eyes is totally blind, the other very weak. Both were ruined in Kiangsi, where he worked every night by candle-light until 3 or 4 in the morning."

Hsiao Ching-kuang with Edgar Snow in Paoan. After the Long March, Hsiao took part in the 1935 Shansi expedition and was credited with recruiting 8,000 volunteers there. (He became Commander of the Navy after 1949.)

Left to right: Hsieh Chueh-tsai, Communist Minister of Education; Huang Hua, Wang Ling, a courier between Peking and Paoan, and Edgar Snow, interviewing Hsieh in his cave in Paoan, 1936.

Edgar Snow with Lin Tsu-han, Finance Commissioner of the Chinese Soviets.

Lin Tsu-han

Lin Tsu-han, the dignified white-haired commissioner of finance, whose task was to make Red ends meet. This interesting old custodian of the exchequer had once been treasurer of the Kuomintang. Son of a Hunanese schoolteacher, Lin was born in 1882, was educated in the classics and later studied in Tokyo. While in Japan, he met Sun Yat-sen, then exiled from China by the Manchus, and joined his secret revolutionary society, the Tung Meng Hui. When Sun merged with other revolutionary groups to found the Kuomintang, Lin became a charter member. In 1922 he joined the Communist party. He continued to work closely with Sun, however, and was in turn treasurer and chairman of the General Affairs Department of the Kuomintang. When Chiang Kai-shek began the extermination of the Communists in 1927, Lin de-

nounced him, fled to Hong Kong, and then to Soviet Russia. On his return to China, he took passage on the "underground railway" and safely reached Kiangsi. At the age of forty-five he had abandoned the comfortable assets of his position and staked his destiny with the young Communists.

Last Days in Paoan

Life in Paoan went on tranquilly enough and you would not have supposed that these people were aware of their imminent "annihilation." A training regiment of new recruits spent their time marching and countermarching all day, playing games and singing songs. Some nights there were dramatics, and every night the whole town rang with song. In the Red Army University the cadets were hard at work on a ten-hour day of study. A new mass-education drive was beginning in the town, even the "little devils" in the Waichiaopu [the Foreign Office] being subjected to daily lessons in reading, politics and geography.

Every morning, as soon as the sun rose above the hills, I played tennis with three faculty members of the Red University. The court was full of stones, it was fatal to run after a fast ball, but the games were nevertheless hotly contested.

I had a pack of cards, unused since my arrival, and one day I taught Commissar Tsai Shu-fan to play rummy. Tsai had lost an arm in battle, but it handicapped him very little at either tennis or cards. He easily beat me with one hand. Even the women began sneaking up to the Waichiaopu gambling club. My mud *kang* became the rendezvous of Paoan's elite, and you could look around at the candlelit faces there at night and recognize Mrs. Chou En-lai, Mrs. Po Ku, Mrs. Kai Feng, Mrs. Teng Fa and even Mrs. Mao. But the real menace to soviet morals didn't appear till Paoan took up poker. Our tennis quartet started this; we dragged in such respectable citizens as Po Ku, Li Ke-nung, Kai Feng, Lo Fu and others. Stakes rose higher and higher. One-armed Tsai Shu-fan finally cleaned up $120,000 from Chairman Po Ku in a single evening, and it looked as if Po Ku's only way out was embezzlement of state funds. We settled the matter by ruling that Po Ku would be allowed to draw $120,000 on the treasury to pay Tsai, provided Tsai would use the money to buy airplanes for the nonexistent soviet air force. It was all in matches, anyway—and, unfortunately, so were the airplanes Tsai bought.

Farewell to Red China

In the middle of October 1936, after I had been with the Reds nearly four months, arrangements were finally completed for my return to the White world. It had not been easy. Chang Hsueh-liang's friendly Tungpei troops had been withdrawn from nearly every front and replaced by Nanking or other hostile forces.

I walked down the main street of Defended Peace for the last time. People popped their heads out of offices to shout last remarks. My poker club turned out en masse to bid the maestro good-bye, and some "little devils" trudged with me to the walls of Paoan.

"Don't forget my artificial arm!" called Tsai.

"Don't forget my films!" urged Lu Ting-yi.

"We'll be waiting for the air fleet!" laughed Yang Shang-kun.

"Send me in a wife!" demanded Li Ke-nung.

"And send back those four ounces of cocoa," chided Po Ku.

The whole Red University was seated out in the open, under a great tree, listening to a lecture. We shook hands, and I mumbled a few words. Then I turned and forded the stream, waved them a farewell and rode up quickly with my little caravan.

On the twentieth I got through no man's land safely. A day later I was in Sianfu. At the Drum Tower I jumped down from beside the driver and asked one of the Reds (who were wearing Tungpei uniforms) to toss me my bag. A long search, and then a longer search, while my fears increased. My bag was not there. In that bag were a dozen diaries and notebooks, thirty rolls of film—the first still and moving pictures ever taken of the Chinese Red Army—and several pounds of Red magazines, newspapers and documents. It had to be found.

Finally it was realized what had happened. Back at Hsienyang, twenty miles behind us, the missing object had been thrown off with the other loads. It was already dusk, and the driver suggested that he wait till morning to go back and hunt for it. Something warned me that morning would be too late. The truck reversed and returned, and I stayed awake all night in Sianfu wondering if I would ever see that priceless bag again.

The bag was found. Early next morning all traffic was swept from the streets, and all roads were lined with gendarmes and troops. Peasants were cleared out of their homes along the road. Some of the more unsightly huts were simply demolished. Generalissimo Chiang Kai-shek was paying a sudden call on Sianfu. This arrival made an unforgettable contrast with the scenes still fresh in my mind—of Mao Tse-tung nonchalantly strolling down a street in Red China. And the Generalissimo did not have a price on his head. But the precautions taken to protect him in Sian were to prove inadequate. He had too many enemies among the very troops who were guarding him.

Back in Peking, Edgar Snow began writing *Red Star Over China*—the first authentic account of the Chinese Communist Party and the first connected story of Mao Tse-tung and the men and women who would make up the history of China's most thoroughgoing social revolution.

Anti-Japanese posters appeared on the walls of the city of Sian—this one on the ancient Drum Tower.

11

THE SIAN INCIDENT 1936 "CHINESE MUST NOT FIGHT CHINESE!"

"Look at the map and note the smallness of Japan compared to China. Can anyone doubt that we shall triumph?"

—*Chiang Kai-shek*

"If our country is subjugated by the enemy, we shall lose everything. We cannot even speak of socialism if we are robbed of a country in which to practice it."

—*Mao Tse-tung*

General Yang Hu-cheng had been undisputed monarch of those parts of Shensi not controlled by the Reds. A former bandit, he rose to authority via the route that had put many of China's ablest leaders in office, and on the same highway he was said to have accumulated the customary fortune. But recently he had been obliged to divide his power in the Northwest. For in 1935 Chang Hsueh-liang had brought his Tungpei (Manchurian) Army into Shensi and assumed office in Sian as supreme Red chaser— Vice Commander of the National Bandit Suppression Commission. Tugging strings behind was the redoubtable Generalissimo himself, who sought to liquidate not only the Communist-led revolution but also the troops of old Yang Hu-cheng and young Chang Hsueh-liang, by the simple process of using each to destroy the other—a politico-military drama the main stratagem of which Chiang evidently believed was understood only by himself. It was that error in calculation which was in a few months to land Chiang Kai-shek a prisoner in Sian.

In October and November 1935, the Tungpei Army suffered serious defeats, and thousands of soldiers "turned over" to the Red Army. Many officers were also taken captive and held for a period of "anti-Japanese tutelage." When released and returned to Sian, those officers brought back to the Young Marshal glowing accounts of the morale and organization in the soviet districts, but especially of the Red Army's sincerity in wanting to stop civil war and unite to oppose Japanese imperialism. Chang Hsueh-liang himself flew up to Yenan, met Chou En-lai, and became convinced of the

Chang Hsueh-liang (*left*), Chiang Kai-shek's deputy commander-in-chief of all China's armed forces, dines with Red Army cadets in Yenan, capital of the Communists' base.

Reds' sincerity. No word of the truce between Chang and the Communists crept into the press. Although Chiang Kai-shek's spies in Sian knew that something was fermenting, they could get few details of its exact nature.

In October [1936] Japanese-led puppet troops began an invasion of Inner Mongolia. Widespread popular demand that this be considered the signal for a "war of resistance" on a national scale was ignored. Many patriotic quarters began to urge that the Communists' proposals for the creation of a national front be accepted by Nanking. Proponents of such opinions were arrested as "traitors."

In November came news of the disaster to Hu Tsung-nan's famed First Army (KMT). General Hu had been moving almost unimpeded into northern Kansu. In various ways the Reds propagandized the Nanking troops about the "united front," trying to persuade them to halt, urging the enemy to join them in resisting Japan. "Chinese must not fight Chinese!" General Hu pushed on. The Reds staged a surprise frontal attack. In zero weather their bare hands were so cold they could not pull the caps from their hand grenades. Hundreds of them went into the enemy lines using their potato-masher grenades for clubs. The fierce onslaught resulted in the destruction and disarming of two infantry brigades and a regiment of cavalry, while thousands of rifles and machine guns were captured, and one government regiment turned over intact to join the Reds. General Hu beat a hasty retreat. The Generalissimo, angered by the humili-

ation of his best army, became determined to destroy his ten-year enemy.

When Chiang Kai-shek arrived in Sianfu it was for the purpose of completing preliminary plans for his sixth general offensive against the Reds.

Chang Hsueh-liang called a joint meeting of the division commanders of the Tungpei and Hsipei armies on the night of December 11. The decision was taken to use these forces to "arrest" the Generalissimo and his staff. The mutiny of 170,000 troops had become a fact.

Twenty-six-year-old Captain Sun Ming-chiu, commander of the Young Marshal's bodyguard, led an assault on the Generalissimo's residence. Chiang had already fled. Sun took a search party up the rocky, snow-covered hill behind the resort. Clad only in a loose robe over his nightshirt, his bare feet and hands cut in his flight up the mountain, and minus his false teeth, Chiang was crouching beside a great rock. His first words were, "If you are my comrade, shoot me and finish it all." To which Sun replied, "We will not shoot. We only ask you to lead our country against Japan. Why do you not fight Japan, but instead give the order to fight the Red Army?"

"I am the leader of the Chinese people," Chiang shouted. "I represent the nation. I think my policy is correct."

In this way, a little bloody but unbowed, the Generalissimo became the involuntary guest of General Yang Hu-cheng and the Young Marshal.

A few days later Chang Hsueh-liang sent to Paoan his personal plane, which returned to Sian with three Red delegates: Chou En-lai, vice chairman of the military council; Yeh Chien-ying, chief of staff of the East Front Army; and Po Ku, chairman of the Northwest Branch Soviet Government.

Shortly after his arrival, Chou En-lai went to see Chiang. Chiang was said to have turned pale when Chou—his former political attaché for whose head he had once offered $80,000—entered the room and gave him a friendly greeting.

The Generalissimo feared, as he revealed in his diary, that he was going to be given a "mass trial" and be executed. Instead, he had to listen to what his Manchurian subordinates as well as the Reds thought of his policies—and the changes they believed necessary to save the nation.

On December 24, Chou went to see Chiang. At the meeting Chiang's first words were, "We must not have any more civil war." It was the chief demand of the Communists that he make such a

Curious Shensi peasants look on while fur-capped northeastern troops guard the plane which brought Chiang Kai-shek to Sian on the morning of December 12, 1936. The crew hoped to rescue the Generalissimo; the plane was promptly captured by the "rebels."

"A pleasure resort ten miles outside Sian, Lintung is famous in song and story as the retreat of beautiful Yang Kuei-fei, the most celebrated courtesan of the Tang period. It was here that Chiang Kai-shek was taken prisoner."

Women were represented in the mass demonstrations in Sian. Madame Yang Hu-cheng, wife of the Shensi leader, marched in front of this group of the Women's National Salvation Union.

promise. After that he merely made some superfluous remarks saying, "All the time we've been fighting I often thought of you. I remembered even during the war that you had worked well for me. I hope we can work together again."

Chiang was released entirely on Chang Hsueh-liang's initiative, according to Po Ku. Mme. Chiang had great influence here on the sentimental Chang. She kept saying she hoped Chang would give them a Christmas present by releasing them and there could be forgiveness all around. Chang Hsueh-liang fell for this.

The chief reason why Chang Hsueh-liang so quickly released Chiang Kai-shek, without having obtained Chiang's acceptance of his demands, was because of the unexpected attitude adopted by the Chinese Reds at Sian. The latter, who had earlier supported a long detention, and even a "public trial" for Chiang, abruptly urged his release after he had verbally agreed to only one of the rebels' eight demands—to end the civil war. There is no doubt that the attitude of Soviet Russia influenced

this quick disposition of the Sian affair, and that Moscow was quite pleased with the peaceful settlement that restored Chiang to power. The Russian Communists feared that the elimination of Chiang Kai-shek would result in a protracted civil war in which the Japanese might succeed in turning the Nanking government into a real Franco regime of the East. China would thereby not only be rendered strategically valueless to, but a potential belligerent against, the Soviet Union.

Whatever Chiang did or did not promise before he was released, the practical result was to end civil war. On Christmas Day the Young Marshal escorted the Generalissimo unharmed back to Nanking. The Generalissimo quietly called off the anti-Red offensive and personally authorized negotiations with the Reds. Officially, the Kuomintang now announced that the first task before the country was "the recovery of the lost territories," whereas formerly Chiang had always insisted upon "internal pacification"—annihilation of the Reds—as "the first task."

Chang Hsueh-liang, 1936.

Chiang Kai-shek never forgave Chang Hsueh-liang and never freed him. Thirty years later Chang was still Chiang Kai-shek's personal prisoner on Taiwan.

During the Resistance War, Yang Hu-cheng offered his services to the Generalissimo. General Yang was put under house detention in Chungking, and toward the end of the war he was secretly executed.

The United Front

Tacit agreement was reached which provided that the Communists could retain their party organization but would abandon the name "Red Army" and become the "Eighth Route Army" as part of the Nationalist Army; that the Communists would cease attempts at violent overthrow of the Nanking government and transform the "soviets" into a "special administration area," and that the Kuomintang would convene the long-delayed "People's Congress," in accordance with the will of Dr. Sun Yat-sen, granting representation to all groups. But

Left: Garbed in flying togs and goggles, Chou En-lai was met by Mao Tse-tung (*left*) at the Yenan airfield after the "settlement" of the Sian Incident. *Right:* Chiang Kai-shek's portrait joined those of Sun Yat-sen, Lenin and Stalin in a northwest village "Save the Country Hall" as the "united front" took effect.

Chou En-lai (*top left*) led a Chinese Communist delegation to Nanking—capital of the Nationalist government until December, 1937—to negotiate a cease-fire with the Kuomintang; he also set up an office of the 18th Army Group (the name given for the combined Communist armies). *First row:* Yeh Chien-ying on left; Chu Teh, far right.

Chiang's negotiations with the Communists had by June 1937 reached a stalemate. The Manchurian army had been peacefully moved out of Shensi by agreement with the Young Marshal's subordinates. Once more the Reds were surrounded and blockaded. Mao Tse-tung and Chu Teh were told that their forces, also, were to be "reorganized" and transferred, as separate elements, to other armies— a process which would have simplified their obliteration. Late in June I received a confidential letter from Mao Tse-tung which expressed "anxiety and dissatisfaction" with the ominous trend of events. Destruction or advance into the northern provinces once more seemed to be their alternatives. In July they were extricated from their precarious position by Japan's "providential" major invasion of China, which gave Chiang Kai-shek no choice but to shelve any and all plans for another annihilation drive.

The Kuomintang government was obliged to tolerate the Communists in the Northwest; elsewhere the party was not legalized. Laws providing capital punishment for membership were never rescinded, but a few Communists were permitted to travel back and forth on recognized war missions, and the Eighth Route Army was allowed offices and a newspaper in the capital.

Communists could, for a brief time, come and go without fear of reprisal. *Left:* Po Ku leans jovially on Li Ke-nung, Wuhan, 1938. *Right:* Among the foreigners and prominent Reds in this group picture are (*front row, from left*) Po Ku, Chou En-lai, Wang Ming; (*middle row, center*) Agnes Smedley; and (*top row, far right*) Mme. Chou En-lai.

When Chou left the Communist areas to become his party's chief of mission in Kuomintang China, some people supposed he had been side-tracked or would be quickly "corrupted by an easy life." I remember visiting him and his wife in a comfortable modern house provided by the Generalissimo, where they had what Teng Ying-chao called "the first real home since we were married." She was then convalescing from a return bout with tuberculosis and that relative peace meant much to her. But Chou's ambitions—and her own—meant more.

Edgar Snow, Chou En-lai and Teng Ying-chao at Wuchang, the Chous' home in Wuhan, 1938. Their marriage was celebrated as a model political partnership as well as a sentimental one.

Wuhan was the last big industrial center still in Chinese hands in the summer of 1938; its streets teemed with soldiers and agitators before the city was abandoned that October. *Above:* Anti-Japanese demonstrators. *Center:* Kuomintang troops. *Left:* A "Propaganda Team" advocating "Support Resistance."

I was in Hankow nearly seven weeks—all of the most blistering heat, made even warmer by the Nips' periodical air raids. The latter generally do little military damage, though they've killed hundreds of poor people, as in Canton. But the people's spirit holds up well nevertheless; in fact that fortitude and patience and philosophic calm of the people in general are the best aspects of an immediate situation which otherwise has little inspiring about it except the nearly incredible courage and heroism of the mass of the Chinese soldiers, who are performing deeds of unexcelled valor every day of the war. But though there are tremendous reservoirs of power in the people, who are ready to be used and to make sacrifices, very little is being done to mobilize them, and all sorts of obstacles are placed in the way of those who wish to do so. If the city masses in Wuhan and Changsha were organized, trained and armed, and if the 20,000,000 people in the environs of these cities were similarly mobilized, there is no doubt in my mind that the Japanese could not take Wuhan—which, properly defended, is virtually impregnable.

During the uprising, the Red forces—then numbering about 40,000—occupied Yenan and other surrounding territory. After that, northern Shensi became the main training base from which the Reds infiltrated the North China plains and carried on guerrilla operations throughout the next eight years of the Sino-Japanese War.

Above: A fighting Chinese soldier.

Below: Japan portrayed as a beast at bay.

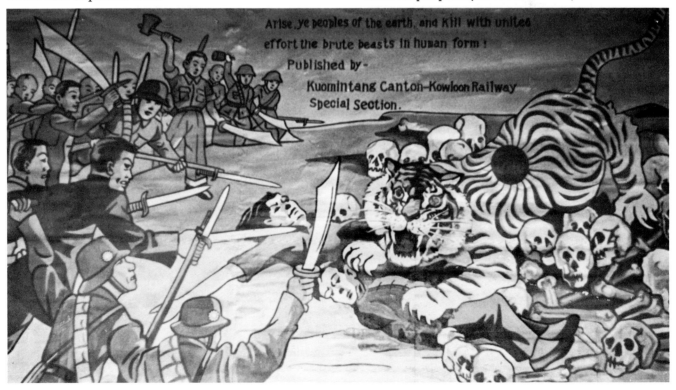

The Marco Polo Bridge, where the Sino-Japanese War began.

THE INVASION OF CHINA 1937

Those guns of July in China opened eight years of Sino-Japanese battle
which heralded the ultimate Communist victory in China.

Lukouchiao was a railway station 15 miles southwest of Peking. The Japanese had illegally occupied the eastern terminus of the shuttle. Possession of Lukouchiao would give them control of all southern rail entries to Peking. A few hundred yards farther east lay the ancient walled town of Wanping, with its marble bridge made famous by Messer Marco Polo.

Late in the night of July 7, on the pretext that one of their soldiers was missing, the Japanese suddenly demanded permission to enter and search the town of Wanping. The morning found the Japanese in occupation of the Lukouchiao Station, exchanging desultory rifle fire with the Chinese troops. For days they faced each other with only a few yards intervening. It would have been very simple to settle the dispute had the Japanese withdrawn to their barracks, but developments proved that Tokyo was prepared to exploit it to the utmost. Japan did not want any agreement at all with a sovereign North China, she simply wanted North China.

The Generalissimo could remain mute no longer. It became manifest that immediate war was certain.

Something had to happen to Peking. It was an anomaly whose days were numbered, a medieval survival where over a million men dwelt among the glitter and loot of centuries accumulated within its wonderful maze of walls. We woke up a little surprised after successive crises to find the towers still manned by Chinese troops. Perhaps it is a little true that even the Japanese felt some affection for Peking, and realizing its

Above: Puppet police searching Chinese citizens in Japanese-occupied Peking, 1938. *Below:* China's "brown, ragged, shining-eyed children" see war at first hand.

value as a museum piece, had always meant to have it whole. As it was, they met more resistance than anticipated, and in the end the city went down not without a certain glory.

Optimism was shared by many who believed that America and Britain would now break off relations with Japan. They were flabbergasted when I suggested that neither government could be expected to give any effective help to China, and that our merchants would continue to arm Japan throughout the war. The next few years were to provide a political education for millions of Chinese.

The Fall of Shanghai

On August 13, fighting commenced in Shanghai and a new front developed in a war destined perhaps to decide the fate of the Pacific for the twentieth century.

We crept up the Whangpoo [River] to Shanghai, passing a row of Japanese warships belching the fury of their guns at the unseen gray lines beyond, while overhead squadrons of planes ferried their shining death across burning Chapei and Kiangwan. It all gave me an odd this-is-where-I-came-in feeling. One battle in a war of a thousand battles loses significance; in my own mind one blurs and telescopes into the next.

Yet its drama was unique in a way not even Hitler's blitzkriegs could duplicate. It was as though Verdun had happened on the Seine, in full view of a Right Bank Paris that was neutral; as though a Gettysburg were fought in Harlem while the rest of Manhattan remained a nonbelligerent observer. People stood on their apartment roofs and watched Japanese dive bombers emptying tons of bombs on the Chinese trenches hidden beyond the horizon of tile and masonry. Guests at the swank Park Hotel, on the security of Bubbling Well Road, could gaze out through the spacious glass façade of its top-story dining room, while contentedly sipping their demitasse, and check up on the marksmanship of the Japanese batteries.

A single bomb, dropped by that sad Chinese aviator who near-missed the Japanese flagship and hit the Settlement, made Nanking Road look like the refuse-laden Whangpoo River suddenly drained dry, or something by Picasso in his Guernica period. Then there was the sick gut when a little Chinese girl whom I heard shrieking in some ruins proved strangely light as I lifted her from a blood-soaked quilt, to find that her legs had been torn off. And now I know why Floyd Gibbons, who arrived and put up at the Cathay Hotel to cover the war from its well-stocked bar, told me that that was the best place to see a war. Gibbons had already seen that little girl, in a previous incarnation, when I was still wet behind the ears.

Soochow Creek, August 14, 1937—Kuomintang planes have tried, and failed to hit a Japanese warship.

Above: Japanese bombing of Shanghai, August 13, 1937.

Below: "One of China's child soldiers."

Widespread and indiscriminate bombing of civilian centers produces in millions of people who *might* have been its victims in every bombed city and town a reaction of profound outrage and disgust. It arouses a peculiarly *personal* hatred of the invader which no one who has not crouched in a cave, or dug his nose in a field to evade dive bombers, or seen a mother looking for the severed head of her son's corpse, or smelled the stench of roasted schoolchildren, can quite understand. This was perhaps Japan's greatest contribution to the unification of China.

The Chinese exhibited an ardor and military skill which most people had not believed they possessed. In the face of point-blank gunfire they drove the Japanese back through the Settlement almost into the river.

Against Chinese troops protected only by hastily erected defense works, it took the Japanese nearly a week to put ashore a landing party, under the protection of a dozen warships and virtually uncontested air support.

Only after two months of steady shelling from naval guns and artillery did they break through the Chinese lines. Yet the tremendous preponderance of fire power, even when often wastefully employed in bombing noncombatant villages and machine-gunning helpless refugees, inevitably told its story, as one Chinese position after another was demolished.

Nationalist troops defending Shanghai against the Japanese, 1937.

People comb through the remains of one of Shanghai's big hotels, August 14, 1937.

Far right: "Old Glory."

Right: U.S. Marines guarding their defense sector of the Shanghai International Settlement.

Below: Exodus from the Hongkew district, August 14, 1937.

Far left: The Shell Building, Shanghai.

Left: Barricaded Chartered Bank of India, Australia and China.

Below: Foreigners leaving the city.

Above: "A moment after the work of a dive bomber."

Right: A Japanese soldier carrying off loot in a baby carriage.

Above: Edgar Snow (*far right*) following a panicked citizen in a leap over a corpse-lined ditch.

Left: "Things you remember after a bombing raid."

The Rape of Nanking

The Japanese entered Nanking on December 12 [1937] as Chinese troops and civilians were still trying to withdraw to the north bank of the Yangtze. Hundreds of people were machine-gunned by planes or drowned while trying to cross the river; hundreds more were caught in the bottleneck at Hsiakuan gate, where bodies piled up four feet high.

The Japanese murdered no less than 42,000 people in Nanking alone, a large percentage of them women and children. Anything female between the ages of ten and seventy was raped. Discards were often bayoneted. Mothers had to watch their babies beheaded, and then submit to raping. One mother told of being raped by a soldier who, annoyed at the cries of her baby, put a quilt over its head and smothered it to death, finishing his performance in peace. Open-air copulation was not uncommon. Some 50,000 troops were let loose for over a month in an orgy of rape, murder, looting and general debauchery.

Stores and houses were stripped and set ablaze. The homes of foreign diplomats were entered and their servants murdered. Privates did as they pleased; officers either participated themselves or excused their men by explaining that the conquered Chinese had no right to expect "special consideration." Japanese embassy officials, aghast at the spectacle, were powerless to do anything about it.

Thousands of men were lined up and machine-gunned. Sometimes groups were used for bayonet exercises. When the victors grew bored with such mild sport they tied their victims, poured kerosene over their heads and cremated them alive. Amazing cases crawled into missionary hospitals: men with their eyes, ears and noses burned away, or with their necks half severed, but somehow still alive.

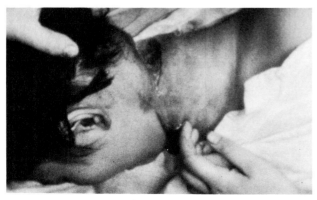

A woman's partially severed head.

Young girls were dragged from American and British missionary schools, installed in brothels for the troops, and heard from no more. One day in a letter written by one of the missionaries in the Zone I read about a strange act of patriotism, concerning a number of singing girls who had sought refuge with their virtuous sisters. The missionary asked them if any would volunteer to serve the Japanese, so that nonprofessional women might be spared. They despised the enemy as much as the rest, but nearly all of them stepped forth. Surely they must have redeemed whatever virtue such women may be held to have lost, and some of them gave their lives in this way, but as far as I know they never received posthumous recognition or even the Order of the Brilliant Jade.

Hankow fell about as expected, at the end of October 1938, a little hastened by the almost simultaneous loss of Canton. Perhaps the worst aspect of the period was the discouraging repetition of Chinese mistakes made elsewhere—the failure adequately to reorganize and evacuate industry and skilled workers, followed by the equally feeble attempts to immobilize these two strategic cities as enemy war bases, before they were abandoned. Japan used the captured resources and industrial plant to push her invasion farther inland.

A most curious thing became manifest. The defeated Chinese were not behaving according to the rules. Although Japan won all the great battles, she could never win a political decision and was never able to conclude the war victoriously. Anyone who acknowledged defeat would simply not be obeyed by the people and would be disowned.

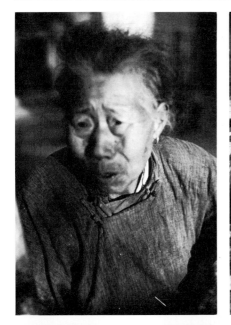

Nanking, 1937.

Top: Bayonet practice. *Bottom:* Burying Chinese prisoners alive.

When Wang Ching-wei, the No. 2 man in the Kuomintang hierarchy, betrayed China and became chief of the Japanese puppet government at Nanking [1938], the people spat on him and his influence vanished. The same thing would have happened to Chiang Kai-shek if he had surrendered. This fact was perfectly understood by Chiang himself. General Stilwell also understood that. Few other Americans did. It was never Chiang's will that kept China in the war. Quite simply, Chiang never had the power to take China out of the war.

From 1938 to the end of World War II the Japanese were never seriously harassed by the defeated generals and politicians in the far west and south of China. It was the peasant who "raised his club" behind their [Japanese] own lines, the tireless guerrilla, seemingly nothing and nowhere, who was the uneasy jest of the conquerors by day and their dread preoccupation by night, the endless drop of water on the back. His unorthodox and irregular attacks provided the front that was never quiet, the enemy never defeated, the peasant partisan who would indeed never win the military decision against Japan but who nevertheless would decide the political future of China.

In 1938 Evans Carlson, then a captain in the U.S. Marine Corps, was the only American officer I knew, besides [Colonel Joseph W.] Stilwell, who grasped the significance of this amazing growth behind the Japanese lines.

Wang Ching-wei, once a leader of the Kuomintang, advocated peace with Japan and in 1938 broke with Chiang. From 1940 to his death in 1944, he headed the Japanese puppet government at Nanking.

U.S. Marine Captain Evans Carlson (*far left*) with Edgar Snow (*right*) during the Japanese occupation of Shanghai, 1938.

The New Fourth Army

In January 1938, following the sack of Nanking, the Generalissimo finally authorized the Kiangsi-Fukien Communists to reorganize as the New Fourth Army, and engage in limited guerrilla activity on the north and south banks of the lower Yangtze River. General Yeh Ting was given chief command and Hsiang Ying became field commander.

Word passed quickly through the former soviet districts that Hsiang Ying and Yeh Ting were building a new anti-Japanese army, and hundreds of peasants began trekking in over great distances. Hundreds of "Red bandits," but recently released from prisons and reform schools, returned to their old leaders. Young Vanguards emerged and old Peasant Guards arrived carrying rusty spears, hand grenades and axes. From the occupied cities came students, factory workers and mechanics, who remembered Hsiang Ying as a leader of labor.

Rich in human faith and spirit, but abysmally poor in money and arms, the New Fourth reoccupied about one third of the provinces of Kiangsu and Anhwei, an area with a normal population of 19,000,000 people, now increased by refugees. Japanese held the cities, roads and railways; the New Fourth took back the hinterland.

Edgar Snow encountered Commander Yeh Ting in Hankow in 1938, a year after the founding of the New Fourth Army, the Communists' major force in east-central China.

Five commanders of the New Fourth Army. *Second from left:* the woman commander Chen Ta-ja. *Fourth from left:* Li Hsien-nien. An early leader in peasant uprisings in his native Hupeh province, Li was sent back there, behind Japanese lines, and by 1941 had built an army of 60,000.

In organizing the masses for war, the New Fourth faced greater difficulties than their comrades in the North. The Kuomintang forbade it institutions to carry out economic and political reforms. If the army reoccupied a county city, the Kuomintang restored the old type of *tangpu* administration; no people's councils or representative government here. Despite these handicaps, local leaders were developed, capable of commanding self-defense corps, which the New Fourth undertook to train and arm. Fallow land was put into production wherever possible, often tilled by army auxiliaries. The New Fourth organized its own cooperative workshops.

The settlement of the Sian Incident left the Communists and their Red Army in control of a region about the size of England. It included northern Shensi, from the outskirts of Sanyuan, a few miles north of Sian, to the Great Wall, and on the west

extended to the edge of the Kansu plain, embracing several counties in Kansu province itself, and one or two in the province of Ninghsia. A special administration was set up, called the Shensi-Kansu-Ninghsia Border Government. It proclaimed itself a democracy, established on a united-front basis, and actually did extend to the people, without regard to classes, the right to elect officials—the first attempt of this kind ever made in China. This border regime was given *pro tempore* sanction by Chiang Kai-shek. Yenan became the capital of the new provisional government, as it had been before. It was rear headquarters for the Eighth Route Army as well, and it remained the political center of the Communist party. As the Communist troops marched eastward and northward, behind the Japanese lines, Yenan's influence extended to wider and wider areas.

Red cavalry beneath the ancient pagoda of Yenan, for ten years (1936–46) the hill-cradled Communist capital.

13

YENAN
1939

At an elevation of about 2,500 feet, Yenan lies athwart the historic invasion route from Mongolia to the Wei Valley; over millennia its environs have seen hundreds of stormy battles. In this century, no territory in China was fought over more continuously nor was more impoverished as a result. Bandits and warlords were followed by Communist intellectuals and army officers who sought refuge in a country ideal for guerrilla warfare.

I returned to Yenan in late September 1939, two weeks after the outbreak of World War II. Chou En-lai had flown to Moscow, ostensibly to seek increased aid for China, and presumably to get a reorientation on Stalinist policy since the Nazi-Soviet Pact.

I found Mao still living in a cave; but a modern and improved version, a three-roomed place with a study, a bedroom and a guest room. The walls were of white plaster, the floor was lined with bricks and there were some touches of feminine decoration, added by Mrs. Mao. But here the signs of affluence ended. I discovered Mao still owned only a couple of uniforms and a single padded coat. He had no personal wealth at all.

The years of war had changed him little. No longer on a starvation diet, he had put on some weight; his hair was clipped short; he was dressed as always in the uniform of an ordinary soldier. He was still the plain man of the people, the queer mixture of peasant and intellectual, the unusual combination of great political shrewdness and earthy common sense. He was just as confident as ever that his Communist party would eventually triumph in China, and he still worked all night toward that end.

Reunion—Edgar Snow meets Mao Tse-tung for the second time. Yenan, 1939.

Veterans from Paoan were always asking me what I thought of the improvements since my last visit. The question at first seemed pure irony. Yenan was in fact that only example I have seen of complete demolition of a sizable town by air bombardment alone. Japan must have spent several million yen on this one pattern of lacework alone.

But even demolished Yenan was a big improvement on the past. Optimism is a permanent habit of these people; they wear it like an armor of the mind.

"Yenan is better than Paoan, isn't it so?" asked Mao Tse-tung. "Give us time. If we keep on improving at the present rate, we shall have something to show you in 1945. We have made progress in every direction since you visited us in 1936." And it had to be admitted that they were enjoying better days. Their army had trebled or quadrupled and now garrisoned thousands of miles of new territory. They were no longer completely blockaded from the rest of China.

Outside the city walls a new metropolis was growing up. Hundreds of buildings were strung along the shadow of the cliffs, while tier upon tier of newly dug caves opened their yawning mouths along the mountainside for miles. About 40,000 people, engaged in all the tasks of wartime life, burrowed in and out of the caverns all day long. Its ingenuity and courage were admirable, if also uncomfortably prophetic of housing that may yet become universal, as the bombing plane circumnavigates the earth.

Mao was able to continue (in relative security) an intensified program of Marxist indoctrination which attracted thousands of young patriots and intellectuals, and prepared the peasant masses for future revolution while they were organized to resist Japan. It was during this period that the Reds in effect seized political control of the national anti-Japanese war in North China.

The Communists became in effect a mobile, armed, ubiquitous propaganda crusade spreading

Left: Yenan, after Japanese air raid.

Middle left: Hillside caves.

Middle right: Yenan's hospital was built deep into the loess-earth hillside.

Bottom left: Youths with back packs walking to join the Reds.

Bottom right: The finish of a girls' fifty-meter race at a Yenan sports meeting.

their message across hundreds of thousands of square miles. To millions of peasants they brought their first contacts with the modern world. To youths and women—for the Reds courted them first and last—they opened up unheard-of vistas of new personal freedom and importance.

Side by side with political reforms have gone economic and social changes. In the case of women the enforcement of laws like monogamy, freedom of marriage at the age of consent, free education, and suffrage at the age of eighteen, has won a surprising response. Many women have been elected to village and town councils, and large numbers of young girls carry serious political and military responsibilities.

Material conditions had improved. Mines and crude industries were developing. North Shensi had an export surplus of cotton, wool, hides, vegetable oil and grain. Industrial and producers' cooperatives were filling many of the needs of the civilian population and the army. Consumers' cooperatives had shelves well stocked with the simple necessities of the farming population. Government control kept prices down and they were generally from 30 to 40 percent less than elsewhere. The Border Government had, in a campaign mobilizing all able-bodied people in the area to take part in planting and tilling, opened about 200,000 acres of wasteland. Local guards and garrison troops took part in this work, as well as all students and "functionaries." Even bankers were not exempt. One morning I found the Border Government Bank

Left: Spinning cotton in a Yenan courtyard. *Right:* Soldiers making sandals, as in the Kiangsi days.

Women graduates of Kang Ta Military Academy, north Shensi.

Mao Tse-tung, Yenan, 1939.

office closed for the day. The whole staff was out harvesting. In food, the region was self-sufficient.

A new publishing house was turning out books, magazines and newspapers, for the front and rear. Many foreign books had been translated. Selected writings of Mao Tse-tung, Chu Teh, Lo Fu and other leaders were offered in cheap editions. There were novels, reportage, essays, military and political books, and translations of works on natural science, art and literature.

Nearly all China's Communist top elite lived and worked here at some time under Mao's leadership. Men trained in the wartime academies in the Yenan hills today enjoy the prestige of veterans of Valley Forge. Here Mao mapped out, tried and perfected the tactics and strategy which he followed to victory in the second civil war, 1946–49.

I saw Mao several times, dropping in to have tea or to play poker. Mao was a big gambler and a poor bluffer, but an entertaining player. He took the whole thing too lightly to be agreeable to any serious player; he enjoyed himself. The stakes were large but entirely fictitious.

Mao asked a number of questions about American geography, climate and people—whether the Negroes had gained any new voting power in the South, and about the American Indians and how they were treated. He was surprised to learn that no Catholic had ever been elected President of the United States. Was there a strong religious conflict in America? He had read about Yellowstone National Park and thought China should have one like that. He seemed greatly interested in every scientific and mechanical aspect of American civilization. He had wanted to travel abroad but felt that he could never do so until he had seen more of China. Although he had walked across a great deal of it, China still held many wonders he had yet to see.

The Third Mme. Mao

Chiang Ching was Mao Tse-tung's third wife (excluding an unconsummated childhood marriage). Her real name was Li Chung-chin, and she was born in 1912, in Taian, Shantung, in the shadow of Tai Shan, one of China's five "sacred mountains." In 1934 Chiang Ching married an actor and they worked in the infant Shanghai film industry, Chiang Ching taking the name of Lan Ping (Blue Apple). They were divorced in 1937. Chiang Ching joined a patriotic propaganda theatrical troupe which took her from Shanghai first to Wuhan, then Chungking. She did some drama and film work and moved on to Sian and thence to Yenan, where she enrolled in the Lu Hsun art institute, which trained theatrical troupes for service at the front. It is not true, as sometimes reported, that Mao Tse-tung was still married to Ho Tzu-chen at the time he met Chiang Ching. They had been divorced in 1937. Mao and Chiang Ching were married late in 1938 or early in 1939. During the war she and Mao had two daughters.

Chiang Ching, an actress with the stage name Lan Ping, arrived in Yenan from Shanghai in 1938. An attentive auditor of Mao's lectures, she soon afterward became his wife.

Posters advertising Chiang Ching's films.

Huang Hua

I knew Huang Hua as a student leader when I taught at Yenching University. He was president of his class—a brilliant idealistic youth with a natural talent for leadership. He was one of the first of many students who left the lovely Northern campus to join the Reds. Huang Hua was the party name of Wang Ju-mei, born in 1912 in an educated family in Kiangsu. He took a leading role in the December 9 student movement, became a national organizer and rose to important posts in the Communist Foreign Ministry. He became outstanding among young diplomat-negotiators trained by Chou En-lai. His wife, Ho Li-liang, was also a prominent party leader.

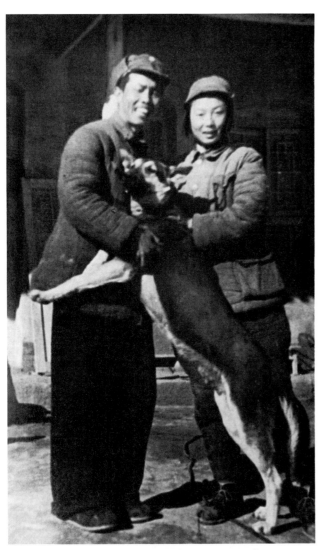

Huang Hua and his wife, Ho Li-liang, play with one of Yenan's rare pets in the courtyard of a cave dwelling.

Jen Pi-shih

Jen Pi-shih was elected to the Politburo in 1930. In 1931 he entered the Hunan-Kiangsi soviet area, where he was chief of the military committee in Ho Lung's forces and also political commissar. He made the Long March and remained in Yenan with Mao Tse-tung.

Liao Cheng-chih

Liao Cheng-chih's father, Liao Chung-kai, and his mother, Ho Hsiang-nin (who held high office in the Chinese government after 1949), were close friends and supporters of Sun Yat-sen. The elder Liao was assassinated in Canton in 1927. Young Liao went to Europe in 1927 to organize strikes against the bad working conditions of Chinese sailors aboard foreign vessels. As a result of frequent imprisonment he learned excellent English and German. In Yenan he was director of the Party newspaper and of the Yenan press agency.

Chu Teh, at net, returns a volleyball during a match in Yenan.

First row, left: Ho Lung with basket-ball team, Yenan.

Mao found time to collect materials for some lectures on basic philosophy for use in the Yenan Anti-Japanese Academy. Some simple and yet fundamental text was needed for the young students being prepared, in brief three-month courses, for political guidance during the years immediately ahead. At the insistence of the party Mao prepared *On Contradiction* and *On Practice* to sum up the experience of the Chinese revolution, by combining the essentials of Marxism with concrete and everyday Chinese examples. Mao said that he wrote most of the night and slept during the day. What he had written over a period of weeks he delivered in lecture form in a matter of two hours. Mao added that he himself considered *On Practice* a more important essay than *On Contradiction*.

Mao Tse-tung—"a rebel who could write verses as well as lead a crusade."

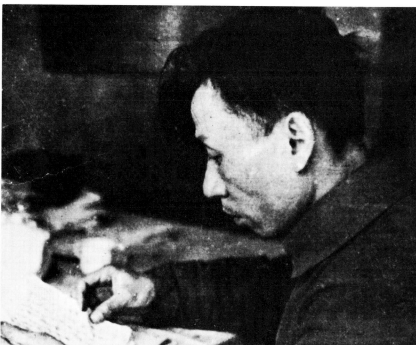

Liu Shao-chi, who "authorized the 'invisible-ink letter' of introduction" which Edgar Snow carried with him as his "passport of entrance" to north Shensi in 1936.

Liu Shao-chi

I did not meet Liu until 1960, having missed him during my first visit to the Northwest; he did not rendezvous with other veterans of the Long March there until late in 1936. Yet it was (I only recently learned) Liu Shao-chi who authorized the "invisible-ink letter" of introduction which I carried to Paoan. At that time Liu was head of the party's North China bureau and was living deep in the political underground.

Five years younger than Mao and a year older than Chou En-lai, Liu was a thin, wiry, gray-haired man with a rather sharp face, and slightly shorter than Mao. He was born only a short distance from Mao's home, in 1898, in Hunan. His father was a primary school teacher. Liu attended Hunan First Normal School (where he enrolled after Mao left) and joined the New People's Study Society founded by Mao. Like Mao, Liu was a rebel against parental control; he was first married by a family arrangement which he refused to recognize. His second wife was executed during the civil war, in 1933. After the Communist victory he married Wang Kuang-mei, a physics teacher in Peking.

Liu was too young to participate in the 1911 revolution. By 1914 he was a radical student; in 1920 he helped form the Socialist Youth League,

precursor of the Communist party. After entering the party, the next year he was assigned to the secretariat of the China Labor Federation and began his career as a labor specialist. Comintern representatives in Shanghai sent Liu to Moscow, where he studied for more than two years. In Canton and Shanghai he worked closely with Chou En-lai during the organization of the revolutionary trade unions, until their suppression in 1927, then led the underground labor movement until, in 1932, he entered Soviet Kiangsi. In Kiangsi he became head of the trade union federation (consisting mostly of rural workers, the "semi-proletariat").

Liu began the Long March and got as far as Tsunyi, where he backed Mao's election as chairman of the party. Then he was sent to contact guerrilla forces north of the Yangtze River and to head the party underground in North China. In 1937 he again joined Mao, in Yenan, and sided with him in the expulsion of Chang Kuo-tao from the Politburo. From this time on, Liu's position as urban spokesman and chief of the North China organization in the "white" areas steadily improved. After the Japanese invasion he took charge of party affairs in enemy-occupied areas.

Throughout the war with Japan and the subsequent civil war, he was Politburo chief among all the Communist forces in East and Northeast China.

The American writer Agnes Smedley, biographer of Chu Teh (*The Great Road*). "Miss Smedley had gradually established contacts with the Chinese Red underground, through whom she got more information about the civil war than anyone else."

Foreigners in Yenan

Agnes [Smedley] was descended from a pre-Revolutionary line of Pennsylvania Quakers, mixed with a few American Indian chromosomes. Childhood was a bitter struggle to get enough to eat, and to learn to read and write, which was made possible by help from her aunt's earnings as a prostitute.

Her life was full of protests not only against man's tyranny toward man but also against woman's tyranny toward man, and vice versa. Her passion for justice and liberation of the human spirit led her into conflicts with important Communists as well as with the Generalissimo and Mme. Chiang. When she was in charge of medical funds in the New Fourth Army she fought a commander who tried to appropriate hospital supplies to sell in order to buy arms. She also had the courage to do verbal and physical battle with no less a personage than Mme. Mao Tse-tung (Ho Tzu-chen), and won a prolonged campaign against the high sisterhood of wives of ranking members of the Chinese Politburo.

Agnes had gone to Yenan soon after the Sian Incident of December 1936. She wrote to ask me to ship from Peking, where I was living, 2,000 rat traps. Then I got a call for hybrid corn seeds, for U.S. government books on public hygiene. chemical farming, pig breeding, poultry raising, medical and hospital data, housing—and literature on birth control. As a lifelong friend of Margaret Sanger, she was a pioneer crusader in Asia. She was writing news stories and taking pictures in Yenan, and spent some of the first money she earned to buy soda crackers and canned milk to "cure" General Peng Teh-huai's ulcers.

Agnes got her portable phonograph up from Shanghai, with a few favorite records like "She'll Be Coming Round the Mountain" and "On Top of Old Smokey." She taught square dancing to Generals Chu Teh, Chou En-lai, Lo Ping-hui, Peng Teh-huai and others. At the end of the evening, Agnes would feel as if the whole army had walked over her feet. She was forty-four then, but had the energy and camaraderie which made dancing with these clumsy country boys more exciting than a sub-deb's night at the Copacabana.

Chu Teh took up dancing like basketball and worked at it furiously. (Chu is the kind of man who will try anything, is always curious, must be active.) Some women did not like these parties,

Left: Ma Hai-teh, an American named George Hatem, was born in Buffalo, New York, the son of Syrian immigrants. He is shown here with his Chinese wife, Chou Su-fei, on their wedding day in Yenan. Mme. Ma was then a young actress who had joined the Communists in the northwest. *Right:* Dr. Hans Muller, who left Nazi Germany and found his way to Yenan; George Hatem *(center)*; and Anna Wang, who married Wang Ping-nan in Germany and went to live with him in China in 1936.

but in time dancing became so popular in Yenan that once a week everyone went to the meeting hall—sometimes it was the former Catholic Church —for square dancing. And Chu Teh led all the rest.

In June of 1936, when I met Dr. Ma Hai-teh in Sian, he began a journey which entirely altered his life. *Ma* means "horse"; why Dr. Hatem was y-clept Horse in Shanghai I do not know, but his nickname is Shag, and something about his thick black hair and dark warm eyes did remind one of a Mongol pony. A healthy, uncomplicated bachelor of twenty-six, he wanted to find some purpose to his work as a doctor. Hitler had also sent him up to Sian—as, in a way, he had sent me. The world was no longer a pretty place for young people who understood where Hitlerism was leading it, and in the East the Japanese, going in the same direction, threatened to take Chiang Kai-shek (who at that time had German and Italian fascist advisers) with them. Since Hitler and Japan hated Communism so much, Shag thought there must be some good in it. In Shanghai a young Red engineer named Liu Ting "awakened" him with accounts of egalitarian life in the forbidden Communist areas. Doctors were desperately needed there. He determined to go to see whether people there really were trying to do something as worthwhile as the engineer had made it sound.

"I don't give a damn for a doctor who lives high by pampering the neurotic rich," he said. "The medical profession is a failure if we can't give all children of even the humblest parentage an equal start in life—the same food and proper care that

only the wealthy can afford now. If that's what these people up there are aiming at, I'm with them. Anyway, I want to see for myself."

His arrival doubled the Western-trained medical force. The only qualified doctor in the whole army then was Fu Jen-chang, a product of a Methodist missionary hospital in Kiangsi. Shag was a much overworked man until the outbreak of the Japanese war, when the Yenan Hospital was set up with the help of funds raised abroad by Mme. Sun Yat-sen.

James Bertram *(right)*, a New Zealand war correspondent, standing beside General Hsiao Ke, a youthful-looking Eighth Route Army commander who was a veteran of the Long March.

Chou En-lai and the American correspondent Anna Louise Strong in Yenan, 1947. It was to Miss Strong that Mao Tse-tung addressed his words: "All reactionaries are paper tigers. In appearance, the reactionaries are terrifying, but in reality they are not so powerful. From a long-term point of view, it is not the reactionaries but the people who are really powerful."

such time as she could return to her native land without losing her passport.

Evans Carlson was the first foreign military observer (by several years) to confirm the paradoxical fact that as fast as the Japanese advanced, the Reds were expanding the physical area of their influence by carrying on a war of attrition far inside the enemy's perimeter of occupation.

Carlson met Chu Teh and all his commanders and walked and rode hundreds of miles with them. He accompanied them on many small battles and saw them organize the peasants and train and arm them with captured guns. After three months he was so full of what he had seen that he came out feeling that he had to wake up America with it. His superiors refused, and Carlson, a man of strong convictions, temporarily resigned his commission in order to write and speak freely.

Evans Carlson was no Communist. He was one of those people whom Dostoyevsky's policeman called "far more dreadful"—a Christian who believed in God and also believed in socialism.

The Communists didn't weaken Carlson's faith in American principles but he was greatly impressed with their army's training and indoctrination methods, its spirit of self-sacrifice and the high standards of personal morality and competence of its officers. Other American military observers in China ridiculed Carlson for his enthusiasm. It particularly irritated them that he thought *we* had anything to learn from *any* Chinese. But he had one intensely interested listener on high. He was sending confidential personal reports to the White House, for the President's very interested eye, alone. Three years later Roosevelt would back Carlson's plan to set up that unique organi-

Perhaps the best known of all American residents of China was Anna Louise Strong, minister's daughter, author and journalist. She once edited the *Moscow News* with Mikhail Borodin, who in 1923–27 was principal Soviet adviser to the Kuomintang. On a revisit to Moscow in 1949, during the last years of Stalin, Miss Strong was suddenly denounced as an "American spy" and expelled from Russia. Soon after Khrushchev's speech which posthumously demolished Stalin, a special Kremlin declaration was issued to withdraw the condemnation of Miss Strong and to "rehabilitate" her. Shortly afterward she left California for Peking and there settled down comfortably, at least until

First row, from left: Anna Wang, Evans Carlson, Yeh Chien-ying, unknown. *Top, from left:* Tung Pi-wu, unknown, Li Ke-nung. In Wuhan, 1938.

zation known as the Marine Raiders. In it he incorporated a spartan physical training regimen and
egalitarian code of brotherhood between officers
and men based on his experiences with the Eighth
Route Army.

Assigned to organize and train battalions of
picked American youths for special tactical tasks,
he incorporated many ideas avowedly borrowed
from the Chinese guerrillas. Marine Raiders led
by this son of a Connecticut clergyman carried the
Chinese cry "Gung ho!" ("Work together") back
across the Pacific.

Revolutionary Theater

I filed out, after the performance of *Huang Ho*,
beside Mao Tse-tung.

"How did you like it?" he asked.

"Excellent. It's the best chorus I've heard in
China since Yenching sang the *Messiah*."

"Yes, it is a big change since our theater in
Paoan."

This building, originally a Catholic church and then the Red Congress Hall, became Yenan's Lu Hsun Academy of Fine
Arts. Here, a delegation of Northwest Youth National Salvation members are shown meeting in April 1937. Hu Yao-pang
(*fourth from left*) was one of the Communists' most important youth leaders. With this Academy, Yenan was as much a
mecca for radicals in art as in politics.

Above: Lenin por-
trayed by a Chinese
actor in a Lu Hsun
Academy produc-
tion.

Right: A make-up
man standing beside
the Chinese actor
he turned into Stalin
for the Russian play
Men With Guns.

Left: Members of the Yenan Chorus of the Lu Hsun Academy.

Below: The Academy's production of the famous *White Haired Girl.*

Yenan's Cultural club (*above*), and the Communists' first film studio workers.

Education

Thousands of youths walked hundreds of miles across enemy-held territory to reach Yenan and study in its institutions.

There was a different approach to all problems, and markedly so in education. The little town was now one of the nation's largest educational centers. Despite its wretched material conditions and almost daily visits from enemy bombers, it offered a wide variety of training and new cultural influences. At the end of 1939 mass education was ahead of any district in Free China.

Hsu Teh-li, the former president of a normal school in Changsha, and famous as the man who became a Communist when he was fifty, laid the foundations for the new educational system. I called him "Old Hsu" because that was what everyone in the soviet districts called him—Lao Hsu, the Educator. Like his sexagenarian crony, Hsieh Chu-tsai (and you could often see this pair of white-haired bandits walking along arm in arm) he had bright merry eyes and a pair of muscular legs that had carried him across the greatest rivers and mountain ranges of China on the Long March. Mao Tse-tung was one of his students in normal school (Hsu said he was terrible in math) and so were many youths who later became Reds.

Fellow artists in Yenan: Ting Ling, prominent in the Communist's literary world, stands between Hu Man, a painter (*right*), and Emi Siao, a poet.

Ting Ling became China's best-known revolutionary woman writer. She studied at Peking University and Shanghai University, began to publish short stories in 1927, and married another noted writer, Hu Yeh-ping. Both were arrested by Kuomintang authorities in 1933. Hu was executed but Ting Ling was released in 1936, and went to Yenan the same year and added her talent to the Red Theater.

Left: Hsu Teh-li. *Right:* Hsieh Chu-tsai, scholar and poet.

Children in Yenan's kindergarten (*above*) were already beginning "military training." *Below:* Grade school children in a gunless rifle drill.

An utter newcomer in Yenan's institutions of learning was the Women's University, a veritable College of Amazons. Most of the women had come by dangerous guerrilla trails, from hundreds of miles behind the Japanese lines. Here was a real hunger for education.

It was nothing less than an earthquake in the lives of north Shensi people to have a school of any kind for women. Before the Reds entered this area they were still hired out as "labor," like donkeys and mares, while the males stayed home and collected their wages.

Outdoor class at the Women's University.

Mrs. Wang Ming was a teacher in the university.

Girl sentry on guard before the Women's University.

The Eighth Route Army fighting against the Japanese on the Great Wall.

14

GUERRILLA CHINA

Great areas of what was nominally occupied territory in North China were not actually controlled either by the Wang Ching-wei government (based in Japanese-occupied Nanking) or by the Japanese troops which maintained it in power. Chinese guerrilla bands fought the enemy in virtually every village in the North China hinterland. These anti-Japanese units ranged far and wide and limited Japan's real control chiefly to the railways, roads and zones around big cities and towns. The guerrillas set up political administrations which exercised all the functions of government, behind the Japanese lines. Under a more or less unified command they had armies totaling perhaps 300,000 men and women, variously trained and armed. Most of the troops either were directly under Chinese Communist commanders or were very friendly to them.

There are regions where war has brought only death and disease and retrogression, and over great areas all the old evils flourish as before.

Still, in other places, often far back in remote villages where you might least expect it, the war set loose an epidemic of ideas and changes which nothing else than revolutionary struggle could have achieved.

One of the most striking achievements of the Border Region was the intimate connection established between the people and the fighting forces. The idea that the civilian owes anything to his armed defenders, and especially to any "useless fellow" who crawls back from the front with an arm or leg missing, is quite recent except among the Reds, who early recognized the importance of enforcing respect and honor for the revolutionary fighter.

The People's War

Right: Women and children check passes in the North-east.

Below: A Red Army truck going down from Yenan to Sian in 1938—accompanied by a baby (*right*) whose traditional split pants serve as an obvious aid to his soldier "nurse."

Above: People's militia remove rails to cut off a Japanese supply line.

Left: A peasant couple contribute their time to defense. Anything that could be used—tin cans, bottles, teapots—was turned into land mines.

Far left: Early on, Mao Tse-tung said, "Women hold up half the sky."

Above left: Children boil water for wounded soldiers.

Left: Emerging from an underground bunker, a soldier receives a welcome meal.

Guerrilla Doctor

A remarkably ingenious Canadian chest specialist, Dr. Norman Bethune, organized front-line guerrilla medical services for the Eighth Route Army. He did the work of twenty men until he died of septicemia for lack of penicillin. Renowned as a surgeon with the anti-Franco forces, Bethune had offered his services to China after Spain was submerged by Hitler and Mussolini. His name is a legend revered and memorialized throughout China. There were years when amputations and other operations on wounded men were performed without anesthesia, as in American Civil War days. After 1940, Chiang Kai-shek's forces had restored a blockade around the guerrilla base in Shensi, and their denial of simple medicines cost the Eighth Route Army thousands of unnecessary deaths, like that of Bethune.

Far left: Dr. Norman Bethune, the Canadian "barefoot doctor."

Left: Bethune at the front.

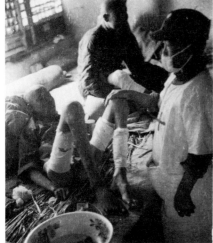

Above: Tending wounded in a mobile hospital.

Left: Bethune operating on the field, aided by the donkey-packed "operating hospital" he had created earlier in service during the Spanish Civil War.

Right: Red soldiers and ancestral guards—an ancient temple is used as a hospital.

Pioneer Reforms

By the terms of the Kuomintang-Communist "reconciliation" of September 1937, the Reds introduced what was called "the new democracy," a united-front system which spread wherever they went behind Japanese lines. This was hateful to the Generalissimo, but it did have a legal basis; years earlier the Kuomintang regime had promulgated a law which provided for establishment of local self-government where and when any provincial governor decided that the people were "ready." No government had ever found the people "ready," however. According to a rule Communists imposed on themselves, their party members in the village, county and provincial councils were not to exceed one third of the total representation. Kuomintang members were also allowed to participate, but as the Communists were the best organized, they easily dominated.

Suffrage was made universal and equal, regardless of sex or class. Many landlords who had fled during the civil war now returned to their homes, where they received new land as tillers; and these men were accorded equal suffrage, including the right to hold office. Merchants and small capitalists were also permitted to take equal part in political life. Even small feet (women with bound feet) and old ladies felt that they must take part and hobbled over long distances to cast their vote.

These "new democratic" regimes won widespread approval even in Kuomintang China, where many liberal intellectuals had long advocated the same program. Rents were reduced, gentry domination was curtailed or ended, usury was abolished, idle land was put under group production, youth and women were brought into politics, unemployed persons were organized, self-defense corps made up of peasant volunteers, and mass education produced new leaders among the non-landlord classes. Corruption was kept to a minimum by collective control and stern punishment, ostracism and disgrace. This experimentation in gradualism was to last nearly a decade. It was to facilitate the relatively swift and smooth transition by which the Communists would later lead the country, stage by stage, from "coalition government" to the state socialism of today.

The Reds were never "agrarian reformers" who believed in land redistribution as an end in itself. They simply saw that only by preliminary "land reform" could they get the peasants to join in a fighting alliance and later win their support for the main program. Remaining the party of the proletariat in theory and doctrine, the Communist intellectuals became in practice the party of the poorer two thirds of the peasantry whom the Kuomintang, wedded to its landlord supporters, could not claim to represent.

Left: Village voting in northwest Shensi. *Right:* Women deputies in a border region.

Here, land is measured for distribution to the peasant "have-nots." Kungchantang, the Chinese word for "Communist Party," literally translates into "Share-Property-Party."

A peasant woman stands on her bound feet in public accusation against a landlord.

Rice fields where there were none before—Nanniwan, 1943.

Nanniwan

Deep in Shensi province lies the narrow valley of Nanniwan, about ninety kilometers southeast of Yenan. In 1941, when the Yenan base areas were blockaded on the south and west by Nationalist troops and westward and northward by the Japanese, Nanniwan was a pilot project begun in response to Mao's call for self-sufficiency and "ample food and clothing" to be produced by the army's own efforts.

"Any soldier or civilian who likes to eat but does not like to work cannot be considered a good soldier or a good citizen," said Mao. "It is simply wrong to demand grain and money from the masses, as the Kuomintang does, without making every effort to help them to increase production."

To lead the way, the army's 359th Brigade, officered mainly by young veterans of the Long March, broke open the wilderness glen of Nanniwan, each soldier armed with rifle, spade and enough seed grain to last one season. Like American pioneers, they cleared enough land to plant a crop; they built caves and lean-tos to survive the severe winter, recruited some landless peasants to help them, made wooden hoes and plows, learned to write on birchbark, brought in a first harvest, replanted, cropped enough to sell a surplus for a few farm animals, built wooden spinning machines, made their own woolen cloth, and fought engage-ments to keep open a smuggling trade with Nationalist territory. After two winters of near-starvation, Nanniwan became a self-sufficient forest community.

Indusco 1938

Among non-party patriots of all descriptions a real faith persisted that a progressive government representative of varied opinion and worthy of the people's spirit of devotion and self-sacrifice would emerge during the war. Out of such faith grew the most original and hopeful experiment of the "united front" period—the Chinese Industrial Cooperative organization [Gung Ho, or the Work-Together Movement: Indusco]. It provided work and an education for tens of thousands of Chinese and proved indeed to be the forerunner of what ultimately became the largest producers' cooperative movement in the world.

I vividly remember the setting in which the idea was born. The war had passed from Shanghai on up the Yangtze River Valley. Behind it lay the ruins of a nation's industry. Except for the tiny oasis of the International Settlement, everything for miles seemed a desert of rubble, charred timbers and twisted iron, beneath which many bodies still lay. Over 70 percent of China's prewar indus-

The triangular Indusco sign appeared far and wide; some mobile cooperative units functioned far behind the Japanese lines in North China. Here two customers bow to each other in front of a cooperative savings bank displaying the Indusco symbol.

---

try was concentrated in a little triangle bounded by the cities of Shanghai, Wusih and Hangchow. By early January 1938, all that plant had fallen to the Japanese, for whom the immobilization of China's industry and labor was a main objective of "total aggression."

Indusco set up several hundred small factories, workshops, power plants, transports and mines. We

had our own training schools, war veterans and war orphans vocational centers, printing and publishing houses, lunch rooms, clinics, nursery schools and character-study schools for illiterate worker-members and their children. Indusco became a reasonably sound prototype of a democratic, cooperative society, producing a wide variety of goods of war value. Some mobile cooperative units functioned far behind the Japanese lines in North China.

Indusco—as the movement was known abroad was primarily the invention of Rewi Alley, Nym Wales and myself. It could never have got off the ground without the initial sponsorship of a strange pair of enthusiasts—Soong Ching-ling and the British ambassador in China, Sir Archibald Clark-Kerr, later to be Lord Inverchapel.

He personally presented the Indusco scheme to Generalissimo and Mme. Chiang Kai-shek and H. H. Kung. They agreed to try it out. He also secured the release of Rewi Alley by the Shanghai Municipal Council, and Chiang appointed him to carry out the plan. Alley knew written and spoken Chinese, and had wide technical knowledge as well as broad experience in China. He was appointed chief technical adviser and quickly gathered together a field staff of able and honest young men. He set up an organization based on modified cooperative principles that provided for low-interest loans and private credits to finance the first coop units, with workers entitled to buy over their shares and take full control as soon as they became technically trained to do so.

Archibald Clark-Kerr, whom Snow described as "a maverick among British diplomats. The first principle of most career diplomats is actively to avoid action; Clark-Kerr succeeded by breaking tradition at least once a day."

Indusco Activities

Rewi Alley with war-orphaned students at his Sandan School in 1939.

I first met Rewi far up in Inner Mongolia in the arid June of 1929. Employed at the time as a factory inspector by the Shanghai International Settlement, he had chosen to spend his annual vacation in the famine region with a handful of foreigners who ran a few soup kitchens and were offering food and shelter to those still capable of working on the irrigation canal near Kueisui. He was a strangely out-of-place figure in that dark sickly crowd, his sunburned face covered with dust beneath a fiery bush of upstanding hair. When he stood with those giant's legs spread apart in a characteristic attitude, he seemed somehow rooted to earth.

That summer Alley adopted his first Chinese orphan, a boy he picked up among the human debris of the famine and took to Shanghai to be educated. Two years later Alley was loaned by the Shanghai Municipal Council to help rebuild the Yangtze dikes after the great flood. Again he came out with a famine orphan. In Municipal Council circles, where few white sahibs would dream of sitting down with a "coolie" at their table, the Family Alley soon became a kind of legend.

Alley was, of course, only the "prime mover" that had started the wheels. He and the unique backing he had were necessary guarantees to Chinese members that the organization would have a chance to develop along true cooperative lines free from the traditional incubuses of bureaucracy, nepotism and graft. Thus reassured, some of China's ablest engineers and technical men had given up highly paid jobs and volunteered for the new industrial army, with an enthusiasm that amazed cynical onlookers.

Virtually free of graft and nepotism, the organization was for a time relatively immune from bureaucratic control. That very circumstance, a historical accident, was soon to mark Indusco as a target for destruction by the most reactionary elements in the regime it might have helped to save.

Ironically, it was the Communists themselves who would see the usefulness of the cooperative method of organizing the people, for their own ends, in a great transitional stage of the consolidation of their revolutionary power.

By 1942 the Yenan depot came to be much the largest regional headquarters in the country, with as many workers as all the others in China combined.

Mao Tse-tung attending an exhibition of agricultural and industrial products, in the Shensi-Kansu-Ninghsia border area.

Chungking street scene, 1940s.

(15)

KUOMINTANG CHINA 1939-1946

If China today had no Kuomintang there would be no China. If the Kuomintang fails it means the failure of the whole Chinese nation. To put it briefly: the destiny of China depends solely on the Kuomintang.
—Chiang Kai-shek

Under Chiang Kai-shek's government some attempt was made to establish rule by constitution and law, some roads were built, modern banks were established, some flood-control work progressed, scientific study was somewhat encouraged, educational facilities improved, and women began to claim legal equality with men. Modernization along such lines was certainly more rapid than under previous regimes; had there been no Japanese invasion, Chiang might have succeeded in unifying the country under right-wing dictatorship. But the whole pace of change was far too slow to cope with the deep crisis inside Chinese society. Increasingly Chiang resorted to despotism to hold back the tidal demand for revolutionary measures.

Beyond the Japanese-controlled area and beyond the guerrilla state, there was the state ruled by the Generalissimo and his party, which had its headquarters at Chungking, Szechuan. Its provinces reached all the way from Sinkiang down to the outskirts of Canton.

Chungking was, when I first arrived in the summer of 1939, a place of moist heat, dirt and wide confusion, into which, between air raids, the imported central government (Kuomintang) made an effort to introduce some technique of order and construction. Acres of buildings had been destroyed in the barbaric raids of May and June. The Japanese preferred moonlit nights for their calls, when from their base in Hankow they could follow the silver banner of the Yangtze up to its confluence with the Kialing, which identified the capital in a way no blackout could obscure.

Above: An officer aboard the American gunboat *Tutuila* in the Yangtze River photographed the bombing of Chungking.
Below: Chungking slums.

The city had no defending air force and only a few anti-aircraft guns. There seemed no likelihood of a cessation of American supplies of war materials to Japan.

Spacious public shelters were being dug, but it was estimated that a third of the population still had no protection. Government officials, given advance warning, sped outside the city in their motor cars—cabinet ministers first, then vice-ministers, then minor bureaucrats. The populace soon caught on; when they saw a string of official cars racing to the west, they dropped everything and ran. A mad scramble of rickshas, carts, animals and humanity blew up the main streets like a great wind, carrying all before it.

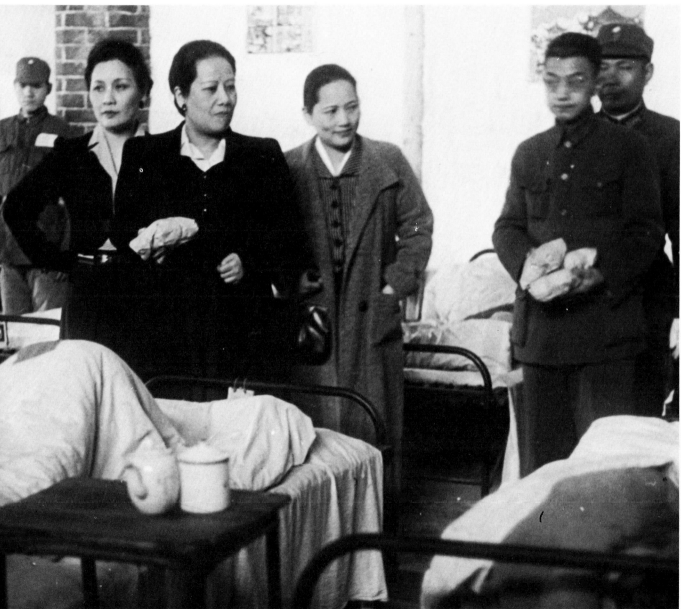

The three Soong sisters visit a military hospital in Chungking in 1939, during the United Front between the Communists and Kuomintang. *Left to right:* Mei-ling (Mme. Chiang Kai-shek); Ai-ling (Mme. H. H. Kung); Ching-ling (Mme. Sun Yat-sen).

The immediate result of the European war was to cut off Chungking's most important source of munitions: Germany. Despite their pact with anti-Comintern Japan, the Nazis supplied China with over 60 percent of her munitions imports as late as July 1939—no more ironic than the fact that Japan still got more than half her imported war materials from China's traditional best friend, Uncle Sam.

Most of the Russian munitions went into China either through Burma or Indochina until in June 1940 Japan compelled the French to close the railway into Yunnan. When the British complied with Japanese demands, and closed the Burma highway, China was left with but one free route of supply—the desert road from Russian Turkestan.

Chengtu, August 20, 1939

In the still uninvaded provinces of China, the Kuomintang selected and appointed all officials. Chiang Kai-shek was the "leader" of that party. He was also the party-elected chief of state. Nobody in China except a minority of the 2,000,000 members of the Kuomintang party ever cast a vote to keep Chiang Kai-shek in power. In this picture neither the Communist party nor any other political party had any *de jure* existence. It is still a fact that the Kuomintang government had never officially rescinded its anti-Communist laws, which made membership in the Communist party an offense punishable by death. Under such a regime no political opposition can exist, except with the support of armed forces.

It was easier to fly from Chungking to Chengtu, the "Peking of West China," than to get a ride by road, but I wanted to see the countryside and some of the industrial cooperatives.

Fourteen passengers in rear of Dodge 2½-ton truck, luggage piled high. Driver with dysentery. Arrived at river too late to cross; had to spend night in a filthy town, lodged in a pigsty-like inn, in a room with three beds and mosquito-cloth canopies. Mine was so covered with blood it looked like a matador's cloth. The town itself was equally miserable. No decent food, only cold stuff exposed to innumerable flies. (The w.c. was a railing outside our room in the inn and emptied into the back courtyard.) While we ate, a horde of small boys, all in rags, stood about and watched us. Apparently orphans, they swarm like flies up and down all village streets, a few selling dirty grapes or peanuts, most of them frankly beggars. The road is lined with them. Thousands of them. Many are diseased with syphilis, beri-beri and other ailments. They say they are the children of opium derelicts. From these lost children the Reds collected hundreds of followers whom they have made into soldiers and men. Szechuan is rich, but the poverty of the people is all the passer-by can see.

Derelicts of war— the orphan children of China.

Doctors and nurses of the New Fourth Army's medical staff in southern Anhwei province.

Betrayal of the United Front

In 1941 some Kuomintang troops engaged the rear echelon of the New Fourth while it was moving to an area entirely behind the Japanese lines to which it was assigned by the Generalissimo. The partisans were reportedly outnumbered eight to one. The little detachment of about 4,000 was not a combat unit and it was easily encircled and annihilated. General Yeh Ting was taken prisoner and General Hsiang Ying was killed, together with many of his staff, some doctors and nurses of the medical battalions, convalescent wounded soldiers, cadets, men and women students, and some industrial cooperative workers attached to the army.

The incident failed to liquidate the New Fourth Army, but it drove a deep wedge between the Communist and Nationalist parties. Observers considered that the refusal of the Communists to retaliate at that time, combined with the sharply unfavorable reaction in foreign capitals, prevented a major recrudescence of civil war which would have greatly simplified Japan's political problem in China. The Generalissimo ruled that the incident was caused by the New Fourth's "insubordination" and henceforth withdrew all aid not only from that army but also from the Eighth Route. From this time on they not only received no pay nor ammunition but were blockaded by a ring of strong government forces from access to supplies in Free China.

Subsequently Chiang Kai-shek stopped paying all the Communist partisans, and imposed a blockade against their bases in North China. Since then Kuomintang-Communist clashes behind the Japanese lines were continuous, at times amounting to major civil war.

Chen Yi

Born in Szechuan in 1901, he went to France (1919–21), where he combined labor (barge loading, washing dishes, and work at the Michelin and Creusot plants) with study at the Institut Polytechnique in Grenoble. In Peking, in 1923, he joined the KMT and the CCP. He worked at Whampoa Academy as political instructor under Chou En-lai. He took part in the Nanchang Uprising, and in early 1928 he accompanied Chu Teh to Chingkangshan. During the Long March, Chen stayed behind with Hsiang Ying to command a Red rear guard in Kiangsi, and from 1934 until 1937 fought bitter battles for survival.

Chen Yi was named acting commander of the New Fourth Army by Mao Tse-tung. Liu Shao-chi soon joined him as political commissar. By 1945 the New Fourth had carved an immense territory from the Japanese conquest and built up the largest Red force in Central China.

Chen Yi (*right*), shown here in 1939 with Yeh Ting outside New Fourth Army headquarters, was one of the top Communist commanders throughout the entire Chinese revolution.

Left: Yeh Chien-ying became a principal Communist military liaison person in Kuomintang territory. *Right:* This photograph, taken at Chungking's airfield in 1940, shows three prominent members of the Communist liaison mission.
From left: A Kuomintang officer who met them; Po Ku, who was propaganda director of the Eighth Route Army's liaison office in Chungking; Teng Ying-chao; and Lin Po-chu, with his hands on Yeh Ting's daughter (killed in 1946, along with her parents, Po Ku and Teng Fa in a plane crash).

American journalists Hugh Deane, Graham Peck and Jack Belden (*top row, left to right*) join (*bottom row, left to right*) Chen Chia-kang (assistant to Chou En-lai), Li Kung-po, Mao Tun (a well-known playwright), Anna Wang, Israel Epstein and Chang Han-fu, at Chungking's foreign press hostel.

Left: Chou En-lai (*center*) at a press conference, Red Crag Village. Red Crag served as headquarters for the Communist delegation stationed in Chungking and was also their office for the Eighth Route Army, and the South China Bureau of the Party Central Committee—which operated clandestinely. *Right:* Chou En-lai stands beside a sign of support from the International Fur and Leather Workers Union, sent from the United States to Yenan.

Chou En-lai.

Few Chinese made a more favorable impression on American officials during the war than Chou En-lai.

Chou knew the idiom of democracy as well as he knew his dialectics. Unlike some of his comrades, he had never been mistreated by foreigners. He could be friends with them as individuals; his "anti-imperialism" was a matter of "historical necessity." Diplomats were often charmed by this attractive, youthful-looking radical who could speak of Paris, London and Berlin. Soldiers were impressed by the force and simplicity of his analysis and judgment.

An interesting consciousness of immensely increased strength was evident in all recent declarations by Chinese Communist leaders. Typical of this new firmness was the speech made by Chou En-lai after his return to Yenan from Chungking late in 1943:

"Has the Chinese Communist Party lost its backing? It is true that during its birth and development the party received help from the Comintern.

But the backbone of the party is not the Comintern but the Chinese people. Our party is a party of the masses. We are firmly supporting national unity. We are still prepared to talk with the Kuomintang, to discuss how to avoid the danger of civil war. However, such negotiations must be sincere, equals meeting equals, mutually making concessions. We hope also to cooperate with all other anti-Japanese parties on a democratic basis in order to wage the war firmly and push on toward progress."

During World War II, Chou was responsible for securing and transporting supplies for Yenan. He directed propaganda among Chinese at home and abroad, organized secret party cells among military groups, and routed volunteers to the guerrilla frontiers in the North. The one open and legal Communist paper in Kuomintang China took its orders from him. He was in touch with Russian and other foreign diplomats and he had valuable contacts inside the Generalissimo's headquarters. He was Mao's main source of "outside" intelligence. The extent of the party nuclei set up by Chou En-lai throughout Kuomintang China became apparent only when, as civil war spread after 1947, ready-made local teams arose to help "liberate" one town and city after another. In the Communists' postwar decision to make a bid for all-out power Chou is believed to have had a decisive influence. Through his intelligence network, he concluded that Chiang Kai-shek could not conquer the Red forces. And he knew by 1946 that the United States would not give the Generalissimo the huge American combat force needed to keep him afloat.

Teng Ying-chao, representative in Chungking for the women's organization in the northwest, with Chou En-lai, chief representative for the Communists to the Nationalist government.

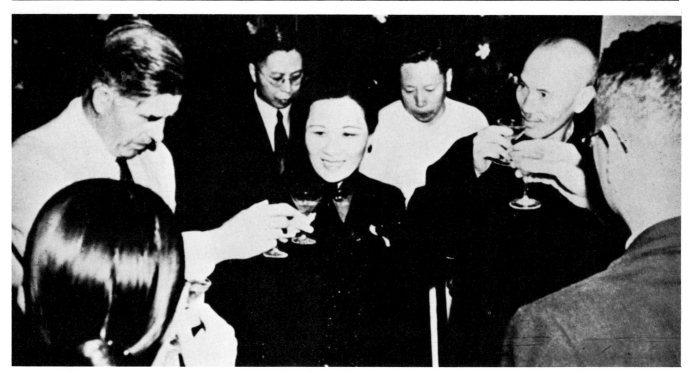

Vice President Henry Wallace, shown with the Chiang Kai-sheks in Chungking, 1944, was sent by President Roosevelt to persuade the Generalissimo to open up negotiations with Yenan.

Courting the U.S.

After Pearl Harbor there was never any possibility that the Chungking government would make a collaborationist peace with Japan. It was our turn; the ruling Kuomintang party understood that we had inherited the major task of defeating Japan. Earlier tendencies toward some modification in the one-party structure of the Kuomintang dictatorship came to a halt. What was the need for "representative popular government"? Was not America going to send Chungking all the airplanes, tanks and guns necessary to build a great army? What internal opposition could then challenge Kuomintang rule? With the half-billion-dollar American loan given unqualifiedly to Chungking, plus promises of Lend-Lease aid on an unlimited scale, efforts to develop China's own resources as a means of waging war against Japan began to wane. Kuomintang bankers spent their time drawing up grandiose schemes for post-war industrialization of the eastern provinces, with the help of American capital. Some dreamed of seizing Japan's lost markets with cheap goods to be produced by American machinery and coolie-level Chinese labor.

There was good reason to suppose that Kuomintang chieftains aimed at 1) the rebuilding and modernization of Kuomintang armies, and the creation of an air force, with American help; 2) the recovery of power in the rich Yangtze Valley and Shanghai and in Canton, behind a vanguard of American air, naval and ground forces; 3) an expedition to recover North China ports, also behind American spearheads. Finally, into Manchuria the same way.

All this the Kuomintang leaders hoped to accomplish without any serious political changes and without any agreement with, or support for, the Communist-led guerrilla forces. Those who might resist would be blockaded and gradually exterminated as "bandits." Chungking counted upon the support of American forces—right up to Manchuria and the Soviet border. Indeed, there were expressions of genuine astonishment by Kuomintang officials upon learning that Americans would like to see the two parties get together.

What the Communists were demanding was simply the withdrawal of Chiang Kai-shek's military blockade, the payment and supply of their troops with Lend-Lease materials on a basis of equality with the Kuomintang armies, modification of the one-party dictatorship, and the setting up of a government in which they, as well as other parties, could be represented. They wanted a minor but a legal position, which would enable them to par-

A toast at Chungking's Eighth Route Army office between U.S. Army officers and Chinese Communist representatives (*far right, clockwise*): Wang Ping-nan, Chiao Kuan-hua, Chou En-lai, Chen Chia-kang and Mme. Kung Peng.

ticipate in councils and in general mobilization for an intensified war effort. The Kuomintang realized that if the legality of the party were once recognized on a constitutional basis, giving it equal privileges with the Kuomintang, it would never be possible to suppress the Communists. The Kuomintang feared that they would win any mass election.

When I came back to China again from Russia in the middle of 1943 I found that the country's economy had become chaotic, its political life more reactionary than at any time since 1936, and its military efficiency was at the lowest level since the

war began. Hoarding of commodities and speculation in grain and land were the chief occupations of landlords, pawnbrokers, merchants and native banks. Many industrialists had lost interest in production; there was more money to be made in hoarding raw materials and waiting for price rises, which averaged better than 10 percent monthly. The cost of living had risen some 200 times above the prewar level. Planes that should have carried in guns or machines were filled with American-made banknotes flown in at the rate of billions of dollars monthly.

Communist leaders gathered at Yenan airfield include (*beginning fifth from left*): Lin Piao, Hsu Teh-li, Mao, Tung Pi-wu, Lo Jui-ching, Chu Teh and Chou En-lai. Yeh Chien-ying and Nieh Jung-chen are at far right.

Stilwell and Chennault

Stilwell had been impressed by the performance of the Chinese Reds against Chiang Kai-shek. "Those Reds may be bandits, as Chiang says they are," Joe burst out to me one day, "but bandits or not, they're masters of guerrilla warfare. I don't know what they're preaching but to me it looks like they've got the kind of leaders who win. I mean officers who *don't* say, 'Go on, boys!' but '*Come on,* boys!' If that's the case and they had enough of them, they could keep the Japs busy here till kingdom come."

Stilwell's orders were "to increase the combat effectiveness of the Chinese army." To do that he had to establish minimum controls over American aid in order to build a reliable, patriotic, well-fed and well-trained *national* army for China out of the coterie of feudal chieftains manipulated in a balance of weakness system by the Generalissimo.

That made Stilwell a "reformer" and that was why he could not be tolerated by the Dynasty, the generals-in-business, and greedy parasites from top to bottom.

He gave me a horrendous account of his troubles with "the Peanut," as he called Generalissimo Chiang, "so that you can tell the American people the truth, when the time comes, about how their money was thrown away in China."

By late 1943 another factor began to rob Japan of the security she had enjoyed on the China flank for five years. This was the rise to supremacy of American air power in the China skies, under Major General Claire Chennault.

Chennault knew China mainly as it looked from the air, not the ground. He really thought he could by-pass both the Japanese occupational forces and the Chinese Communists to decide matters by machines and air power. Had he possessed atom bombs this might have made sense, but the truth was that he never possessed nor had the possibility of disposing of anything more than tactical air

Above: Lieutenant General Joseph Stilwell ("Vinegar Joe"), Commander of American Forces in China, Burma and India, decorates Chiang Kai-shek with the Legion of Merit on behalf of President Roosevelt, August 3, 1943.

Right: Chiang Kai-shek greeted by U.S. Major General Claire Chennault at Kunming, 1945.

power which depended for its continued existence entirely on land bases which Japan could at any time eliminate by ground forces if necessary. Chennault had only contempt and impatience with Stilwell's aim of giving priority to the creation of effective ground forces capable of defending and advancing his air bases—and the wholesale reforms needed to accomplish that task. If Chennault had been a Greek naval commander during Cyrus' war against Athens, the equivalent of his behavior toward Stilwell would have been for him to persuade the Athenian League to withhold supplies and weapons from the Greeks preparing to defend Marathon in order to divert everything to a naval attempt to knock out the Persians' supply line over the Bosporus—*after* the Persian army had already taken possession of virtually the whole of Attica.

There never was anything like this winged transport line Americans built into China from India, which began as a Toonerville trolley of the air and ended up carrying more cargo than the Burma Road ever handled and more than the combined air freight delivered by all the airlines of the United States. The whole miracle was made possible, basically, by a wonderful cluster of airfields built in one of the wettest spots on earth by the hand labor of women and children. They made an unforgettable sight: long lines of barefoot, bangled women, with heavy silver and gold anklets and bracelets, and some with rings of gold in their noses, stretching as far as you could see, coming from rock piles in the distance. A brief pause in the stately walk, a nod of the head, and off rolled the single stone balanced on top of each head. Nearly all the airfields and military buildings we had in India grew up in the same way, rising literally from millions of nodding Indian heads. As a month-to-month proposition it was one of the worst spots an airman could be sunk in. Most of them eventually got dengue or malaria and dysentery, if no worse. The odds piled up with the number of trips a pilot made over the 17,000-foot passes that lead into Yunnan. We lost more planes in transport service here than in combat with the Japanese.

The Hump—the trans-Himalayan air route between East India and Yunnan province, China.

Kunming, Yunnan.

Flying Tigers

Many of the Flying Tigers were still there, having exchanged their fancy Chinese-looking uniforms for American khaki. But while the Tigers volunteered to fight for China—and for $600 a month plus $500 for each enemy plane downed—the new boys who came in made no more than pencil pushers in Washington, and they were in China because it was then an American battlefield and the President wanted them there. They got no bonuses for plunking enemy planes and they had no special personal reasons for being in the place. Many of them just knew that yesterday you were home where you could drink good beer, smoke plausible cigarettes and date a blonde, while today you have got a map, a plane and an order to fly the Himalayas for the Chinese, and not a blonde or a good smoke in the whole country.

Besides carrying military freight, the ferry command saved the lives of hundreds of wounded soldiers and civilians rescued from Upper Burma during the Japanese advance.

The Stars and Stripes in China.

The Flying Tigers, a group of American volunteer pilots who, in 1937, began working under Chiang Kai-shek's air adviser, Claire Chennault. They were incorporated into the U.S. Army's 14th Air Force, after the Japanese bombed Pearl Harbor in December 1941.

Kunming street scene, 1940s.

Far from wishing to discourage Japanese visitors, Chennault tried to make it easy for them to come in. Over in Africa I noticed that airdromes often would not answer routine calls from our planes for weather and direction signals, the explanation being that the enemy might ride in on the beam and bomb the airport. In Yunnan no effort was made to hide the radio frequency, and during an air fight animated conversations were often held between the combatants. Listening in at his operations base, Chennault could follow a whole engagement.

Foreign Service Officers in China

The China career service had been made possible by the Foreign Service Act of 1924. That far-seeing piece of legislation was intended to free the foreign service from partisan politics along lines of the British career service. Candidates were selected by tough competitive examinations, and on the basis of merit, aptitude and general competence alone.

After 1941 our China-language officers were to prove beyond any doubt their superiority over political appointees who sometimes could not even pronounce the names of the high officials to whose government they were accredited.

As the best of them had to become conspicuous for their judgment in matters affecting the war years and the revolution, in contradiction to views

Foreign Service officer John Service (*third from right*) resided in Yenan in 1944 and 1945 as a member of Stilwell's staff and subsequently as political adviser to General Albert C. Wedemeyer (who replaced Stilwell in the autumn of 1944). Shown here (*right to left*) are: Yang Shang-kun, director of the general office of the Central Committee; Chen Yi; U.S. Captain Whittlesey; Chu Teh; Wu Yu-chang; and Nieh Jung-chen. They were known as the "fellow provincials" because all had been born in Szechuan province.

held by certain congressmen at home who lived in dense ignorance about China, the corps was destined to ultimate dissolution. Within two decades they would be rewarded for their hard work by slanderous attacks from McCarthy and the China Lobby until not a Chinese-speaking officer from the senior career service was left in the chambers where vital United States policies and decisions on Asia were made.

Sino-American Cooperative Organization

In 1941, the United States and Chiang Kai-shek signed a secret agreement to set up the Sino-American Cooperation Organization (SACO), under which the United States helped train and dispatch secret agents for the Kuomintang government. The chief of SACO was Tai Li, head of the Kuomintang military secret service; its deputy chief was a commodore in the U.S. Navy named M. E. Miles. —L.W.S.

Chiang Kai-shek's government never accorded the Communist party a legal position. It recognized only the army. Civilian Communists, like members of all other non-Kuomintang parties, remained subject to the old repressive laws which, though not widely enforced, were never rescinded. Today [1941] hundreds of political prisoners are held in the Kuomintang areas, and Communists allege that many have recently been murdered or executed.

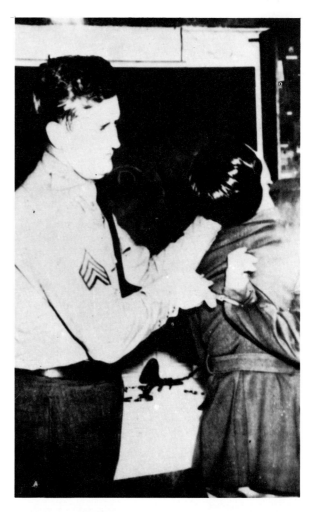

Site of Chungking's political prison. It was here that Yeh Ting was imprisoned for five years following the New Fourth Army Incident of 1941.

U.S. military personnel supervised classes and trained Kuomintang secret agents used against the Communist forces.

The "Dixie Mission"

Mao Tse-tung, at Yenan airfield, greets Colonel David Barrett (*right*), head of the U.S. Military Observations Group chosen to evaluate the Communist position in terms of American aid and collaboration against the Japanese. Called the "Dixie Mission" (for the "rebel" side), it consisted of nine members representing the U.S. air corps, medical corps, signal corps and infantry. *Left:* Chu Teh and John Service.

Kang Ke-ching with Colonel Barrett.

Early in the war Japan seized over 90 percent of China's modern industry. But for six years thereafter the government continued to have at its disposal greater natural wealth than Japan proper, and unlimited labor power. It failed to combine these assets to replace lost production and it never devised a rational scheme of distribution. The Kuomintang imposed no adequate controls over capital, raw materials, commodities or food, the market became dominated by hoarding and speculative influences and the highest officials and their offspring were numbered among the foremost profiteers. The government increasingly resorted to the printing press for a solution rather than to production.

The result was vicious uncontrolled inflation and vastly increased burdens passed on to the principal producers in the country—the debt-carrying peasants who till the land but as a rule do not own it. Widespread famine often resulted not from genuine overall shortages but from speculative hoarding. By 1944 probably as many people had died of famine in Free China as in India. Even the army was gravely undernourished; nutritional diseases accounted for about 70 percent of the incapacitated, and wounded for only 30 percent.

I thought of Agnes Smedley's letter, telling how twenty Red soldiers, fighting in Shensi, had their hands frozen black, so that they had to be amputated. Fighting for what? For sleek-haired scum like these, whose dance tickets for a night would buy them gloves, if they thought about it, which they don't. It was like this, too, when Nanking soldiers were dying like squashed bugs outside the Settlement. They went on dancing and whoring and spending and having a fine opinion of themselves. Their elders continued to gorge on big feasts.

Chungking furnished these warriors no blankets, no winter uniforms, no shoes or socks, no doctors, nurses or medicines. In the bitter subzero weather many attacks were carried out by men who tramped barefoot across the frozen hills and streams leaving crimson stains behind them on the icy paths; wounded youths shivered in thin blood-clotted jackets of cotton cloth; hundreds lost toes, fingers and ears from frostbite.

The Kuomintang used this photograph as propaganda accusing the Communists of causing widespread starvation.

Anti-Kuomintang cartoon, with Chiang Kai-shek
(*middle, bottom*) in the never-ending circle of
war profiteers.

Japanese propaganda shows corrupt Kuomintang
capitalists enjoying life while the Chinese people
starve and slave.

The Recall of Stilwell

There was pretty general agreement that in 1944 the United States gave up its real chance to influence the political fate of China in an enlightened way. That was when General Joseph Stilwell was withdrawn as head of the American military, after he had made a Homeric struggle for imperative reforms. Thenceforth our vast unconditional aid enabled Generalissimo Chiang Kai-shek to reestablish his internal monopoly of military power sufficiently to prevent the drastic changes which alone could have stopped a violent social revolution.

General Stilwell's recall was, of course, closely connected with the central question of war and politics in China. Stilwell knew China too well. He knew the language and he knew the psychology of the warlords he was dealing with; he knew the weaknesses, as well as the potential strength, of the Chinese armies. Stilwell had for some time regarded the Communist forces with respect; he had wanted to use some of their partisan leaders and troops in Burma and Thailand, but the Generalissimo had stubbornly refused. Then General Chu Teh wrote a formal letter in which he offered to place his entire command under the American, and appealed for Lend-Lease aid against Japan. On orders from Washington, Stilwell went to the Generalissimo and asked permission to use Eighth Route and New Fourth troops in the offensive plans, and to equip them with Lend-Lease goods under American command.

Chiang flew into a rage and sent a message to President Roosevelt asking for Stilwell's recall. Stilwell came home and General Patrick Hurley became the new ambassador [November 17, 1944] and introduced a policy of appeasement of Chungking.

"The basic trouble with Chiang," said Joe, "is just his plain dumb ignorance. One of the worst disservices done to the American people is the overselling of Chiang Kai-shek. We've made a hero out of him and he believes all the crap he's read in our press about him and thinks he hasn't got anything to learn. Actually he has little power—far less than people at home suppose. He couldn't get his generals to obey him if he ordered one; they don't want to move. They're making money now—hoarding food for speculation, selling our supplies on the black market, lending money; by God, they're not soldiers, they're speculators . . . each general has settled down on his own little dunghill and doesn't want to disturb the peace."

The Generalissimo had had his way, but at the expense of bringing to the President's close scrutiny the most noisome details of inner corruption, demoralization and incompetence of Chiang's military, economic and political household.

"After all, you saved the Kuomintang," a Chinese intellectual in Chungking said to me. "It's your baby now and you cannot avoid responsibility for its actions."

In the spring of 1945, Hurley had come to the conclusion that the Chinese Communists were being supported by Russia. He went to the Kremlin and asked Stalin what he would "settle for" in China. Stalin replied in time-worn phrases that "the Soviet government is determined not to interfere in the

U.S. economic and military mission to Chungking, September 28, 1944. *Left to right:* T. V. Soong, Foreign Minister of Kuomintang China; U.S. War Production Board Chairman Donald Nelson; Chiang Kai-shek; U.S. Major General Patrick J. Hurley; Clarence E. Gauss, U.S. Ambassador to China; and General Ho Ying-chin, Chief of Staff of China's National Military Council. Ambassador Gauss resigned his post after President Roosevelt ordered Stilwell's recall that October.

internal affairs of China," but said that he would like to see the Communists enter a coalition government with the Nationalists under Chiang Kai-shek, whom he recognized to be head of the legal Chinese government. Hurley apparently interpreted Stalin's remarks as an "undertaking" that Moscow would repudiate the Communists if they did not come to terms with the Kuomintang, and he wired the White House that he and Uncle Joe were in complete agreement. Our Moscow embassy understood Stalin's language, however. Men present at the interview told me they had, after reading Hurley's extravagant claims, hastily informed the State Department that he was under serious misapprehensions.

In a private conversation with me, President Roosevelt showed considerable impatience with Chungking's attitude in the negotiations which had been dragging on for months, in an effort to solve the internal deadlock. He said that he had had hopes, for a while, that Hurley might be able to bring the two parties together; that a formula had been sent up to Yenan and that the Communists had made some amendments to it. "Now everything seems to have fallen down," he said. "The Kuomintang has raised some perfectly absurd objections to the amendments of the Yenan government." He also told me that he was anxious to see organization of guerrilla forces in North China, to aid our

landings there. "I've been working with two governments there and I intend to go on doing so until we can get them together."

Roosevelt died the next month. Soon afterward all talk of a North China landing or any serious military collaboration with Yenan abruptly ended, as all our support was thrown behind Chiang Kai-shek and the big gamble on the survival of one-man rule. Nevertheless, back in Chungking, General Hurley continued to assure [Vice President] Truman that he had the Chinese Communists in his pocket—till political explosions after V-J Day demonstrated they were anywhere else but.

Chu Teh and Patrick Hurley in Yenan, 1944.

Japanese Surrender, Moscow Betrayal

The Sino-Soviet Treaty of 1945, concluded between Chiang's regime and the Kremlin, clearly demonstrated the latter's skepticism concerning the postwar future of the Celestial Marxists. That treaty completely deprived Yenan of Soviet diplomatic support at the very moment when the former had obviously intended to intensify an open struggle for power.

Once German defeat became manifest, it had been the nightmare of Chiang Kai-shek that the Russians would attack Japan, without any understanding with him. He feared that they would then promptly install the Chinese Communists in power, in the wake of their own advance in Manchuria. The Kremlin chose, instead, to sign a treaty of alliance with Chiang, which promised to aid his troops exclusively, and to recognize his authority, and his alone, in a Manchuria where neither he nor the United States then had any forces. It was considered good diplomacy by both Chinese Nationalists and American official observers. It was believed that the treaty had definitely disposed of the Chinese Reds, "once and for all."

Japanese troops give themselves up.

There is no evidence to indicate that the Kremlin thought otherwise or was interested in more than Russian national aims in Manchuria. It offered no other advance interpretation to Chinese Communist headquarters, then still at Yenan, where the treaty came as a complete surprise.

Yenan's political line had clearly reflected quite other expectations. Several days after the treaty was signed but before it was published—Japan had already surrendered—the Chinese Communists issued a proclamation to their forces which demanded: 1) immediate seizure of Nanking, and establishment of a "people's government" there, and 2) seizure of the cities of North China and Manchuria, and disarming of Kuomintang troops in repudiation of the Generalissimo's authority. Yenan heaped scorn upon Chiang Kai-shek as a "fascist," a "traitor," and an enemy of the people no better than Japan's puppets at Nanking.

It was nearly a week after V-J Day before the treaty [with Moscow] was made public. Finally convinced that the text was authentic, the Yenanites realized that both Stalin and the United States were committed to support the Kuomintang regime. They had no alternative but to compromise, in the first round of the postwar struggle.

Within a month Mao Tse-tung was in Chungking for negotiation—at the instigation of American Ambassador Patrick Hurley—with Chiang Kai-shek.

The discussions lasted some forty-two days and resulted in the "October 10th Agreements," which Mao described as "words on paper."

Besides underestimating Mao's chances of victory, Stalin had reason, before the end of World War II, to be skeptical of his ability to fit Mao into his pattern of revolutionary power. The alliance he signed with Chiang Kai-shek in 1945, the day after Russia attacked Japan in Manchuria, plainly advanced Russian national interests. By terms of the treaty Chiang in effect abandoned China's claims to Outer Mongolia by agreeing to a Soviet-sponsored plebiscite. He agreed to restore Russia's former rights in Manchurian railways and enterprises which Stalin, to avoid a conflict, had earlier sold to Japan. The treaty even restored Russian control over the old Czarist Port Arthur naval base on the Pacific. (The Yalta Pact—1945

Mao Tse-tung on plane from Yenan to Chungking, August 28, 1945, for Nationalist-Communist negotiations.

General George C. Marshall, U.S. mediator at Chungking, with Wang Ping-nan (*middle*), top assistant to Chou En-lai. "Wang Ping-nan was born in Sanyuan, Shensi. His father was a blood brother of General Yang Hu-cheng (who sided with Chang Hsueh-liang in the Sian Incident). Yang sent Wang Ping-nan to Germany to prepare him as his secretary. When he returned to China in 1936, he was underground liaison between the Chinese Communist Party, Chang Hsueh-liang, and Yang Hu-cheng." He was of important help to Snow on his trip to Shensi at that time.

—had left Chiang Kai-shek small choice in most of these matters.) In sponsoring this treaty the United States recognized a Soviet sphere of influence in Manchuria and tacitly drew a line at the Great Wall beyond which American nationalism might not intervene.

It is probable that in 1945 Stalin believed—as did most observers on the spot—both that Chiang Kai-shek's well-equipped 2,500,000-man army would quickly disperse the poorly armed and heavily outnumbered Communist troops, and that if necessary the United States would massively intervene to save Chiang from destruction. Stalin's advice to the Communists to dissolve their armies and collaborate as a minority in Chiang's government was probably based on those beliefs. Even in Manchuria, according to General George Marshall, who headed America's mediation mission in China, "In the opinion of all my advisers and intelligence, they [the Russians] were not supporting them [the Chinese Communist forces]." The swift and total disintegration of Chiang's armies following initial disasters in Manchuria, and the emergence of the Chinese Communists as victors over all China in 1949, made any regional Soviet hegemony in the north an impossibility.

Meanwhile, the American Air Force flew Chiang's troops into the key cities of the north to take over from the defeated Japanese. In accordance with the treaty, our Air Force and our Navy also ferried thousands of Kuomintang troops into Manchuria. The Soviet Russian command gradually handed over the principal cities and railways to Chinese Nationalists.

But the Chinese Reds were already too formidable a power to be liquidated by any mere scrap of paper signed in Moscow. Over 1,000,000 members had a vested interest in the party. Nearly 1,000,000 troops which surrounded the big walled cities depended upon it for survival. They all saw golden opportunities slipping away as Chiang Kai-shek rapidly replaced the Japanese and the Russians. So they, too, began a rush for Manchuria, on foot.

While the Generalissimo took over the railways and cities, the Communists sent in some of their best troops and cadres to infiltrate the towns and villages, reinforcing local guerrillas. All this competition went on in the field, from the Yellow River to Manchuria, while at Chungking both sides negotiated questions of constitutional government and military reorganization, with General Marshall acting as mediator.

Communist troops read an appeal to General Marshall.

When Stalin recognized and agreed to support only Chiang's government in Manchuria, he probably foresaw events differently from the way they occurred. Sound strategy required that the Generalissimo return to power in eastern China after first smashing the Chinese Reds south of the Great Wall or driving them into Manchuria. Against the advice of the commanding American officer in the China war theater, Lieutenant General Albert C. Wedemeyer, Chiang foolishly attempted to take control of Manchuria before consolidating his rear, and while the Reds were still thoroughly saturating North China. Events then developed in reverse order. Manchuria became the independent base from which the Chinese Reds swept southward.

Sent to Manchuria in 1945, Lin Piao became commander in chief of Red forces there. To him, in 1946, Mao Tse-tung addressed his now celebrated "general concepts" of military operations for renewed KMT-CP civil war. Lin held command of the main Communist forces in Manchuria. Within a year he entrapped the core of Chiang Kai-shek's American-armed and American-trained armies, capturing or killing a total of thirty-six generals. Following victory in Manchuria, Lin encircled Chiang's main forces in northern China.

Kuomintang representative Chang Chun with General Marshall and Chou En-lai (*center*) signing the cease-fire agreement in Chungking, January 10, 1946. "Chou led the Communist Party's delegation in peace negotiations with the Kuomintang, until all-out civil war was resumed in 1946. Back in Yenan, he worked side by side with Mao in the supreme command."

Dinner with Chairman Mao, January 9, 1965

The Chairman recalled that when I had first visited him, in Paoan, they had just begun preparing for war against Japan. The Japanese had been of great help. They created conditions which made it possible for Communist-led guerrillas to increase their troops and expand their territory. Today when Japanese came to see Mao, and apologized, he thanked them for their help. Later on, the United States government also helped by siding with Chiang during the civil war. During the liberation war they had relied mainly on United States weapons turned over to them by the troops of Chiang Kai-shek. The Generalissimo had always been their teacher. In truth, it was Chiang and the Japanese warlords who directly taught them how to fight, while the United States had been their indirect teacher.

Snow and Mao, Peking, 1960.

Mao Tse-tung in Yenan, winter of 1946.

THE SECOND CIVIL WAR 1946-1949

By July 1946, heavy fighting had spread to most of the country. Meanwhile, formal attempts to achieve a truce and create a coalition government preoccupied American policy makers in China until 1947. By then the two Chinese armies were locked irrevocably in a final struggle for power which engulfed the whole country.

"Mao Tse-tung gave us a picture of Chiang Kai-shek's strategy, and his own [said George Hatem]. We had already lost Kalgan and were evacuating most of the cities and railways we held. The Nationalists were bombing the hell out of us in their American planes. After Mao finished listing all the places we were giving up, things looked pretty grim to me.

" 'We're winning!' Mao said. 'If Chiang goes on making mistakes like this, he will be finished in three to five years.' "

Years ago the "four principles" of guerrilla warfare which the Red Army evolved from its early struggles were elaborated by Mao Tse-tung in the following set of paradoxes:

"Defense, in order to attack; retreat, in order to advance; flanking, in order to take a frontal position; curving, in order to go straight. These are inevitable phenomena in the process of development of any event or material matter."

Such was the general strategy which Mao used to defeat Chiang Kai-shek's forces when they launched a major attack against Yenan in March 1947. Under Hu Tsung-nan and other top commanders, picked Nationalist troops numbering 230,000 invaded the Red bases in northern Shensi, Kansu and Ninghsia. Most of the Red troops were east of

the Yellow River, scattered across the North China plain to Manchuria, where Chiang had already suffered heavy reverses. Yenan had only 30,000 regular troops at its disposal and did not call for reinforcements from the east.

One month before the Nationalists attacked, the Politburo and Central Committee decided to withdraw from Yenan if the enemy advanced in force, but to "defend and expand" the Northwest base as a whole; to keep army general headquarters in the hills close to the Yenan region; and to follow tactics of "wear and tear," "wearing down" and "completely exhausting" the enemy.

The enemy arrived well armed but found a dearth of food, animals and able-bodied men in the towns. If he went foraging in the countryside and spread out, he was ambushed and quickly wiped out. If he pursued in force, the Reds broke contact, countermarched and bit off his tail. Four times the Nationalists circled the province chasing the Reds; each time they dropped a few more brigades isolated and outnumbered in sudden, surprise attacks. By the end of the year [1947] the Nationalists were completely defeated and withdrawing in great confusion. Yenan then began sending directives for general offensives on a nationwide scale.

Far left: 53,000 U.S. Marines occupied Peking, Tientsin and the vital port of Tsingtao after VJ day. Some are shown here in Tientsin, working with the Kuomintang army.

Left: Demonstration in Peking, December 1946, against the rape of a Chinese girl by a U.S. soldier.

Far left: December 18, 1946, Yenan. Celebration of Field Commander Chu Teh's sixtieth birthday.

Middle: Mao An-ying, Mao's first son by Yang Kai-hui, is shown here with his father in 1946. Born in 1920, he was arrested in Changsha along with his mother in 1930. After her execution he was taken into hiding with his brother, Mao An-ching. During World War II he studied in the Soviet Union. Mao An-ying was killed in battle in Korea in 1950.

Left: Mao leaving Yenan, 1947.

Left: Chou En-lai on horseback (*left*), north Shensi, 1947.

Right: Captured Kuomintang troops in Shantung, January 1947. The Chinese characters on the gate read: "Put into effect the Three Principles and quickly establish a new China and unite the country. Put down internal rebellion. Support the People's Nationalist government."

Below left: People join the Liberation Army in northeast China.

Below middle: A schoolboy in Honan knits his own sweater as the war goes on.

Below right: In Peking, students march against starvation, civil war and persecution.

Above: Rocks and boulders serve as militia ammunition.

Left: Guerrilla fighters wait in a field.

Below: Kuomintang prisoners of war guarded by militia.

Above: Payday in Shanghai, 1948.

Right: By April 1949, one U.S. dollar was worth 9.5 million Chinese yuan in bank vouchers. The official rate of 4 million "gold" yuan to one old Chinese silver dollar went as high as 9 million to one on the open market.

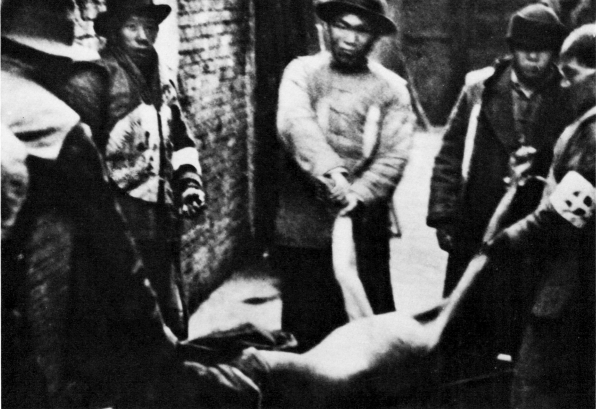

As battles pushed on, people scrambled for grain spilled on the street (*top*). In Shanghai, ninety-nine bodies were picked up from the city's streets on January 25, 1948, the day this photo was taken.

In 1947, Mao Tse-tung sent Lin Piao his famous "general concepts" of the campaign to destroy the Nationalists. Adhering to their basic principle—striking at the human forces and ignoring urban defense concentrations—Lin took over the countryside. He isolated Chiang's city-based armies and pinched off their flanking units one by one. Within a few months the Nationalists were devoured, as Mao put it, "mouthful by mouthful"—or, general by general; Lin eliminated thirty-six of Chiang's best division commanders. He then moved into North China to repeat the meal.

Lin Piao.

Top left: Liberation of Yenan, April 22, 1948.

Bottom left: A unit from the Northwest Field Army joins the people in celebration as the Communists recovered their almost destroyed capital.

In Jack Belden's *China Shakes the World* the story of "Gold Flower" is as stark and poignant as an Erskine Caldwell tale—but with what a different resolution! Cowed and hopeless, Gold Flower had been full of suppressed resentments against a loafer husband who alternately whipped and used her,

against a mother-in-law and father-in-law who literally treated her as a slave. In her own words she tells how she revolted after the "turning-over" movement (the revolution) reached her village. Of all the exciting changes none had such astonishing reality for her as the Women's Association, set up

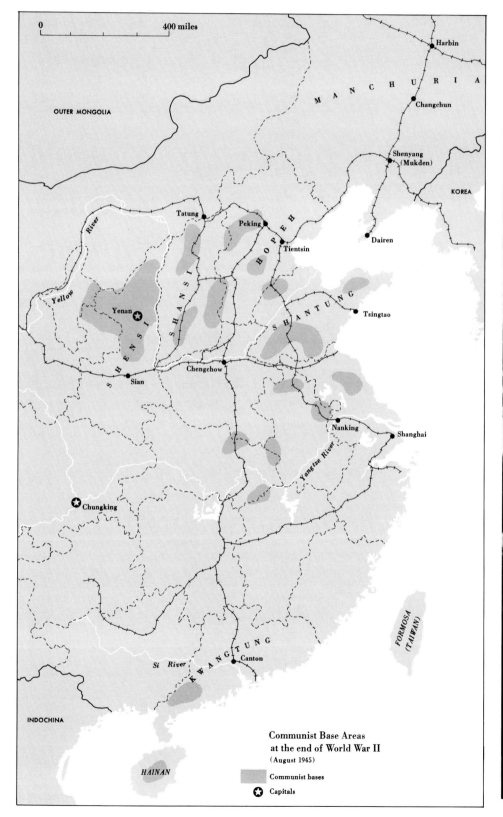

Communist Base Areas
at the end of World War II
(August 1945)

[grey] Communist bases

⊛ Capitals

to teach, produce and to defend woman's rights as an equal of man. We see this association gain meaning in Gold Flower's life until at last her female allies drag her husband before a village court, accuse him and end by beating him to a pulp. Disgraced and ostracized, he flees from the village, to leave Gold Flower in peace, ready to take a mate of her own choosing. Such stories, scattered through the book, make clear the little-known but enormously important role of women in China's civil war and the many ways in which they shaped its result.

Women in central Hopei province dig tunnels behind enemy lines.

The Final Battles 1948-1949

"Throughout the civil war Liu Shao-chi was the Politburo chief among all the Communist forces in eastern and northeastern China."

"Following Japan's surrender and the death of Yeh Ting, in 1946, Chen Yi became full commander of the New Fourth Army—renamed the East China People's Liberation Army." *Above:* Commander Chen Yi (*center*) sits astride a captured tank in East China.

Captured Kuomintang officers and soldiers after the Tsinan battle in Shantung, northeast China, September 1948.

The 38th Nationalist Division fighting in Manchuria.

Communist prisoners are guarded by Kuomintang during the Manchurian campaign.

Kuomintang troops at drill, Mukden, 1947. The city fell to the Communists on November 1, 1948.

In June 1948 Chen Yi's army captured Kaifeng, capital of Honan province. Soon afterward Chen Yi assumed a new "general front command" which included Liu Po-cheng, Su Yu, Tan Chen-lin, and as chief political commissar, Teng Hsiao-ping. In the Huai-Hai campaign, in November 1948, Chen defeated the main forces of Chiang Kai-shek so decisively that the Kuomintang lost East Central China. As the Third Field Army, Chen Yi's troops pushed on to Nanking, Shanghai and the provinces of Fukien and Chekiang, south of the Yangtze River.

Communist troops cross a river during the Huai-Hai campaign, which lasted sixty-five days (November 6, 1948, to January 10, 1949), cost the Nationalists over 555,000 troops, and paved the way for the Communist capture of Nanking.

Kuomintang prisoners leave the battlefield during the Huai-Hai Campaign.

Left to right: Su Yu, Teng Hsiao-ping, Liu Po-cheng, Chen Yi and Tan Chen-lin, leaders of the Huai-Hai Campaign.

Top photo shows a defense line of American trucks set up by the Nationalists during the Huai-Hai battles, and below, an open-air field hospital, both captured by the People's Liberation Army.

Chiang Wei-kuo (*in turret, left*) a son of Generalissimo Chiang, rides in an American tank during the Civil War.

Nationalist troops, captured during Huai-Hai battles.

"We won't kill you if you put down your arms."

During the war Mao was supreme commander in chief and sometimes made critical decisions alone. In September 1948, when it became apparent that national power was within grasp, the Central Committee passed a resolution, under Mao's chairmanship, which declared:

> The Party-committee system is an important Party institution for ensuring *collective leadership and preventing exclusive control by any individual.* It has recently been found that the practice of exclusive control . . . by individuals prevails in some leading bodies. . . . This state of affairs must be changed. Hereafter . . . all important matters must be submitted to the committee and fully discussed by the members present.

Six months later another Central Committee meeting, "at the suggestion of Comrade Mao Tse-tung," made the decision prohibiting birthday celebrations for party leaders and the use of party leaders' names to designate places, streets and enterprises.

Mao Tse-tung in conference with Chou En-lai, at Hsipaipo, where they and the Party Central Committee commanded battles during the last campaigns of the civil war.

The fall of Tientsin,
January 15, 1949.

Far left: Mao Tse-
tung reviewing
tank units of the
People's Liberation
Army in Hsiyuan,
on the outskirts of
Peking, March
1949.

Left: Chiang Kai-
shek resigned as
President, in Nan-
king, on January
21, 1949. Kuomin-
tang Vice President
Li Tsung-jen took
over the office to
negotiate with the
Communists,
March–April 1949.

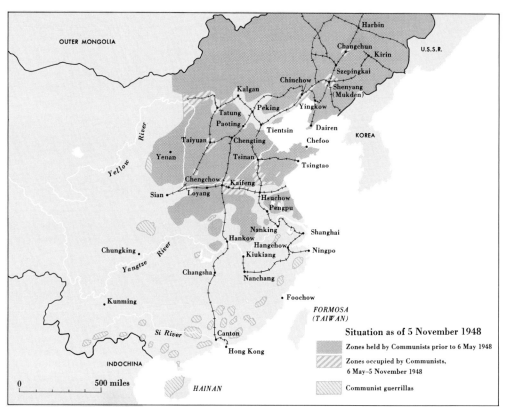

Situation as of 5 November 1948

OUTER MONGOLIA

U.S.S.R.

Harbin

Changchun

Kirin

Szepingkai

Chinchow

Shenyang (Mukden)

KOREA

Kalgan

Peking

Yingkow

Dairen

Tatung

Paoting

Tientsin

Chefoo

Taiyuan

Chengting

Yenan

Tsinan

Tsingtao

Chengchow

Kaifeng

Sian

Loyang

Hsuchow

Pengpu

Nanking

Shanghai

Hankow

Hangchow

Kiukiang

Ningpo

Chungking

Nanchang

Changsha

Kunming

Foochow

FORMOSA (TAIWAN)

Canton

Hong Kong

INDOCHINA

HAINAN

Yellow River

Yangtze River

Si River

0   500 miles

Zones held by Communists prior to 6 May 1948

Zones occupied by Communists, 6 May–5 November 1948

Communist guerrillas

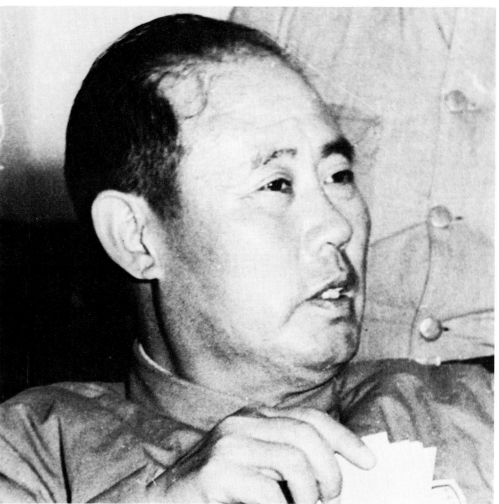

"Kuomintang General Fu Tso-yi, the commander of the Peking garrison, was the last old North China warlord to surrender. He held on to Peking for a month while he bargained for a peaceful turnover and good conditions for his men and himself. (Peking, like Paris, is always surrounded first, then peacefully surrenders.) He crossed over to the Communist side shortly after the city fell."

People's Liberation Army troops taking over from Kuomintang sentries after entering Peking on January 31, 1949.

Celebration as the Liberation Army enters the capital.

The Last Days of the Kuomintang

Above: Communist troops on top of Chiang Kai-shek's presidential palace in Nanking, April 23, 1949. The Communist troops walked into the city unopposed.

Right: "Chu-Mao," at Hsipaipo, Hopei, March 1949, before going to Peking.

Above: Hsu Hsiang-chien, the Red commander of Taiyuan, capital of Shansi province. *Left:* Nationalist officers under guard at Taiyuan.

Kuomintang planes, captured at the fall of Sian, the largest city in northwest China.

Right: "Teng Hsiao-ping served as chief of the General Front Committee, the supreme staff of all the People's Liberation Army on the Central Plains, and was also political commissar of Liu Po-cheng's army of victory in Sze-chuan." Liu Po-cheng (*right*) and Teng Hsiao-ping, just before one million Red troops crossed the Yangtze River in 1949.

Below: Crossing the Yangtze, April 1949.

Far left: "Chiang Ching-kuo, the Generalissimo's son, made the final days of the Kuomintang's rule in Shanghai memorable by the wholesale arrest, torture or murder of alleged 'traitors'—rich men, not Communists —to extract from them the last of the hidden gold, to carry off to the new democracy in Formosa."

Left: A woman weeps over the corpse of a relative. *Below:* Mob flees Shanghai.

Above: Demonstrations in Chungking.

Left: While Nationalist troops look on in the background, a Shanghai municipal policeman kills two political prisoners during street executions before the city fell to the Communists.

Below: Chiang Kai-shek prepares to fly out of Chungking, leaving his capital in flames. On May 3, 1949, it was reported that he had arrived in Formosa (Taiwan).

Taiwan province [Chinese territory seized by Japan in the war of 1895 and promised to China at the Cairo, 1943, and Potsdam, 1945, conferences] became Chiang Kai-shek's sanctuary [December 19, 1949] when he fled from the mainland in 1949. Truman put a naval blockade around Taiwan in 1950, thus intervening to prevent unification. In 1955 Eisenhower formalized the de facto American protectorate in an alliance with Chiang —while the United States recognized and financed Chiang's Nationalist government as the pretended sovereign over all China, keeping Chiang seated in the United Nations and the People's Republic out of it until 1971.

Right: Veteran mounted troops of Chen Yi entered Shanghai on May 25, 1949. By 10 A.M. they had taken over the city down to the Bund on the west bank of the Whampoa River and as far as Soochow Creek to the north.

Below: Tired Red troops declined the use of beds, saying they did not want to impose on the public and slept, instead, on the streets of Shanghai.

Above left: Kuomintang General Chang Chih-chung, who decided to stay on the mainland with the Communists, is shown with Mao Tse-tung and Chou En-lai at the Peking railway station after the city had changed hands.

Above right: A senior cadres meeting in Peking, July 1949, presided over by Peng Teh-huai.

Left: Mao Tse-tung was elected Chairman of the People's Republic of China at the First Plenary Session of the Chinese People's Political Consultative Conference, Peking, October 1, 1949.

Mao, Chou and Chu at the October 1st celebration 1949, on Tien An Men, "Heavenly Peace Gate," in the heart of Peking.

Victory

In 1949 the Communists summoned a meeting in Peking of the Chinese People's Political Consultative Conference—which had first been organized with Kuomintang permission, but with tireless promotion by Chou En-lai and other Communists. Attended by 662 delegates nominally representing all the anti–Chiang Kai-shek forces, classes, professions and nationality groups in China, and excluding only landlords and "bureaucratic capitalists" (those directly linked with the Kuomintang hierarchy), that conference adopted an Organic Law for its own existence, a preliminary Organic Law of the People's Republic, and a "Common Program." These three documents were the fruit of many earlier discussions between the Communists

and their own non-Communist supporters. They embodied Mao's concepts of a future constitution to provide for the state superstructure of a "democratic dictatorship." The term "The People's Republic of China" had been used in Mao's address to the preparatory committee of the "New People's Political Consultative Conference" in June 1949.

"China has stood up," Mao proclaimed on the birthday of the People's Republic in 1949. The People's Republic had eliminated foreign economic and political control, and was united under a single government for the first time since the collapse of the empire.

By 1949 history had proved Chou and Mao right in their strategy and—presumably—Stalin wrong. At the end of innumerable battles, countless hours of wrangling, cunning and deceit known as "negotiations," years of youth and middle age dedicated

on the map, could never understand. In the end it was the people living in the space who decided.

That alone explains the collapse of Chiang Kai-shek and a political organization seemingly at the peak of its might and prestige. It explains the futility of the elaborate waste of more than $5 billion in American arms and services put at Chiang's disposal. It explains the complete destruction of the best-equipped, best-financed military force that China had ever seen, by ragged hordes of men, women and children roused to fury and murderous desperation by a regime that symbolized corruption and oppression.

The revolt of the peasant against the authority of the landlord has become the most important political fact in Asia. How often must it be said that the victory of the Chinese Communists was before anything else the victory of farmers claiming title to the land they till?

Raising the first five-star flag of the People's Republic of China, October 1949.

to the insurgent quest for power—violence, devastation, millions of casualties—Chou had his reward. The foreign devils had been eliminated—with one notable exception, the "northern barbarians," the Russians. The Kuomintang was in full flight. As he stood beside Mao and Chu Teh, before the imperial palaces at Peking, a vast sea of faces turned to hail Chou En-lai as one of a triumvirate, the architects of a new dynasty—the People's Republic.

Not the Communist party, not the Kremlin and its Red Army, not a series of devices or narrow conspiracies manipulated by either one of them, created the new power now entrenched in Peking. The revolution made that power; a revolution that consisted of people and derived its energy from the will and struggle of the millions. That is something which the makers of American policy, who saw China as a hunk of territory, a strategic area

Edgar and Lois Snow with Mao Tse-tung on Tien
An Men, October 1, 1970.

*The truth is that if I have written anything useful
about China it has been merely because I listened
to what I thought I heard the Chinese people saying
about themselves. I wrote it down, as honestly and
as frankly as I could—considering my own belief
that it was all in the family—that I belonged to the
same family as the Chinese—the human family.*

Photographic Credits

COURTESY OF JOSEPH ABELES
COLLECTION

45, bottom; 218, right top & bottom;
219, top & bottom; 221, top

COURTESY OF REWI ALLEY

34, top right; 39, bottom; 44, bottom
left; 96–97; 203, left top & bottom;
204, top left & right, bottom left;
205, top, bottom left & right; 206;
217, bottom

COURTESY OF JAMES BERTRAM

73; 102, top; 144; 147, top; 148;
183, bottom; 211, bottom

THE BETTMANN ARCHIVE, INC.

45, top left

CHINA PHOTOS, PEKING

8, top; 9, top; 20; 22, bottom right;
23, bottom; 24, top; 25, bottom
right; 26, top; 27, top, bottom;
28, top, bottom; 30, top; 31, top,
middle right, bottom right; 32; 33;
36; 39, top; 44, bottom right; 46,
top; 48; 49, top; 52, right; 54, top
& bottom; 66, bottom; 68, left; 71,
left & right; 72, top; 75, top; 90,
bottom left; 95, top; 98, top; 135,
top; 136, bottom; 139, bottom; 156,
top left & right; 166, top & bottom;
170; 174, top left, bottom; 180;
184, top; 186, top & bottom; 187,
top & bottom; 188, top & bottom;
190, top; 192; 194, top; 196; 197,
bottom; 198, bottom; 199, top; 201,
top; 207; 214, top right, bottom left;
216; 234, bottom left; 234–235,
bottom; 236, top; 242, top &
bottom; 250, bottom; 253, bottom;
254, top; 255, bottom right; 258,
bottom; 260, top & bottom; 264,
bottom; 265, top left, bottom; 266,
right; 267, top left

China Pictorial Magazine, PEKING

181, right; 246, top

CHINA PUBLISHING COMPANY, PEKING

143

China Reconstructs Magazine,
PEKING

49, bottom

COURTESY OF CHOU SU-FEI

103, top right; 178, bottom left; 183,
top left; 198, top; 228

CHUNGKING PHOTO ARCHIVES

208; 210–211, top; 210, bottom; 215,
bottom; 222, top, bottom left &
right (all photos); 224; 225, top &
bottom; 261, top right; 263, top
right, bottom right

COURTESY OF FREDERIC DAHLMANN

16, bottom; 22, bottom left; 23, top
left & right; 29, top, middle left,
bottom; 157; 159, bottom; 160,
bottom

RIGHTS RESERVED BY SOPHIA DELZA

29, middle right

PRIVATFOTO DES AUTORS, DIETZ VERLAG,
BERLIN

89, top

COURTESY OF ISRAEL EPSTEIN

146

COURTESY OF HAO PO

116, bottom; 266, left

Hong Kong Evening Standard

xii

KEYSTONE, PARIS

13, top right, bottom right; 57, bottom

MERL LA VOY, LIBRARY OF CONGRESS
COLLECTION, WASHINGTON, D.C.

11

LIBRARY OF CONGRESS, WASHINGTON,
D.C.

10

COURTESY OF LIU CUI

100

COURTESY OF DR. KLAUS LOEFFLER

24, bottom; 34, top left; 46, bottom;
47

COURTESY OF DR. MA HAI-TEH
(GEORGE HATEM)

199, bottom left & right

COURTESY OF ANNA MARTENS

22, top right; 25, top right, bottom
left; 26, bottom; 27, middle; 30,
middle; 40–41; 183, top right; 184,
bottom right; 214, middle; 215,
top; 217, top; 229

MILITARY MUSEUM, PEKING

52, left; 55, top; 62; 70, top; 77, left;
80, bottom; 84; 138; 149, top;
173, bottom right; 178, top right;
179, top & bottom; 189, middle,
right; 190, bottom; 195, bottom;
201, bottom; 204, bottom right;
227; 235, bottom right; 236,

bottom; 237, top, bottom left; 238–239; 239, top right, bottom right; 243, top left; 244–245; 246, bottom; 247, bottom; 232; 250, top; 251, top & bottom; 252, bottom; 253, top; 254–255, bottom; 257, top & bottom; 259, top left, bottom; 265, top right

INGE MORATH

18; 50; 147, bottom

MUSEUM OF REVOLUTIONARY HISTORY, PEKING

7; 9, bottom; 31, bottom left; 34, bottom; 35, top left & right, bottom; 42, top & bottom; 44, top; 53, bottom; 58, top; 65, top; 67; 68, right; 70, bottom; 74, top & bottom; 77, right; 92–93; 135, bottom; 149, bottom left; 150, top; 154; 158, top; 159, top; 173, middle left; 174, top right; 195, top; 197, top; 200, left & right; 202; 213, bottom; 214, bottom right; 221, bottom; 231, top; 234, top left; 234–235, top; 237, bottom right; 243, bottom; 249; 255, top; 258, top; 264, top; 267, bottom right

NATIONAL ARCHIVES, WASHINGTON, D.C.

12; 13, top left, bottom left; 43; 60; 85; 181, left; 223, top & bottom; 226, top; 230; 240; 240–241; 247, bottom; 248, top & bottom; 252, top; 261, bottom

COURTESY OF AGNES SMEDLEY COLLECTION, PEKING

30, bottom; 169; 213, top

EDGAR SNOW

38, top & bottom; 41, right; 55, bottom; 102–103, bottom; 104, left & right; 105, top; 110; 111; 112, top, middle, bottom (all photos); 113; 114, top & bottom; 115; 117, top left & right; 118, top, bottom left & right (all photos); 119, top & bottom; 120, top & bottom; 121, top & bottom; 122, left & right; 123, top left & right, bottom left & right (all photos); 124, top, bottom left & right (all); 125, top left & right, bottom (all); 126, top; 127, top; 128, bottom left & right; 132, right; 133; 136, top; 137, top; 139, top left & right; 163, bottom; 175; 176, bottom; 212; 214, top left

EDGAR SNOW COLLECTION

2; 8, bottom; 14; 16, top; 17; 19, left & right; 45, top right; 50, inset; 53, top; 56; 57, top; 58, bottom; 59, top & bottom; 61; 65, bottom; *66, top; 69; 72, bottom; 75, bottom; *76; 79; *80, top and middle; *81, top & bottom; *82, top & bottom; *83, top & bottom; *86; *98, bottom; 99; 103, top left; 106; 108, bottom; 109; 116, top; 117, bottom; *126–127, bottom; 127, bottom right; 128, top, bottom right; 129; 130; 132, left; 134; 137, bottom left & right; 140, bottom & top; 141, left & right; 149, bottom right; 150, bottom left & right; 151; 152, top, middle, bottom (all); 153, top & bottom; 156, bottom; 158, bottom; 160, top left & right; 161, top left & right, bottom (all); 162, top & bottom; 163, top; 164, top & bottom; 165, top left & right, bottom (all); 167, top & bottom; 168; 172; 173, top, middle right, bottom left; 176, top; 178, bottom right; 182; 185; 189, top left; 191, top, bottom left & right (all); 194, bottom; 203, bottom right; 231; 259, top right; 268–269

* Reproduction by Edgar Snow from an old Chinese soviet photograph

LOIS SNOW COLLECTION

177, top left & right, bottom

UPI

94, bottom; 256; 261, top left; 262–263

COURTESY OF SUE WARREN

226, bottom

WIDE WORLD PHOTOS

78; 218, left; 220, bottom; 243, top right

Books by Edgar Snow

(Material for *Edgar Snow's China* has been taken from these editions)

Far Eastern Front. New York: Smith and Haas, 1933.
Living China. London: Harrap, 1938.
Red Star Over China. New York: Bantam Books, 1971.
The Battle for Asia. New York: Random House, 1941.
People on Our Side. New York: Random House, 1944.
The Pattern of Soviet Power. New York: Random House, 1945.
Stalin Must Have Peace. New York: Random House, 1947.
Random Notes on Red China (1936–1945). Cambridge, Mass.: Harvard U. Press, 1957.
Journey to the Beginning. New York: Random House; Vintage, 1972.
The Other Side of the River. New York: Random House, 1961.
Red China Today: Revised and updated edition of *The Other Side of the River.*
New York: Random House, 1970.
The Long Revolution. New York: Random House, 1971.

Source Notes

(Abbreviations used in references listed below)

AM	*American Mercury* magazine	N.Y. H T	New York *Herald Tribune*
ASIA	*Asia* magazine	OSOTR	*The Other Side of the River*
BFA	*The Battle for Asia*	POOS	*People on Our Side*
DIARY	Snow diary (unpublished)	POSP	*The Pattern of Soviet Power*
FEF	*Far Eastern Front*	RCT	*Red China Today*
JTTB	*Journey to the Beginning*	RNORC	*Random Notes on Red China*
K.C. J-P	Kansas City *Journal-Post*	RS	*Red Star Over China*
LC	*Living China*	RS, bio.	*Red Star Over China*, biography section
LR	*The Long Revolution*	SEP	*Saturday Evening Post*
NATION	*The Nation* magazine	SMHP	*Stalin Must Have Peace*

1 Background to Revolution

3–7 "To attempt to condense . . . republican government." OSOTR, 59–65

7 "When, in 1912 . . . 'Who is George Washington?'" FEF, 151

8 *Box:* "She was born in . . . in Chiang Kai-shek's government." RS, bio.

8 "Mme. Sun . . . to her by history." JTTB, 82

8 "'How, exactly' . . . coding and decoding." *Ibid.*, 88

8 "'Everything he planned . . . to unify our country.'" BFA, 122

8 "The China Ching-ling believed in . . . merited in the world." JTTB, 83–84

7, 9–10 "Sun Yat-sen lacked armed forces . . . as his successor." OSOTR, 67

10 "Chiang Kai-shek . . . a powerful ally in Soviet Russia." BFA, 120

10 "Nationalist troops . . . joined in the struggle." FEF, 158

10, 13 "In 1927 the Nationalist revolution . . . labor power." OSOTR, 68

13 "Chiang Kai-shek and his bureaucracy . . . not Christians." *Ibid.*, 59–69

12 *Box:* "Because the men . . . control of policies." FEF, 164

12 "Chiang had a wife . . . 'just the same.'" JTTB, 85

12 "It is not unfitting . . . consumed him. *Ibid.*, 137

12 "The 'palace clique' . . . income tax report." POOS, 282

12–13 "Usually either Dr. Kung . . . reformer." JTTB, 216

13 "Dr. Kung . . . on top." *Ibid.*, 217–18

2 Arrival in China

15 "When I first . . . *Chicago Tribune*." JTTB, 3

15–16 "'Why don't you' . . . in the modern world." *Ibid.*, 4

19 "Before my first task . . . town of Mencius." *Ibid.*, 4–5

19 "Finally Peking . . . oldest dust of life." *Ibid.*, 119

19 "I did a series . . . had begun." *Ibid.*, 4–5

3 Shanghai

21–22 "Shanghai seemed . . . deadly pollution." JTTB, 16–17

22 "In this river . . . in the world." FEF, 178

23 "There were . . . Greater Shanghai." BFA, 45

23 "The French Concession was run . . . register." JTTB, 21

23 "The Settlement was still . . . burden." *Ibid.*, 17

23 "In Shanghai . . . jurisdiction." FEF, 123

24 "At first I mistook Shanghai . . . wonder." JTTB, 16

25 "All the leg work . . . unlimited." *Ibid.*, 18

25 "In the Shanghai Settlement . . . planes." FEF, 176–77

26 "the beggars on every . . . plaintive cries." OSOTR, 504

28 "the hundred . . . alleyways." *Ibid.*, 503

32 "The cities of China . . . procurers." *Ibid.*, 46

32 "Shanghai has been accused . . . repletion." AM (Aug. 1930)

32 "North of Soochow Creek . . . daily." FEF, 177

32 "I remembered . . . they could not feed." RS, 260

32 "There is . . . country." DIARY, June 17, 1936

32 "There are thousands more . . . demand for bread." FEF, 177

32 "During the thirties . . . her stepson also." JTTB, 86

32 "Ching-ling was not easy . . . he had died a poor man." *Ibid.*, 83

33 "She embraced . . . Corinthians." *Ibid.*, 87

33 *Box:* "Already revered as a scholar . . . satire and humor." *Ibid.*, 131

33 "His message . . . intelligent order.'" LC, Intro., 25

33 "When I was living in Shanghai . . . running the country.'" JTTB, 132

34 "Opium is sold . . . deathly sick." AM (Aug. 1930)

34 "Tu Yueh-sheng . . . first names." FEF, 240

34 "It was Lin Yu-tang . . . its price." JTTB, 27

34–35 "I also learned . . . Nationalists." *Ibid.*, 26

35 "Chiang overthrew . . . execution." BFA, 79

35 "The counterrevolution . . . underground." OSOTR, 152

4 Rural China

37 "I believe . . . trouble." JTTB, 174

37–38 "Vast libraries exist . . . bankruptcy." OSOTR, 96–97

38–39 "At the end . . . seven million people." JTTB, 3

39 "Saratsi . . . China." K.C. J-P (Sept. 11, 1929)

39 "It was . . . would bring." JTTB, 9

39 "Last-ditchers . . . not noticing them." *Loc. cit.*

39 "For many blocks . . . were watery." K.C. J-P (Sept. 11, 1929)

39, 41 "But these were not . . . rainy days." RS, 217–18

42 "An agonizing death . . . dark embrace of death." N.Y. H T (Dec. 6, 1930)

42 "Paralysis . . . perhaps years." FEF, 4–5

44 *Box:* "The Kochin mines . . . upright." DIARY, 1929

44 "There are nearly . . . offspring." Letter to R. Walsh, ASIA

45 "Confucius taught . . . her own." BFA, 249

46 "In most districts . . . poor." N.Y. H T (Dec. 17, 1933)

46 "In places . . . poor peasants." Letter to brother Howard, May 5, 1934

47 "Tax collectors in advance." BFA, 136, 217

47 "Probably . . . American." N.Y. H T (Dec. 17, 1933)

47 "Children . . . day was done." DIARY II

47–48 " 'Why don't they revolt?' . . . *and arms.*" RS, 218

48–49 "Of all Mao's writing . . . 'vanguard.' " OSOTR, 150–51

49 "Mao's faith . . . working class." Also caption. *Ibid.*, 100

50 "Nothing . . . of China." FEF, 14

5 Manchuria

51 "For the Japanese generals . . . Asia." FEF, 310

51–52 " 'Blood and Iron' . . . indicated." *Ibid.*, 46–49

52 "Chang . . . authority." *Ibid.*, 65–66

52 "To comprehend . . . Manchuria." *Ibid.*, 55–56

52 "Following . . . Great Wall." *Ibid.*, 56–57

52 "The Old Marshal . . . Tokyo did not." *Ibid.*, 58–59

52–53 "It was uncertain . . . Nanking." *Ibid.*, 59

53 "On September 18 . . . wrongs." JTTB, 98

53–54 "The Mukden invasion . . . Shanghai." FEF, 171

54 "When General Honjo . . . advisers." *Ibid.*, 89–90

54–55 "When the invasion . . . China proper." RS, 18

54 *Box:* "I had an interesting trip . . . trenches." Letter to brother Howard, Dec. 7, 1931

55 "It was dark . . . beginning." JTTB, 95

55 "Outrage . . . interfere." FEF, 214–15

55 "There was the fresh corpse . . . sanctuary." JTTB, 97

57 " 'The Chinese' . . . Army." *Ibid.*, 100

57 "I had met . . . voluntarily." FEF, 222–25

103   "The names . . . against Japan." *Ibid.*, 142
103   "The students . . . pro-China." *Ibid.*, 146
103–4   "For most of them . . . to the government." *Ibid.*, 143
104   "It was . . . eight years." *Ibid.*, 143
104   "Caught unprepared . . . save China!' " *Ibid.*, 144
104   "Within . . . resist Japan." *Ibid.*, 144–45
104–5   "As a face-saver . . . purposes." BFA, 12–13
105   "The student rebellion . . . camp." JTTB, 145
105   "Among . . . last hope." *Ibid.*, 146

9   Red Star Over China

107–8   "Fighting . . . come out alive." RS, 2–7
108   "Then in June 1936 . . . parts of China." SEP (Nov. 6, 1937)
108   "I went to Shanghai . . . singular journey." JTTB, 152
108   "It is true . . . too high to pay." RS, 7
108   "Both the eastern . . . of China." Caption. *Ibid.*, 10
109   "One midnight . . . at Sianfu." *Ibid.*, 8–11
109   "A curtained car . . . I am living with him." *Ibid.*, 24
110   "We left Sian . . . in Central Asia." *Ibid.*, 26–28
110   "To state . . . Chinese manner." *Ibid.*, 30
111   "Chou En-lai . . . even white teeth." OSOTR, 105
111   " 'Hello . . . Chou En-lai.' " JTTB, 157
111   " 'I have a report . . . districts.' " RS, 44
111   "He told me . . . 'for Chiang Kai-shek.' " OSOTR, 105
111   "Chou ended . . . Mao Tse-tung." JTTB, 159
111   "Northern Shensi . . . an acre." OSOTR, 462
111–12   "It was . . . located." RS, 64
112   "A curious crowd . . . Paoan." OSOTR, 141
112   "It was the first time . . . those mountains." DIARY 12, p. 27
113   "I met Mao . . . strategist alive." RS, 64, 65, 68
113   "I was quartered . . . sour plums." OSOTR, 141
113   "There would never . . . great man." RS, 66
113   "I often wondered . . . concerned." *Ibid.*, 71
113–14   " 'Revolution' . . . materials about it." RS, 181, with part of fn. 2 on p. 470
114   "The truth is . . . fashion." JTTB, 176–77 "
114 *Box:*   "Mao's second wife . . . a daughter." RS, bio.
114   "Mao had met . . . mother hen." From "The Divorce of Mao Tse-tung." Unpublished story.
114   "The great mass . . . twenty-four." RS, 265–66
114, 116   "There is nothing grim . . . join the Reds in singing." DIARY 12, p. 14
115   "The Chinese Communist armies . . . any salary." Caption. Written on back of photo.
116   "The majority . . . the Reds." RS, 266
116   "I have seen . . . meanwhile." DIARY 17, p. 45
116   " 'What' . . . 'that's bitter!' " RNORC, 120
117   "The Reds . . . troops." RS, 269

118   " 'Sound Heart' . . . in China." Caption. Written on back of photo.
119   "These Red Army . . . 'bandit' in turn." Caption, bottom. Written on back of photo.
120   "They were youths . . . geography." RS, 342
120   "They wash . . . anew in China." DIARY 17, p. 43
120   "Their simple text books . . . 'By our Red Army.' " DIARY 12, p. 17
120–21   "I sat down . . . 'a thing like that!' " RS, 43
121   "The Reds saw to it . . . social life." *Ibid.*, 229
121   " 'Child slavery . . . some rent.' " DIARY 15, p. 17
121   "The myths . . . soviet law." RS, 230
122   "There was a Lenin Club . . . illiterates." *Ibid.*, 291–92
122   "There was a wall newspaper . . . productions." *Ibid.*, 293
124   "There was no more powerful weapon . . . peasantry." *Ibid.*, 101
125   "By what legerdemain . . . as navy." Caption. Written on back of photo.
125   "Latinized signs . . . ideograph." Caption *"Far left."* RS, 107
125   "Wei Kung-chih . . . from Kiangsi." Caption *"Middle."* *Ibid.*, 105
125   "Barefoot . . . at Juichin." Written on back of photo.
126   "Although . . . Paoan." RS, 264
126   "As I traveled . . . companions. *Ibid.*, 246
127 *Box:*   "I was traveling . . . good friends." *Loc. cit.*
127   "(Fu joined . . . five years ago.)" DIARY 17, p. 37
128   "Eight 'divisions' . . . Peng Teh-huai." RS, 271
128   "I found Peng . . . superficially." *Ibid.*, 272–73

10   The Communist Leadership

131   "If China had not . . . iron age." JTTB, 164
131–32   "Most of what . . . his land." *Ibid.*, 161
132   " 'Consult others' . . . 'out of mud.' " *Ibid.*, 162
132 *Box:*   " 'You were the only . . . Museum." OSOTR, 266
"Mao was forty-three . . . to my two." Caption. JTTB, 164
133   "There was a kind of magnetism . . . insurrectionist." SEP (Mar. 27, 1954)
133   "He did not seem . . . fatherly arm." *Ibid.*
133   "From the highest . . . any formality." RS, 268
135   " 'I like babies . . . in the army.' " Caption. BFA, 273
135   "Stronger . . . to the Reds.)" DIARY 17, p. 28
135   "Tsai Chang . . . the Long March." RNORC, 138
136   "Po Ku was one . . . poker." *Ibid.*, 15

136 "Born in 1908 . . . soviet government." RS, bio.

136 "Lui Chun-hsien . . . her interpreter." Caption. DIARY 12, p. 46

137 "Lin Piao . . . for power." RS, 96

137 "When Generalissimo Chiang . . . modern armies." RS, bio.

138 "Teng Hsiao-ping . . . in Kansu." *Ibid.*

139 "Nieh Jung-chen . . . Army." *Ibid.*

139 "As a member . . . in 1921." Caption. RS, 554

140 "One-eyed Li Ke-nung . . . in the morning." Caption. DIARY 12, p. 8

141 "Lin Tsu-han . . . young Communists." RS, 235

141–42 "Life in Paoan . . . Tsai bought." *Ibid.*, 373–74

142 "In the middle . . . guarding him." *Ibid.*, 394–96

11   The Sian Incident

145 "Look at the map . . . triumph?" BFA, 40

145 "If our country . . . practice it." *Ibid.*, 281

145 "General Yang Hu-cheng . . . prisoner in Sian." RS, 11–12

145–46 "In October . . . exact nature." *Ibid.*, 20, 23

146 "In October [1936] . . . 'traitors.'" *Ibid.*, 399

146 "In November . . . the Reds." *Ibid.*, 400

146 "Chang Hsueh-liang . . . become a fact." *Ibid.*, 403, 406

146 "Twenty-six-year-old . . . the Young Marshal." *Ibid.*, 408–9

146 "A few days later . . . greeting." *Ibid.*, 416

146 "The Generalissimo feared . . . nation." JTTB, 186

146, 148 "On December 24 . . . Chang Hsueh-liang fell for this." RNORC, 12

147 "A pleasure resort . . . taken prisoner." Caption. OSOTR, 459

148 "The chief reason . . . Soviet Union." BFA, 296–97

148 "Whatever Chiang . . . 'first task.'" JTTB, 186

149 "Chiang . . . Taiwan." RS, 478

149 "During . . . executed." *Ibid.*, 561

149–50 "Tacit agreement . . . annihilation drive." JTTB, 186–87

150 "The Kuomintang . . . in the capital." *Ibid.*, 197

151 "When Chou left . . . one." SEP (Mar. 27, 1954)

152 "I was in Hankow . . . impregnable." Letter to J. B. Powell, Aug. 28, 1938

152 "During the uprising . . . of the Sino-Japanese War." OSOTR, 452

12   The Invasion of China

155 "Those guns . . . in China." RS, preface. Rev. ed.

155 "Lukouchiao . . . war was certain." BFA, 16, 17

155–56 "Something . . . glory." *Ibid.*, 9–10

156 "Optimism . . . Chinese." *Ibid.*, 4, 5

157 "On August 13 . . . century." *Ibid.*, 17

157 "We crept up . . . into the next." *Ibid.*, 45

157 "Yet its drama . . . batteries." *Ibid.*, 45, 52

157 "A single bomb . . . behind the ears." JTTB, 98

158 "Widespread . . . unification of China." BFA, 162

158 "The Chinese . . . demolished." *Ibid.*, 48, 49, 50

164 "The Japanese . . . four feet high." *Ibid.*, 57–58

164 "The Japanese murdered . . . about it." *Ibid.*, 57

164 "Thousands of men . . . still alive." *Ibid.*, 59

164 "Hankow fell . . . inland. "*Ibid.*, 146

164 "Young girls . . . Brilliant Jade." *Ibid.*, 58

164, 167 "A most curious thing . . . future of China." JTTB, 193–94

167 "In 1938 Evans Carlson . . . Japanese lines." *Ibid.*, 194

168 "In January 1938 . . . the hinterland." BFA, 134–35

169 "In organizing . . . workshops." *Ibid.*, 138

169 "The settlement . . . wider areas." *Ibid.*, 252–53

13   Yenan

171 "At an elevation . . . warfare." OSOTR, 451

171 "I returned . . . Pact." RNORC, 69

171 "I found Mao . . . wealth at all." BFA, 282

171 "The years . . . that end." *Ibid.*, 283

172 "Veterans . . . mind." *Ibid.*, 266

172 "Yenan . . . rest of China." *Ibid.*, 267

172 "Outside the city . . . the earth." *Ibid.*, 266

172 "Mao . . . in North China." OSOTR, 467

172, 174 "The Communists . . . importance." JTTB, 174

174 "Side by side . . . responsibilities." POOS, 295

174–75 "Material conditions . . . self-sufficient." BFA, 267

175 "A new publishing house . . . literature." *Ibid.*, 268

175 "Nearly all . . . 1946–49." OSOTR, 452

175 "I saw Mao . . . to see." RNORC, 72

176 *Box:* "Chiang Ching . . . two daughters." RS, 499–500

178 "I knew Huang Hua . . . party leader." *Ibid.*, 516

180 "Mao found time . . . *On Contradiction.*" LR, 174

181 "I did not meet . . . China." OSOTR, 333–34

182 "Miss Smedley . . . else." Caption. *Ibid.*, 264

182 "Agnes . . . Copacabana." From an unpublished story by Snow.

182–83 "Chu Teh . . . rest." DIARY 54.

183 "In June . . . Mme. Sun Yat-sen." OSOTR, 261–67

184 "'All reactionaries . . . powerful.'" Caption. From *Selected Works*, Vol. IV, p. 99

184 "Perhaps . . . passport." OSOTR, 104
184 "Evans Carlson . . . speak freely." JTTB, 196–97
184 "Evans Carlson . . . socialism." RNORC, 129
184–85 "The Communists . . . Army." JTTB, 197
185 "Assigned . . . the Pacific." POOS, 288
185 "I filed out . . . 'Paoan.' " BFA, 272
189 "Ting Ling . . . Red Theater." RS, bio.
189 "There was a different . . . in Free China." BFA, 271
189 "Hsu Teh-li . . . became Reds." RS, 239
191 "An utter newcomer . . . their wages." BFA, 276

14 Guerrilla China

193 "Great areas . . . to them." From "War and Change in China," a talk by Snow
193 "There are regions . . . achieved." BFA, 249
193 "One of the . . . fighter." Ibid., 322
198 "A remarkably ingenious . . . Bethune." OSOTR, 268
200 "By the terms . . . dominated." JTTB, 225
200 "Suffrage . . . their vote." BFA, 318
200 "These 'new democratic' . . . of today." JTTB, 226–27
200 "The Reds were never . . . represent." OSOTR, 100
202 "Deep in Shensi . . . community." LR, 111–12
202 "Among . . . the world." JTTB, 198
202–3 "I vividly . . . 'aggression.' " From "China's New Industrial Army," an article by Snow.
203 "Indusco . . . in North China." JTTB, 202
203 "Indusco . . . Lord Inverchapel." Ibid., 198
203 "He personally . . . to do so." Ibid., 202
203 "a maverick . . . once a day." Caption. Ibid., 198
206 "I first met Rewi . . . legend." BFA, 92, 93
206 "Alley was . . . onlookers." Ibid., 200
206 "Virtually free . . . helped to save." JTTB, 203
206 "Ironically . . . power." Ibid., 225
206 "By 1942 . . . combined." Ibid., 233

15 Kuomintang China

209 "If China today . . . on the Kuomintang." POOS, 281
209 "Under Chiang . . . measures." JTTB, 137
209 "Chungking was . . . could obscure." BFA, 155
211 "The city . . . to Japan." Ibid., 160
211 "Spacious public shelters . . . before it." Ibid., 156
212 "The immediate result . . . Turkestan." Ibid., 180–81
212 "In the still uninvaded . . . forces." From "China to Lin Yutang," in NATION (Feb. 17, 1945)
212 "It was easier . . . cooperatives." BFA, 216
212 "Fourteen passengers . . . can see." DIARY
213 "In 1941 some Kuomintang troops . . . Free China." POOS, 298

213 "Born in Szechuan . . . survival." RS, bio.
213 "Chen Yi . . . Central China." RS, 497
215 "Few Chinese . . . Chou En-lai." OSOTR, 105
215 "Chou knew the idiom . . . judgment." SEP (Mar. 27, 1954)
215 "An interesting . . . 'toward progress.' " POOS, 300
215 "During World War II . . . afloat." SEP (Mar. 27, 1954)
216 "After Pearl Harbor . . . Chinese labor." POOS, 278
216 "There was good reason . . . together." POSP, 128
216–17 "What the Communists . . . election." Ibid., 132
217 "When I came back . . . monthly." POOS, 279
218 "Stilwell . . . kingdom come." JTTB, 152
218 "Stilwell's orders . . . to bottom." Ibid., 219
218 "He gave me . . . in China." Ibid., 382
218 "By late 1943 . . . Chennault." POOS, 278
218–19 "Chennault knew . . . of Attica." Letter to John Hart, Feb. 29, 1960
219 "There never was . . . the Japanese." POOS, 274–75
220 "Many of . . . Japanese advance." "China's Flying Freighters"
221 "Far from wishing . . . engagement." Ibid.
221 "The China career service . . . were made." JTTB, 148, 149
222 Box: "Chiang Kai-shek's government . . . executed." "Is It Civil War in China?" in ASIA (1941)
224 "Early in the war . . . 30 percent." POOS, 279–80.
224 "I thought . . . big feasts." DIARY 21, p. 7
224 "Chungking . . . frostbite." BFA, 341
225 "There was . . . for its actions." POOS, 297
225–26 "In the spring of 1945 . . . misapprehensions." SMHP, 58
226 "In a private conversation . . . 'together.' " POSP, 140
226 "Roosevelt died . . . one-man rule." RNORC, 130
226 "Nevertheless . . . else but." SMHP, 59
227–28 "The Sino-Soviet Treaty . . . Chiang Kai-shek." SEP (Apr. 9, 1949)
228–29 "The discussions . . . an impossibility." OSOTR, 616–17
229 "Meanwhile . . . mediator." SEP (Apr. 9, 1949)
231 "When Stalin . . . southward." OSOTR, 652
231 "Sent to Manchuria . . . Lin Piao . . . China." RS, bio.
231 "Chou led . . . supreme command." Caption. RS, bio.
231 Box: "The Chairman recalled . . . teacher." LR, 198

16   The Second Civil War

233   "By July 1946 . . . country." OSOTR, 452
233   " 'Mao . . . five years.' " *Ibid.*, 268
233, 235   "Years ago . . . from the east." *Ibid.*, 453
235   "One month . . . the enemy." *Ibid.*, 468
235   "The enemy . . . scale." *Ibid.*, 454
243   "In 1947 Mao . . . repeat the meal." NATION (Dec. 3, 1966)
244–45   "In Jack Belden's . . . its result." Snow review of *China Shakes the World*, in NATION (Nov. 7, 1949)

246 *Box:*   "Throughout . . . Liu Shao-chi . . . China." Caption. OSOTR, 334
   "Following Japan's surrender . . . Chen Yi . . . Army." Caption. RS, bio.

249   "In June 1948 . . . Chen Yi . . . Yangtze River." *Ibid.*
254   "During the war . . . enterprises." OSOTR, 329

256   "[Kuomintang] General Fu Tso-yi . . . surrenders.)" *Ibid.*, 489
260 *Box:*   "Teng Hsiao-ping . . . in Szechuan." RS, bio.
261   "Chiang Ching-kuo . . . Formosa." JTTB, 17
263   "Taiwan . . . until 1971." LR, 11
265   "Mao Tse-tung . . . 1949." Caption. Hsinhua Press, Peking
266   "In 1949 . . . in June 1949." OSOTR, 317–18
266   "China has . . . the empire." *Ibid.*, 135
266–67   "By 1949 history . . . People's Republic." SEP (Mar. 27, 1954)
267   "Not the Communist party . . . oppression." NATION (Nov. 7, 1949)
267   "The revolt . . . land they till?" NATION (Jan. 28, 1950)
269   "The truth is . . . the human family." From "I Heard the Chinese People," speech given by E. Snow in California, July 1949

Index

Page numbers in italics refer to illustrations.